SISTERS

AN ANTHOLOGY

PARIS
PRESS   Ashfield, Massachusetts 2009

SISTERS

AN ANTHOLOGY

EDITED BY **Jan Freeman, Emily Wojcik, and Deborah Bull**

First Paris Press edition, 2009.

Library of Congress Cataloging-in-Publication Data
Sisters : an anthology / edited by Jan Freeman, Emily Wojcik, and Deborah Bull.
-- 1st Paris Press ed.
   p. cm.
 ISBN 978-1-930464-12-4 (alk. paper)
 1. Sisters--Literary collections. I. Freeman, Jan. II. Wojcik, Emily. III. Bull, Deborah.
 PN6071.S425S59 2009
 808.8'03522--dc22

                        2009035253

Please see page 281 for acknowledgments and permissions.
978-1-930464-12-4
1-930464-12-6

a c e g i j h f d b

Printed in the United States of America.

For Eva, Naomi, and in memory of Miriam Schocken

✳

For Carla and Nancy
For Molly
For Zane

CONTENTS

A Note from the Publisher / xi

Joan Baez   *from* Daybreak / xvii

I   DON'T TELL MOTHER

Wendy Wasserstein   Don't Tell Mother / 3

Marilyn Chin   Parable of the Cake / 9

Margaret Atwood   The Headless Horseman / 12

Tsipi Keller   Shlug da Kleine / 37

Joyce Armor   Sweet Dreams / 44

Jeanne M. Leiby   Docks / 45

Rita Dove   The House Slave / 58

Claire Bateman   Reprieve / 59

Simone de Beauvoir   *from* Memoirs of a Dutiful Daughter / 61

Beverly Jensen   Idella's Dress / 67

Mary Karr   *from* The Liars' Club / 79

II   SISTER—SISTER

Lan Samantha Chang   The Eve of the Spirit Festival / 87

Edwidge Danticat   *from* Caroline's Wedding / 101

C.D. Wright   Yellow Dresses / 110

Gwendolyn Brooks   Sadie and Maud / 111

Ana Maria Jomolca   Twin Bed / 112

Alice Walker   Everyday Use / *123*

Catherine Chung   Hannah / *134*

Marie Luise Kaschnitz   Sister—Sister / *146*

Jane Hirshfield   Red Scarf / *147*

Julia Glass   *from* I See You Everywhere / *148*

Misty Urban   A Lesson in Manners / *158*

Cynthia Hogue   The Seal Woman / *174*

Martha Rhodes   Without Gloves / *176*

Ali Smith   *from* Girl Meets Boy / *177*

Lucille Clifton   sisters / *186*

Delia Ephron   *from* Hanging Up / *187*

III   HAVING OUR SAY

M.F.K. Fisher   Not Enough / *195*

Dorothy Parker   Letter to Helen Rothschild Droste / *199*

Robin Becker   Borderline / *206*

Daisy Zamora   Letter to a Sister Who Lives in a
Distant Country / *209*

Barbara Kingsolver   *from* The Poisonwood Bible / *211*

Jane Bowles   A Quarreling Pair / *221*

Clare Coss   Recollections of a
79-Year-Old Sister / *227*

Audre Lorde   A Family Resemblance / *230*

Barbara L. Greenberg   Close to the End / *231*

Myra Shapiro   Basque Guide / *232*

Ruth Prawer Jhabvala   Pagans / *233*

Contents

Maxine Kumin   The Last Good War / *260*

Grace Paley   I Needed to Talk to My Sister / *261*

Sarah and   *from* Having Our Say:
A. Elizabeth Delany   The Delany Sisters' First 100 Years / *262*

✳

Muriel Rukeyser   Two Years / *271*

Dedications to Sisters / *273*

About the Authors / *276*

Acknowledgments and Permissions / *281*

About the Editors / *284*

About Paris Press / *285*

NOTE FROM THE PUBLISHER

Several years ago, I traveled to Emory University for a celebration of Elizabeth Cady Stanton and her speech *Solitude of Self*. Vivian Gornick and I presented the keynote address, and my youngest sister, a professor of anthropology and women's studies, introduced us. Following the tribute, many of my sister's colleagues commented on how much we look alike, and they remarked on our shared interest in the lives of girls and women. As we stood beside a table that was covered with wine, cheese, and copies of *Solitude of Self*, my sister said to me, "I always wanted hands like yours, with long tapered fingers, and oval nails. Your hands are beautiful."

I looked at my small squat hands and short fingers and said, "You're crazy. My hands are exactly like yours." "No," she said, "I've envied your hands all my life. My hands are like Dad's." "So are mine," I replied. We held up our hands, and they were identical. The same shaped nails, fingers, the same shaped palms.

"But I've always been so jealous of your hands," she said. "They're the same as yours," I replied. And at our father's hospital bed, before he died, we noted that our hands were in fact exactly like his. Our mother and our other sister have the long elegant fingers, *they* have the beautiful hands.

Returning from Atlanta, I found myself thinking about sisters, and I asked Emily Wojcik, the assistant editor at Paris Press, if she might be interested in working together on an anthology about sisters. She has one sister. I have two.

We talked about possible stories, poems, essays, and started to look for books about sisters. I had copies of the wonderful photo-essay book, *Sisters,* and some out-of-print anthologies. But soon, we became immersed in current projects, and the sisters idea drifted away.

During the next few years, after family gatherings or phone calls, the subject resurfaced; each time, enthusiam rekindled, we uncovered more poems and stories, and then returned to the work at hand—Muriel Rukeyser or Zdena Berger or Virginia Woolf.

Then a good friend's sister died. My friend is the youngest of three girls, and they have always appeared in my mind as a unit, a perpetual threesome, similar and different, like most of the sisters I know. When her eldest sister died, I wanted to give my friend a book about sisters. Novels weren't exactly right. Photo-essays weren't quite right either. There were no anthologies in print. So Emily and I decided we would create one, and at last we began this book.

❋

Many voices, emotions, writing styles, and cultural backgrounds live in these pages. We received many submissions that we admired but were unable to include, due to space limitations and the prevalence of certain subjects, which easily could have overpowered the book. The topic addressed most frequently: the death of a sister.

One issue that we discussed in the early stages of the project was combining sisters in "family" with "sisterhood." We decided to focus on sisters within families, since present or absent, they are with you forever: You may love each other, resent each other, care for or burden each other. Some may remember the day a sister was born; and many learn the primal ways life changes when a sister dies.

When given the opportunity, nearly everyone who has a sister immediately has a story to tell about her. Sisters are subjects in literature throughout history, but they are overlooked in literary criticism.

Perhaps as a genre the relationship is too complex to untangle, yet simultaneously taken for granted.

In this anthology, Emily Wojcik, Deborah Bull, and I have attempted to include a variety of experiences and relationships, as well as cultural backgrounds, ages, and geographies. And since we were unable to offer a representation of everything and everyone we hoped to include, we view *Sisters: An Anthology* as a beginning for Paris Press. Our goal is to give readers a taste of work by contemporary and modern women writers who have explored the pivotal role that sisters play in each other's lives, whether they are enemies or the best of friends, filled with venom or with love.

※

On behalf of Paris Press I thank Emily Wojcik and Deborah Bull for the joy of creating *Sisters.* I am deeply grateful for the guidance that Deborah Bull offered and the knowledge she shared; without her, *Sisters* would not exist. And I am indebted to Emily Wojcik. She is a tireless researcher, editor, and an inspiration of organization. Immense gratitude to Jane Lund for her intricate and moving collage, "Sisters Dresses," which graces the cover of the anthology. A sky full of thanks to Rosemary Ahern for her help in the selection and review of material for the anthology. Gratitude to Linda Weidemann, Judythe Sieck, Bob Bull, Amy Mann, Patricia McCambridge, Betsy Stone, Barbara Alfange, Patricia Lee Lewis, and Sonja Goldstein. And thanks to all the writers who submitted their work.

Special thanks to Bruce Slater and Eleanor Lazarus for their bountiful advice. Paris Press is indebted to its Board of Directors and to its Advisory Board for help in all stages of *Sisters,* and for keeping the Press afloat in this challenging time.

SISTERS

AN ANTHOLOGY

I began to grow very fond of the bearded guru with the goat laugh. I felt he might have answers that no one else had. I asked him how I could learn to get along with my sister Mimi. She was twelve then, and very beautiful, and we fought all the time. Not in a big way, but by nasty little put-downs and ugly faces, and once in a while nail marks left in each other's arms. It seemed so endless and unkind. Ira said to pretend that it was the last hour of her life, as, he pointed out, it might well be. So I tried out his plan. Mimi reacted strangely at first, the way anyone does when a blueprint is switched on him without his being consulted. I learned to look at her, and as a result, to see her for the first time. I began to love her. The whole process took about one summer. It's curious, but there is perhaps no one in the world as dear to me as Mimi.

Joan Baez, FROM DAYBREAK

I

DON'T TELL MOTHER

DON'T TELL MOTHER

BY *Wendy Wasserstein*

I HAD A TEMPERATURE OF 104 and tonsillitis at my oldest sister Sandra's first wedding. I was six years old at the time, which made her nineteen. My mother tells me that all I wanted was to get out of bed and put on my pearls and white gloves. In fact, my mother repeats this story whenever she feels that I no longer accessorize enough. All I remember from the entire nuptials, which took place in our home in Brooklyn, a sizable red brick corner Dutch Colonial, was my older siblings, Bruce and Georgette, racing upstairs into my sickroom to let me know that Cousin So-and-so had just fallen through the floor while freely interpreting the hora.

My sister Sandra—known to the world as Sandra, never Sandy, from the day she left the Flatbush Dutch Colonial—has always preferred that I not dwell on the wedding story. Frankly, my older sister prefers not to dwell on Brooklyn, our parents, anyone's former marriages, or anything personal, including health and religion—and especially not the cousin who fell through the floor. (I never saw the hole, I never heard of any broken limbs, but I still choose to believe the story.) Even now, Sandra, from behind her desk at the penthouse offices of Clark & Weinstock, management consultants, advises, "If you really want to talk about me as a serious person, you have to think about how that story sounds and looks."

3

It would be impossible not to talk about my sister as a serious person. She started college at sixteen and graduated with honors at nineteen. Over the course of three decades in mainstream—or, as she prefers, "blue-chip"—corporate America, Sandra was the first female product-group manager at General Foods, in 1969; the first female president of a division of American Express, in 1980; and the first female to run corporate affairs as a senior officer at Citicorp, in 1989. In other words, she never had the luxury of not demanding to be taken seriously.

Two years after her first marriage, Sandra disappeared from my life: she moved to London. She was twenty-one and separated, and she began a career in advertising at the London Press Exchange. For me, "Sandra in London," and even the very tasteful name of Meyer she'd acquired from her husband, became a mythical, glamorous alternative to the bouffant-hair-sprayed mothers at the parent-teacher association, and even to our own mother, Lola, the Polish-born dancer, predestined to plié while broiling lamb chops in Brooklyn. I bragged to the girls' baseball team that my big sister in Europe wrote the "little dab will do ya" Brylcreem jingle. Later, of course, I found out that she was actually an account executive, but it all certainly seemed far more desirable than growing up to chaperon the school trip to the Horowitz Margareten matzo factory.

Around the time that Sandra returned permanently from London, my family moved from Brooklyn to the Upper East Side. When I was in high school, she had a career-gal pad in the East Fifties and was commuting daily to General Foods, in White Plains. Shortly after the Civil Rights Act, the corporate food giant hired the first female associate product manager/Postum and Toast'em Pop Ups—my sister Sandra. Our family had cases of unopened Toast'ems in the kitchen cabinets, and Sandra Meyer moved up to marketing manager/

Maxwell House. In that position, she was in charge of the Maxwell House–Folgers coffee wars.

As far as I was concerned, my oldest sister personally sent Tang to the moon and plumped every raisin in Post Raisin Bran. When I visited her in her ever larger offices, she was always the only woman along her corridor who wasn't sitting outside an office glued behind a typewriter and a telephone. Very grown-up, very Darien-looking men named Ed, Rick, and Jim were always popping in and out. Somehow, the love-ins of the late sixties seemed to be eluding them. I always politely shook the gentlemen's hands and couldn't wait for them to leave so I could talk to my sister some more about my prospects at the Horace Mann prom, which were surely more interesting than the marketing potential of Brim.

My mother often asked me if I thought Sandra would marry one of these Eds, Ricks, or Jims. I remember dinners at places like Le Pavillon with my parents, Bruce, Georgette, myself, and Sandra accompanied by various General Foods suits. Afterward, Lola would press me to determine whether the fella meant anything special to her eldest daughter. I never told her that I personally loved it that Sandra was single—partly because I knew those inspection dinners would stop as soon as she married again. I also never told her that my big sister advised me while I was still in high school to stay single until I was thirty unless I fell madly in love. Sex was one thing, and marriage was another, she said.

Sandra finally married the handsomest man who came to dinner, a Robert Redford look-alike. When she gave birth to her first daughter, Jenifer, there was mandatory unpaid maternity leave at General Foods. Therefore, my sister hid her pregnancy until her next promotion was confirmed. Her efficiency in life management, however, never undermined her maternal commitment. In fact, if you asked my mother, the domestic dancer, and my oldest sister, the corporate player, what was the most important thing they'd done with their lives, they'd both say, "Having children." However, my mother would say the answer was obvious, because "there's no children like my children," which I always thought should have been sung by Ethel Merman, while Sandra would clip, "Jenifer and Samantha are such capable and independent women."

I wish that my sister would tell me what toll her life has taken on her. Rather, I wish I could get an illogical, nonpositioned answer. But I suppose it's no different than when I'm asked if I think of myself as a woman playwright. Frankly, there's really no discussion in either case. My sister would say that life takes its toll, male or female, period. I heartily disagree. I can't help but wonder what difference it would have made in my sister's personal or corporate life if she had been a man. Of course, Sandra would say that if you're a player, gender shouldn't be an issue. But for my generation, gender *is* the issue.

After my sister's second marriage dissolved, she went to American Express as vice president, worldwide card product marketing. In my mind, she and Lou Gerstner, now the chairman of IBM, spent lunches at the Four Seasons devising new uses for the gold card. At that time, my sister fell madly in love—the sort of love she advised me to wait for—with Andrew Kershaw, then the chairman of Ogilvy & Mather, North America. Andrew died in her house in Pound Ridge six weeks before the wedding. I waited with Sandra in her Madison Avenue apartment while lawyers arrived to take the paintings he'd brought with him back to his first wife, in Toronto. Like a good baby sister, I remained in the background for the entire event. I wanted to take care of her without her knowing what I was doing. My sister and I stay within our defined boundaries. She's capable. I'm funny. Except for when I'm surprisingly capable and she's inexplicably funny.

Our mother referred to Sandra when we were growing up as "Strazac," which means "fireman," but which Mother, for reasons of her own, translated as "a general in the Polish army." Even as a child, Sandra liked to be in charge. For the record, I was called Epidemic, because I was always hanging around and was impossible to send off to bed. Georgette was known as Gorgeous, for the obvious reasons, and Bruce remained Bruce. When I look at pictures of Sandra from college, I see a rather delicate-looking young American girl with beaming brown eyes and lovely tapered hands. No one would mistake her for a Polish general, but, of course, I'm not often confused with black cholera or influenza, either. A few years ago, when Sandra was a senior corporate officer at Citibank, she broke her leg, and a day after surgery, when a nurse came into her hospital room to change her IV, Sandra snapped at her, "Can't you see I'm busy? I'm on a business call!" This sort of will is beyond any *strazac*, or Poland would never have divided. This sort of determination, I'm sure, is responsible for a very well-placed corporate lawyer's telling me that my sister saved John Reed's job at Citibank during its financial crisis. John Reed is—"of course," as my sister would say—the chairman. What my sister won't discuss is why so many of her male corporate contemporaries have become chairmen and she has not. My sister is a strong woman but not an angry one. Ultimately, she's a team player.

My favorite Sandra story is another one she would prefer I not tell. Sandra came home twice from Europe during her five years away. During one of those visits, I was a third grader at the Yeshiva Flatbush. (I feel Sandra already blushing.) Every Saturday, I took dancing lessons in Manhattan rather than attend temple services. In order for Sandra and me to get to know each other, my mother suggested that Sandra pick me up from school and take me to Howard Johnson's for a grilled cheese sandwich and on to Radio City for the stage spectacular and a Doris Day film.

My phantom neo-British sister in her gray flannel suit arrived at the dancing school, immediately warned me "Don't tell Mother," and hustled me off to the House of Chan for spareribs and shrimp with lobster sauce. Neither dish was on the rabbi's recommended dietary list at the yeshiva. I was terrified that a burning bush or two stone tablets would come hurtling through the House of Chan's window. But I was with my glamorous big sister, who everyone told me was so brilliant, so I cleaned my plate.

After lunch, we skipped Radio City; Sandra had no interest in the Rockettes or Doris Day. We went to the Sutton Theatre, on East Fifty-seventh Street, which seemed to me the ultimate in style: they served demitasse in the lobby. The feature film was *Expresso Bongo,* starring Laurence Harvey as Cliff Richard's tawdry musical agent. All I remember is a number in a strip joint with girls dancing in minikilts and no tops. I knew that in whatever Doris Day movie we were meant to be going to she would be wearing a top.

I never told my mother, but I loved everything about that afternoon. My big sister Sandra showed me that women, especially a female general with an epidemic, could go anywhere.

PARABLE OF THE CAKE
BY *Marilyn Chin*

The Neighborwoman said to us, "I'll give you a big cake, little
Chinese girls, if you come to the Christmas service with me and
accept Jesus Christ, our lord, into your heart." We said, "Okay,"
and drove with her to the other side of the city and sat through a
boring sermon when we should have taken the bus to Chinatown for
our Cantonese lessons. Afterward, she gave us a big cake that said
"Happy Birthday, Buny" on it. She must have got it for half price
because of the misspelling. My sister and I were really hungry after
the long sermon, so we gulped down the whole cake as soon as we got
home. I got sick and threw up all over the bathroom and my sister
had to clean it up before Granny got home. Then my face swelled
up for two days on account of my being allergic to the peanut butter
in the frosting. My sister was so afraid that I would croak that she
confessed everything to Granny. First, Granny gave me some putrid
herbal medicine, then she whipped us with her bamboo duster. She
whipped us so hard that we both had red marks all over our legs.
Then she made us kneel before the Great Buddha for two hours
balancing teapots on our heads.

On Christmas Eve, Granny went to Safeway and bought a big
white cake with Santa's face on it and made us go with her to the
Neighborwoman's house. She placed the cake into the woman's
hands and said, "Peapod, translate this, Malignant Nun, we do not
beg for your God." I didn't know how to translate "malignant" and
said politely, "Dear Missus, No beg, No God."

My sister and I both wept silently, embarrassed that Granny made us into a spectacle and ashamed that we had to lie to get out of it. Meanwhile, Granny was satisfied that we learned our lesson and decided to take her two favorite peapods to Chinatown for sweet bean dessert. We were the only riders on the bus that night; everybody else was probably home with their families preparing for a big meal. "Merry Christmas, ho ho ho, I am Santa's helper!" said the Bus Driver. He was wearing a green elf's hat, but we knew that he was really Mr. Rogers the black bus driver. He gave us each two little candy canes. Granny scowled, "Tsk, tsk, ancient warrior in a fool's cap!" Then we sat way in the back of the bus and Granny began singing our favorite song:

"We will go home and eat cakies, little lotus-filled cakies," Granny sang. "We will eat sweet buns, sweet custard sweet buns!" she sang. "We will eat turnip squares, salty white turnip squares," she sang. "We will eat grass jelly, tangy green grass jelly. We will eat dumplings, soft, steamy dumplings." She was so jolly that we forgot our embarrassing episode and we sang with her, clapping hands—we sang and sang.

Granny would die a few years later, leaving us 3,000 dollars under her mattress and a brand-new cleaver, still wrapped in Chinese newspaper from Hong Kong. We would grow up into beautiful, clear-skinned young women. We would become born-again Christians and get a complete makeover at the mall. We would work hard in our studies, become successful and drive little white Mercedes. We would remember *nothing, nada,* nothing that our grandmother taught us. We would learn nothing from our poverty, but to avoid poverty at all cost.

Fa la la la la, little cakies, little cakies, little cakies... We would drive around in our little white Mercedes all over southern California eating little cakies. Yes, let's put on the Ritz, sisters: little petit-fours in pastels and rainbows... booze-soaked baba au rhums, oooh yes, nuttynutty Florentines on little white doilies... Oh sisters! Let's ghetto it! Ho Hos, Ding Dongs, pink and white snowballs, let's suck the creamy hearts out of the twinkies. Come hither, come yon, young Chinese girls. Come, let's drive around in our little white Mercedes eating cakies, little cakies. Come, let the crumbs fall down our chins and dance on our laps. Come, light light airy madeleines, come, creamy creamy trifles. Come, little cakies, little cakies. Come, the sweet, sweet hereafter....

THE HEADLESS HORSEMAN
BY *Margaret Atwood*

FOR HALLOWEEN THAT YEAR—the year my sister was two—I dressed up as the Headless Horseman. Before, I'd only ever been ghosts and fat ladies, both of which were easy: all you needed was a sheet and a lot of talcum powder, or a dress and a hat and some padding. But this year would be the last one I'd ever be able to disguise myself, or so I believed. I was getting too old for it—I was almost finished with being thirteen—and so I felt the urge to make a special effort.

Halloween was my best holiday. Why did I like it so much? Perhaps because I could take time off from being myself, or from the impersonation of myself I was finding increasingly expedient, but also increasingly burdensome, to perform in public.

I got the Headless Horseman idea from a story we'd read in school. In the story, the Headless Horseman was a grisly legend and also a joke, and that was the effect I was aiming for. I thought everyone would be familiar with this figure: if I'd studied a thing in school I assumed it was general knowledge. I hadn't yet discovered that I lived in a sort of transparent balloon, drifting over the world without making much contact with it, and that the people I knew appeared to me at a different angle from the one at which they appeared to themselves; and that the reverse was also true. I was

12

smaller to others, up there in my balloon, than I was to myself. I was also blurrier.

I had an image of how the Headless Horseman was supposed to look. He was said to ride around at night with nothing on top of his shoulders but a neck, his head held in one arm, the eyes fixing the horrified viewer in a ghastly glare. I made the head out of papier mâché, using strips of newspaper soaked in a flour-and-water paste I cooked myself, as per the instructions in *The Rainy Day Book of Hobbies*. Earlier in my life—long ago, at least two years ago—I'd had a wistful desire to make all the things suggested in this book: animals twisted out of pipe cleaners, balsa-wood boats that would whiz around when you dropped cooking oil into a hole in the middle, and a tractor thing put together out of an empty thread spool, two matchsticks, and a rubber band; but somehow I could never find the right materials in our house. Cooking up paste glue was simple, however: all you needed was flour and water. Then you simmered and stirred until the paste was translucent. The lumps didn't matter, you could squeeze them out later. The glue got quite hard when it was dry, and I realized the next morning that I should have filled the pot with water after using it. My mother always said, "A good cook does her own dishes." But then, I reflected, glue was not real cooking.

The head came out too square. I squashed it at the top to make it more like a head, then left it down by the furnace to dry. The drying took longer than I'd planned, and during the process the nose shrank and the head began to smell funny. I could see that I should have spent more time on the chin, but it was too late to add on to it. When the head was dry enough, at least on the outside, I painted it what I hoped was a flesh colour—a wishy-washy bathrobe pink—and then I painted two very white eyeballs with black pupils. The eyes came out a little crossed, but it couldn't be helped: I didn't want to make the eyeballs grey by fooling around with the black pupils on the damp white paint. I added dark circles under the eyes, and black eyebrows, and black enamel hair that appeared to have been slicked down with brilliantine. I painted a red mouth, with a trickle of shiny enamel blood coming down from one corner. I'd taken care to put a neck stub on the bottom of the head, and I painted this red—for where the head had been severed—with a white circle in the middle of the bottom part, for the neck bone.

The body of the Horseman took some thought. I made a cape out of a piece of black fabric left over from a now-obsolete puppet stage of mine, gathering it at the neck end—designed to sit on top of my head—and sewing buttons down the front, and cutting two inconspicuous holes at eye level so I'd be able to see out. I borrowed my mother's jodhpurs and riding boots, left over from before she was married—she hadn't ridden a horse since her wedding day, she was in the habit of saying, proudly or regretfully. Probably it was both. But I didn't pay much attention to my mother's tone of voice, then: I had to tune it out in order to charge full speed ahead with what I myself was doing.

The riding boots were too big, but I made up for that with hockey socks. I safety-pinned the jodhpurs around the waist to keep them from falling down. I got hold of some black winter gloves, and improvised a horse whip out of a stick and a piece of leather I'd scrounged from the box of archery materials. Archery had once been popular with my father, and then with my brother; but my father had given it up, and the box had been abandoned in the trunk room in the cellar, now that my brother had to study so much.

I tried on the entire outfit in front of my mirror, with the head held in the crook of my arm. I could scarcely see myself through the eyeholes, but the dark shape looming in the glass, with two sinister eyeballs staring out balefully from somewhere near the elbow, looked pretty good to me.

On the night itself I groped my way out the door and joined my best friend of the moment, whose name was Annie. Annie had done herself up as Raggedy Ann, complete with a wig of red wool braids. We'd taken flashlights, but Annie had to hold my arm to guide me through the darker patches of the night, which were numerous in the badly lit suburb we were traversing. I should have made the eye-holes bigger.

We went from door to door, shouting, "Shell out! Shell out!" and collecting popcorn balls and candy apples and licorice twists, and the Halloween toffees wrapped in orange and black waxed paper with designs of pumpkins and bats on them of which I was especially fond. I loved the sensation of prowling abroad in the darkness—of being unseen, unknown, potentially terrifying, though all the time retaining, underneath, my own harmless, mundane, and dutiful self.

There was a full moon, I think; there ought to have been one. The air was crisp; there were fallen leaves; jack-o-lanterns burned on the porches, giving off the exciting odour of singed pumpkin. Everything was as I'd imagined it beforehand, though already I felt it slipping away from me. I was too old, that was the problem. Halloween was for little children. I'd grown beyond it, I was looking down on it from my balloon. Now that I'd arrived at the moment I'd planned for, I couldn't remember why I'd gone to all that trouble.

I was disappointed, too, at the response of the adults who answered the doors. Everyone knew who my friend Annie was portraying—"Raggedy Annie!" they cried with delight, they even got the pun—but to me they said, "And who are you supposed to be?" My cape had a muffling effect, so I often had to repeat the answer twice. "The Headless Horseman." "The headless what?" Then, "What's that you're holding?" they would go on to say. "It's the head. Of the Headless Horseman." "Oh yes, I see." The head would then be admired, though in the overdone way adults had of admiring a thing when they secretly thought it was inept and laughable. It didn't occur to me that if I'd wanted my costume to be understood immediately I should have chosen something more obvious.

However, there was one member of the audience who'd been suitably impressed. It was my little sister, who hadn't yet gone to bed when I'd made my way through the living room en route to the door. She'd taken one look at the shambling black torso and the big boots and the shiny-haired, frowning, bodiless head, and had begun to scream. She'd screamed and screamed, and hadn't been reassured when I'd lifted up the cape to show that it was really only me underneath. If anything, that had made it worse.

※

"Do you remember the head?" I ask my sister. We're in her rackety car, driving over to see our mother, who is now very old, and bedridden, and blind.

My sister doesn't ask, "What head?" She knows what head. "It looked like a pimp," she says. "With that greaser hair." Then she says, "Smart move, Fred." She talks out loud to other, inferior drivers when she's driving, a thing she does adroitly. All of the other drivers are named Fred, even the women.

"How do you know what a pimp looks like?"

"You know what I mean."

"A dead pimp, then," I say.

"Not completely dead. The eyes followed you around the room like those 3-D Jesuses."

"They couldn't have. They were sort of crossed."

"They did, though. I was afraid of it."

"You played with it, later," I say. "When you were older. You used to make it talk."

"I was afraid of it anyway," she says. "That's right, Fred, take the whole road."

"Maybe I warped you in childhood," I say.

"Something did," she says, and laughs.

※

For a while after that Halloween, the head lived in the trunk room, which contained not only two steamer trunks filled with things of my mother's from her previous life—tea cloths she'd embroidered for her trousseau, long kid gloves she'd saved—but also a number of empty suitcases, and the metal box of fly-tying equipment, and the archery materials, and an assortment of miscellaneous items I used to rummage through and pilfer. The head was on an upper shelf, the one with the battered skates and the leather boots—my father's, also my mother's. Foot, foot, foot, foot, head, foot, foot, foot—if you weren't ready for this arrangement and happened to glance up at it, the effect could be disconcerting.

By that time we had a second phone in the house so I could talk with my boyfriends, or go through what passed for talking, without exasperating my father too much—he thought phone conversations should be short, and should convey information. The door to the trunk room was right beside the phone. I liked to keep that door closed while I was talking; otherwise I could see the head staring out at me through the gloom, blood dribbling from the corner of its mouth. With its sleek black hair and minimal chin, it looked like a comic-book waiter who'd got into a fight. At the same time it seemed malignantly attentive, as if it was taking in every word I said and putting a sour construction on my motives.

After its period of retreat in the trunk room, the head migrated into my sister's dress-up box. By now, I was fifteen and my sister was four. She was still an anxious child—if anything, she was more anxious than ever. She didn't sleep through the night—she'd wake up five or six or seven or nine or ten or eleven times, according to my mother. Although I had the room right next to hers, I never heard her plaintive calls and frightened wailing. I slept through it all as if drugged.

But sleeping mothers hear the cries of their own children, we've been told. They can't help it. Studies have been done. My mother was no exception: she'd hear the little voice calling to her across the blankness of sleep, she'd half wake, then stumble into my sister's room, soothe her mechanically, bring her drinks of water, tuck her in again, then go back to bed and fall asleep, only to be wakened once more and then once more and then once more. She'd grown thinner and thinner in the last four years, her skin pale, her hair brittle and greying, her eyes unnaturally large.

In actuality, she'd caught a disease of the thyroid from the hamster we'd foisted on my sister as a pet in the vain hope that the sound of it creaking round and around on its exercise wheel at night would be calming to her. It was this disease that accounted for my mother's scrawniness and staring eyes: once diagnosed, it was easily cured. But that detail tended to get sidelined during the later recountings of this story, both by my mother and by me. The fairy child, the changeling who didn't follow the convenient patterns of other children, who sucked up its mother's energy in an uncanny and nocturnal manner—this is a theme with more inherent interest to it than a hamster-transmitted thyroid disease.

My sister did look a little like a fairy changeling. She was tiny, with blond braids and big blue eyes, and a rabbity way of nibbling on her lower lip as if to keep it from trembling. Her approach to life was tentative. New foods made her nervous, new people, new experiences: she stood at the edge of them, extended a finger, touched gingerly, then more often than not turned away. *No* was a word she learned early. At children's parties she was reluctant to join in the games; birthday cake made her throw up. She was particularly apprehensive about doors, and about who might come through them.

Thus it was probably a bad idea of my father's to pretend to be a bear, a game that had been a great success with his two older children. My sister was fascinated by this game as well, but her interest took a different form. She didn't understand that the bear game was supposed to be fun—that it was an excuse for laughing, shrieking, and running away. Instead, she wanted to observe the bear without being spotted by it herself. This was the reason she'd snipped two holes at eye level in my mother's floor-to-ceiling drapes. She'd go in behind the drapes and peek out through the holes, waiting in a state of paralyzed terror for my father to come home. Would he be a bear, or would he be a father? And even if he looked like a father, would he turn into a bear without warning? She could never be sure.

My mother was not delighted when she discovered the holes cut in her drapes. They were lined drapes; my mother had pleated and hemmed them herself, not because she liked sewing but because it was a good deal cheaper that way. But there was nothing to be done. With a child like that, punishment was beside the point: the poor little thing was in a constant state of suffering anyway, over one thing or another. Her reactions were always in excess of the occasion for them. What was to be done? What was to be done, in particular, about the waking up at night? Surely it wasn't normal. My sister was carted off to see the doctor, who was no help. "She'll grow out of it," was all he would say. He didn't say when.

Because of her sensitivity, or perhaps because my mother was so worn down, my sister was allowed to get away with things I would never have been allowed to do, or so I felt. She spent most mealtimes underneath the table instead of on a chair drawn up to it, and while down there she tied people's shoelaces together.

✳

"Remember the shoelace thing?" I say to her. "We never knew exactly why you did that."

"I hated sitting at the dinner table," she says. "It was so boring for me. I didn't really have a brother and a sister. I was more like an only child, except with two mothers and two fathers. Two and two, and then me."

"But why the shoelaces?"

"Who knows? Maybe it was a joke."

"You weren't very joke-prone at that age."

"I wanted the two of you to like me. I wanted to be funny."

"You are funny! We do like you!"

"I know, but that was then. You didn't pay much attention to me. You always talked about grown-up things."

"That's hardly fair," I say. "I spent a lot of time with you."

"You had to," she says. "They made you do it."

"They had this idea that I was good with you," I say. "That's what they used to say: 'You're always so good with her.'"

"Way to go, Fred, you moron!" says my sister. "Did you see that? Nobody ever signals. Yeah, well, it let them off the hook."

"I made you those moss gardens," I say defensively. These had been a special thing for her: I put them together in the sandbox, with moss for the trees and bushes, picket fences made of sticks, wet sand houses trimmed with pebbles. Paths paved with flower petals. She'd watch, enraptured: her face would brighten, she'd become very quiet, as if listening. The real garden had that effect on her too. It was at its height then. She'd stand among the irises and poppies, stock-still, as if enchanted. "Moss gardens," I say. "And gardens with little shells in them—you loved them. I made those too."

"Not at the dinner table, though," she says. "It's okay, the light's green, you can go! And then after dinner you used to shut me out of your room."

"I had to study. I couldn't play with you all the time."

"You just didn't want me messing up your stuff. Anyway you weren't always studying. You were reading Perry Mason books and trying on lipstick. And then you left, when I was eight. You abandoned me."

"Nine," I say. "I didn't *abandon* you. I was twenty-one! I left home and got a job. That's what people do."

"It's no left turn before six, Fred, you creep! I wish I had a camera. The thing is," says my sister, "I couldn't figure out who you were supposed to *be*."

＊

My sister had a friend who was a lot like her—another quiet, shy, anxious, big-eyed fairy child, dark where my sister was fair, but with the same china fragility. Leonie was her name. They both insisted on wearing flouncy skirts instead of jeans, they both chose *The Twelve Dancing Princesses* as their favourite story. They longed to have me doll them up in outfits improvised from the dress-up box: I'd pin up their hair and put lipstick on them and let them wear my clip-on earrings. Then they'd prance around solemnly in my high-heeled shoes, holding up their too-long play skirts, keeping their red mouths prim.

"Remember the cut velvet?" my sister says. We're in her car again, going to see our mother again. We prefer to do it together. The rundown house with its flaking paint, the tangle of weeds that used to be the garden, our shrivelled mother—we can deal with these better together. We both have soggy raisin-studded muffins in paper bags and takeout coffees in evil Styrofoam cups: we buy ourselves snacks and bribes, we need to be bolstered up.

"She should never have let us have that," I say. "She should have saved it."

The cut velvet was an evening gown, black, white, and silver in colour, dating from the 1930s. Why had our mother given it to us? Why had she cast away such a treasure, as if abdicating from her former life—her life as a young woman who'd enjoyed herself and had adventures? We'd each admired this gown in turn; we'd each ruined it in the course of our admiration.

"*We* wouldn't have done that," I say. "Wasted it."

"No. We wouldn't. We'd have been selfish. Just throw the garbage in the back seat, I keep it strewn with trash back there to deter burglars."

"I wouldn't call it selfish, as such," I say.

"Not that they'd want to steal this rust bucket. Hoarding, then. We're going to be those old ladies they find in houses full of stacks of newspapers and pickle jars and cat-food tins."

"I'm not. I have no interest in the cat-food tins."

"Old age is the pits," says my sister. "I kept a piece of it."

"You did?"

"And that skirt of yours with the big red roses—I kept some of that. And a bit of your blue brocade formal. I thought it was so glamorous! I thought everything you did was glamorous. Fred, you asshole! Did you see how she cut me off?"

"What about the pink tulle?"

"I think Mum used it for dusters."

"No great loss," I say. "It looked like a cake."

"I thought it was great—I was going to have one just like it when I grew up. But by the time I got to high school, no one went to formal dances any more."

※

My sister and Leonie played decorous games together in which life was agreeable, people were gentle and fastidious, and time was divided into predictable routines. They adored miniatures: tiny glass vases with midget flowers in them, eensy-teensy cups and spoons, minute boxes—anything small and dainty. Stuffed-bunny tea parties and doll-dressing absorbed them. All the stranger, then, that they found the Headless Horseman's head in the trunk room, and got it down from the boot shelf, and adopted it.

There it would be, eyes crossed, mouth drooling blood, set in its place between the flop-eared white bunny and the rubber-skinned Sparkle Plenty doll that had led a far riskier and more disreputable life when it had been mine. The head looked out of place but comfortable: everything was done to make it feel at home. A table napkin would be tucked around its neck stump, and it would be served cups of water tea and imaginary cookies just as if it had a body. Better still, it answered when spoken to—it said, "Thank you very much" and "Could I have another cookie, please" and replied to the white bunny and the Sparkle Plenty doll when they asked it if it was having a good time. Sometimes it was made to nod. When the party had been too tiring for it, it was put to sleep in the dolls' bed, with a crocheted quilt pulled up over its receding chin.

Once, I discovered it propped up on my sister's pillow, its neck wrapped in one of our mother's best linen dishtowels. Cookie fragments on dolls' plates were laid out around it, mixed with berries from the prickly-berry hedge, like offerings made to appease an idol. It was wearing a chaplet woven of carrot fronds and marigolds that my sister and Leonie had picked in the garden. The flowers were wilted, the garland was lopsided; the effect was astonishingly depraved, as if a debauched Roman emperor had arrived on the scene and had hacked off his own body in a maiden's chamber as the ultimate sexual thrill.

"Why do you like it so much?" I asked my sister and Leonie. I still took some interest in the head: it was, after all, my creature, though I'd been so young—it seemed to me now—when I'd made it. I regarded it critically: the thing was really unconvincing. The nose and chin were way too small, the skull too square, the hair too black. I should have done a better job.

They gazed up at me with distrust. "We don't *like* him," said my sister.

"We're taking care of him," said Leonie.

"He's sick," said my sister. "We're the nurses."

"We're making him feel better," said Leonie.

"Does he have a name?" I asked.

The two little girls looked at each other. "His name is Bob," said Leonie.

This struck me as funny. I tried not to laugh: my sister was affronted when I laughed at anything to do with her. "Bob the Head?" I said. "That's his name?"

"You're not supposed to laugh at him," said my sister in an injured tone.

"Why not?" I said.

"Because it's not his fault," she said.

"What's not?"

"That he's got no, got no..."

"Got no body?" I said.

24

"Yes," said my sister in a stricken voice. "It's not his fault! It's only the way he is!" By this time the tears were trickling down her cheeks.

Leonie gave me an indignant stare; she picked up the head and hugged it. "You shouldn't be so mean," she told me.

"I know," I said. "You're right. I shouldn't be so mean." But I had to go into my room and close the door, because I had to either laugh or choke.

❋

Yet at other times the two of them demanded meanness from me. They'd pester me ceaselessly because they wanted me to play a game called Monster. I was supposed to be the monster—stalking around the house and out into the yard, legs and arms stiff like a zombie's, calling in a toneless voice, "Where *are* you? Where *are* you?" while they held hands and ran away from me, and hid behind the shrubs or the furniture, twittering with fright. When I got home from school they'd be waiting; they'd turn their delicate little pansy-eyed faces up to me and plead, "Be a monster! Be a monster!" Their appetite for my monstrousness was boundless; as long as the two of them were together, holding hands, they could tough it out, they could escape, they could defy me.

Sometimes my sister would be alone when I got home. By "alone," I mean without Leonie, for of course my mother would be there. Not for long, however: she'd grab the opening provided by my arrival and be off like a shot, heading for the grocery store or some other equally spurious destination, leaving me as impromptu babysitter. Really she wanted the open road; she wanted speed and exercise, and her own thoughts. She wanted to be free of us—all of us—if only for an hour. But I didn't recognize that then.

"Okay," I'd say. "I have to do my homework. You can play over there. Why don't you have a dolly tea party?" But no sooner would I have settled myself with my books than my sister would start up.

"Be a monster! Be a monster!" she would say.

"I don't think it's a good idea. Leonie isn't here. You'll cry."

"No, I won't."

"Yes, you will. You always do."

"I won't this time. Please! Please!"

"All right," I'd say, though I was quite sure how it would end. "I'll count to ten. Then I'm coming to get you." I said this last in my flat monster voice. By the time I'd reached ten, my sister would already have shut herself into the front hall closet with the winter coats and the vacuum cleaner, and would be calling in a muffled voice, "The game's over! The game's over!"

"All right," I would say in a reasonable but still eerie tone. "The game's over. You can come out now."

"No! You're still being a monster!"

"I'm not a monster. I'm only your sister. It's safe to come out."

"Stop it! Stop it! Stop the game!"

"Stop what? There isn't any game."

"Stop it! Stop it!"

I shouldn't have done that. A sister pretending to be a monster, or a monster pretending to be a sister? It was too much for her to decipher. Small children have trouble with ill-defined borders, and my sister had more trouble than most. I knew perfectly well, even while I was speaking in my duplicitous voice, what the results would be: sobbing and hysteria and then, many hours later, nightmares. In the middle of the night, screams of terror would issue from my sister's bedroom; my mother would be dragged from unconsciousness, hoisting herself grimly out of bed, shuffling across the hall to mollify and soothe, while I slept through it all, conked out like a slug drowning in beer, evading the fallout from my crimes.

"What did you do to her?" my mother would say when she got back from her shopping excursion. My sister would still be in the front hall closet, weeping, afraid to come out. I'd be sitting at the dining-room table, placidly doing my homework.

"Nothing. We were playing Monster. She wanted to."

"You know how impressionable she is."

I'd shrug and smile. I could scarcely be blamed for being obliging.

Why did I behave this way? I didn't know. My excuse—even, on some level, to myself—was that I was simply giving in to an urgent demand, a demand made by my little sister. I was humouring her. I was indulging her. Of more interest to me now is why my sister made the demand, again and again. Did she believe she'd finally be able to face down my monster self, deal with it on her own terms? Did she hope that I would finally—at last—transform myself, on cue, into who I was really supposed to be?

※

"Why did you like the monster game?" I say to her.

" I don't know," she says. "Drop dead, Fred, the light was red. Do you want lunch before Mum, or after?"

"If we have it before, we'll get depressed with no treat to look forward to. On the other hand I'm starving."

"So am I. Let's go to Satay on the Road."

"Or we could go to Small Talk. They have good soup."

"I make a lot of soup at home. I need some of that peanut sauce. Should I dye my hair red? I'm getting a lot of grey."

"It looks good," I say. "It looks distinguished."

"But what about red?"

"Why not?" I say. "If you like. I could never handle red, but you can."

"It's bizarre, because we're both yellow/orange, according to the colour charts."

"I know. You can do lime green too. It makes me look bloodless. You used to agitate and agitate for that monster game and then shut yourself up in the front hall closet as soon as it began."

"I remember that. I remember that feeling of being completely terrified. Warm wool, vacuum cleaner smell, terror."

"But you kept on wanting to do it. Did you think you could make it come out differently?"

"It's like saying, 'Tomorrow morning I'm going to get up early and work out.' And then the time comes and you just can't."

"Mother used to think it was her fault," I say.

"What, me hiding in the coat closet?"

"Oh...and other stuff," I say. "The whole picture. Remember when you were going through that total honesty period?"

"I've stopped?"

"Well, no. I never went in for it, myself—total honesty. I preferred lying."

"Oh, you never lied much."

I duck that one. "Anyway, you were halfway through high school when you really got going on the honesty. You were going to tell Mum and Dad about drugs, and skipping school, and kids your age having sex, because you thought Mum and Dad led a protected life and were too repressed."

"Well, they did and they were," she says. "I did tell them about some of it. I told them about taking LSD."

"What did they say?"

"Dad pretended he hadn't heard. Mum said, 'What was it like?'"

"I didn't know you took LSD."

"I only took it once," she says. "It wasn't that great. It was like a really long car trip. I kept wondering when it would end."

"That's what happened to me too," I say.

※

When my sister was sixteen and I was twenty-eight, my parents called me home. This had never happened before: it was in the nature of an SOS. They were becoming increasingly desperate: my sister had added anger to her repertoire of emotions. She still cried a lot, but she cried from fury as well as from despair. Or she'd go into thick, silent rages that were like a dense black fog descending over everyone. I'd witnessed these at family Christmas dinners—events I now tried to avoid as much as possible.

My parents persisted in their belief that I was particularly good with my sister—better than my brother, who did not take emotional outbursts seriously. They themselves certainly weren't good with her, my mother told me. They wanted her to be happy—she was so bright, she had such potential—but she was so immature. They just didn't know what to do. "Maybe we were too old to have another child," my mother said. "We don't understand these things. When I was that age, if you were unhappy you kept it to yourself."

"She's a teenager," I said. "They're all like that. It's hormones."

"You weren't like that when you were a teenager," said my mother hopefully.

"I was more furtive," I said. I didn't go on to say that she could hardly have any idea of what I'd been like then because she'd been in a coma most of the time. I'd done a lot of things she'd known nothing about, but I wasn't going to reveal them now. "She's right out in the open," I said.

"She certainly is," said my mother.

My parents had wanted me to come home because they had a chance to go to Europe—it was some sort of group trip, it wouldn't cost much—and they had never been there. They wanted to see castles. They wanted to see Scotland, and the Eiffel Tower. They were like excited kids. But they were afraid to leave my sister on her own: she took things too hard, and she was going through a bad period. ("Over some boy," said my mother, with slight contempt. As a young woman she'd have let herself be boiled in oil before admitting to a bad period over some boy. The thing then was to have lots of beaus, and to treat them all with smiling disdain.)

They'd only be gone for two weeks, said my father. A little more than that, said my mother, with a mixture of guilt and anxiety. Eighteen days. Twenty, counting the travel.

I didn't see how I could deny them. They were getting old, or what I thought of as old. They were almost sixty. They might never have another chance to see a castle. So I said yes.

It was the summer—a Toronto summer, hot and humid. My parents had never bothered with air conditioning or fans—physical discomfort didn't mean much to them—so the house got progressively warmer as the day advanced, and didn't cool off until midnight. By this time my sister was living in my former bedroom, so I found myself in hers.

Our days fell into a strange pattern, or lack of pattern. We got up when we felt like it and went to bed at irregular hours. We ate our meals here and there around the house, and let the dirty dishes pile up on the kitchen counter before doing them. Sometimes we took our lunches down to the cellar, where it was cooler. We read detective stories and bought women's magazines, which we leafed through in order to rearrange ourselves, though only in theory. I was too tired to do much of anything else; or not tired, sleepy. I'd fall asleep on the chesterfield in the middle of the day, sink down into cavernous dreams, then wake up groggily toward suppertime, feeling hungover. Ordinarily I never took naps.

Once in a while we'd make forays into the blazing-hot garden, to water it according to the meticulous instructions left by our parents—instructions we did not follow—or to yank out the more blatant weeds, the deadly nightshade vines, the burdocks, the sow thistles; or to snip fragments off the exuberant prickly-berry hedge, which was threatening to take over the entire side border. The phlox was in bloom, the dahlias, the zinnias: the colours were dizzying. We made an effort at mowing the lawn with the elderly push mower that had been around forever. We'd left it too long: the mower blades got clogged with crushed grass and clover.

"Maybe it's time they entered the twentieth century and got a gas mower," I said.

"I think we should mow the whole garden," said my sister. "Flatten it right out."

"Then it would all be lawn. More to mow. Let's anyway trim the edges."

"Why bother? It's too much effort. I'm thirsty."

"Okay. So am I." And we'd go inside.

At unpredictable moments, I heard many instalments about a boy called Dave, who played the drums and was unobtainable. It was always the same story: my sister loved Dave, Dave didn't love her. Maybe he'd loved her once, or had begun to, but then something had happened. She didn't know what. Her life was ruined. She could never possibly ever be happy again. Nobody loved her.

"He sounds like a drip," I said.

"He's not a drip! It was so great once!"

"I'm just going by what you told me. I didn't hear about any great parts. Anyway, if he's not interested, he's not interested."

"You're always so fucking logical!" My sister had taken up swearing at a much earlier age than I had, and was fluent in it.

"I'm not, really," I said. "I just don't know what I'm supposed to say."

"You used everything up. You used up all the good parts," said my sister. "There was nothing left over for me."

This was deep water. "What do you mean?" I said carefully. "What exactly did I use up?"

My sister was wiping tears from her eyes. She had to think a little, pick something out from the overflowing pool of sadness. "Dancing," she said. "You used up dancing."

"You can't use up dancing," I said. "Dancing is something you *do*. You can *do* whatever you want."

"No, I can't."

"Yes, you really can. It's not me stopping you."

"Maybe I shouldn't be on this planet," said my sister grimly. "Maybe I should never have been born."

I felt as if I were groping through brambles in a night so dark I couldn't see my own hands. *At my wit's end* had been, before this, merely an expression, but now it described a concrete reality: I could see my wits unrolling like a ball of string, length after length of wits being played out, each length failing to hold fast, breaking off as if rotten, until finally the end of the string would be reached, and what then? How many days were left for me to fill—for me to fill responsibly—before the real parents would come back and take over, and I could escape to my life?

Maybe they would never come back. Maybe I would have to stay here forever. Maybe both of us would have to stay here forever, trapped in our present ages, never getting any older, while the garden grew up like a forest and the prickly-berry bush swelled to the size of a tree, blotting the light from the windows.

In a state of near-panic I suggested to my sister that we should go on an excursion. An adventure. We would go to the town of Kitchener, on the Greyhound bus. It was only about an hour. Kitchener had some lovely old houses in it; we would take pictures of them with my camera. I'd been taking a lot of pictures of architecture around that time—nineteenth-century Ontario buildings. It was an interest of mine, I said, not lying very much. Oddly enough, my sister agreed to this plan. I'd been expecting her to refuse it: too complicated, too much effort, why bother?

We set off the next day supplied with oranges and digestive biscuits, and made it to the bus station without incident, and sat through the bus trip in relative calm. Then we ambled around in Kitchener, looking at things. I took pictures of houses. We bought sandwiches. We went to the park and watched the swans.

While we were in the park, an older woman said to us, "Are you twins?"

"Yes," said my sister. "We are!" Then she laughed and said, "No, we're not. We're only sisters."

"Well, you look like twins," said the woman.

We were the same height. We had the same noses. We were wearing similar clothes. I could see how the woman might have thought that, supposing she was a little nearsighted. The idea alarmed me: before that moment, I'd viewed the two of us in terms of our differences. Now I saw that we were more alike than I'd imagined. I had more layers on, more layers of gauze; that was all.

My sister's mood had changed. Now she was almost euphoric. "Look at the swans," she said. "They're so, they're so..."

"Swanlike," I said. I felt almost giddy. The afternoon sun was golden on the pond where the swans floated; a mellow haze suffused the air. Suffused, I thought. That was how I felt. Maybe our parents were right: perhaps I alone had the magic key, the one that would open the locked door and free my sister from the dungeon that appeared to be enclosing her.

"It was great to come here," she said. Her face was radiant.

But the next day she was more unhappy than ever. And after that it got worse. Whatever magic I thought I might have—or that everyone thought I might have—proved useless. The good times became fewer, the bad times worse. They became worse and worse, for years and years. Nobody knew why.

❇

My sister sits on the bottom step of my stairs, biting her fingers and crying. This doesn't happen once, but many times. "I should just leave," she says. "I should just check out. I'm useless here. It's too much effort." She means: *getting through time.*

"You've had fun," I say. "Haven't you? There's lots of things you like."

"That was a while ago," she says. "It's not enough. I'm tired of playing the game. This is the wrong place for me to be."

She doesn't mean my house. She means her body. She means the planet Earth. I can see the same thing she's seeing: it's a cliff edge, it's a bridge with a steep drop, it's the end. That's what she wants: *The End.* Like the end of a story.

"You aren't useless, you shouldn't leave!" I say. "You'll feel better tomorrow!" But it's like calling across a wide field to a person on the other side. She can't hear me. Already she's turning away, looking down, looking down over, preparing for dark flight.

She'll be lost. I will lose her. I'm not close enough to stop her.

"That would be a terrible thing to do," I say.

"There's no other door," she says. "Don't worry. You're really strong. You'll handle it."

We turn a corner and then another, pass a willow tree and then a weeping mulberry, pull into the driveway of our mother's house. "Look at Fred," says my sister. "Parked right in the middle of the street. If I was a snowplow, I'd plow him right into the prickly-berry hedge."

"That's the spirit," I say. We clamber out of the car, which is getting harder for me to do. Something happens to the knees. I stand, one hand on the car, stretching myself, surveying the ruined garden. "I need to tackle that yew tree," I say. "I forgot my pruners. There's deadly nightshade vine all through it."

"Why bother?" says my sister in full honesty mode. "Mum can't see it."

"I can," I say. "Other people can. She used to be so proud of that garden."

"You worry too much about other people. Was I a really horrible child?"

"Not at all," I say. "You were very cute. You had big blue eyes and little blond braids."

"According to the stories I whined a lot."

"It wasn't whining," I say. "You had a sensitive nervous system. You had an enhanced reaction to reality."

"In other words, I whined a lot."

"You wanted the world to be better than it was," I say.

"No, that was you. You wanted that. I just wanted it to be better than it was for *me*."

I sidestep that. "You were very affectionate," I say. "You appreciated things. You appreciated them more than other people. You practically went into trances of rapture."

"But I'm all right now," she says. "Thank God for pharmaceuticals."

"Yes," I say. "You're all right now."

She takes a pill every day, for a chemical imbalance she was born with. That was it, all along. That was what made the bad times for her. Not my monstrousness at all.

I believe that, most of the time.

⁂

Now we're at the door. The persistence of material objects is becoming an amazement to me. It's the same door—the one I used to go in through, out through, year after year, in my daily clothing or in various outfits and disguises, not thinking at all that I would one day be standing in front of this very same door with my grey-haired little sister. But all doors used regularly are doors to the afterlife.

"I lost track of that head," I say. "The Headless Horseman head. Remember when it lived in the trunk room? Remember all those boots, and the archery supplies?"

"Vaguely," says my sister.

"We'll have to go through that stuff, you know. When the time comes. We'll have to sort it out."

"I'm not looking forward to it," says my sister.

"Where did it go, in the end? That head? Did you get rid of it?"

"Oh, it's still down there somewhere," says my sister.

SHLUG DA KLEINE*

BY *Tsipi Keller*

for J.B.F.

ONE OF MY VERY FIRST MEMORIES, and one that comes back to me every so often, is of my sister pushing me onto the road and nearly under the hooves of a horse. She was about four years old at the time, and I was five. I don't know how she managed it, I was taller and probably stronger—she was a scrawny little thing with large ears—so I assume she pushed me with all the vehemence a four-year-old can muster.

It's hard to tell who resented whom more, but I'm fairly certain that I never pushed her, and that I never tried to harm her physically. My resentment was purer and more abstract, having to do with fairness and justice. After all, she had arrived thirteen months after I did, she took my crib (my parents, Hitler survivors and remnants of an Eastern European shtetl, didn't bother with childrearing literature), and the little creature I called sister had no obvious respect for the one who came before her.

But I also know that I was not an innocent bystander, and it could very well have been anger, rather than deep resentment, that made her push me. Defending my own turf, I saw her as a nuisance and was probably in the habit of belittling her, so it is entirely

---

* Yiddish for "Beat up the little one."

37

possible I had said something right before she pushed me. We were standing at the curb, my mother, my sister and I, waiting for my father. Something in me tells me that my sister, usually passive and quiet until provoked, was standing near my mother, and that I, claiming precedence, tried to take her place at my mother's side, and that she, negating that birthright and claiming her own, pushed me onto the road in retaliation.

Still, it is also fair to say that she was born with an attitude, and she often astonished me—and my parents—in her sudden outbursts. When she was barely eight years old she screamed at them, declaring that she did not ask to be born, and since they chose to bring her into the world, they owed her the dress or whatever else she demanded from them. It was such an amazing and novel claim, I remember looking at her with a new awareness, an awareness that made me admire her, if only for a split second, and also envy her, as I asked myself how she, the little one, had come up with such an argument.

Let me pause here a minute. Born with an attitude? Maybe, just as plausibly, she had to fight for her dignity? My father and mother, more than once, talked about my sister having been the result of an unexpected and an unwanted pregnancy. They talked about how difficult it was for my mother to carry her in her belly on the long and torturous journey from Czechoslovakia to Israel. In addition, my sister's large ears were a source of merriment and family jokes, and my father always liked to repeat the funny story about how I ran to him every night when he returned from work with the plea: *Shlug da kleine!*

It is also true that my parents, unwittingly, encouraged my belittling of my sister. In their innocent and affectionate bantering about her, they gave me license to do the same, and running up to my father and telling him to beat up my sister was yet another way to make them laugh and ingratiate myself; I was the smart daughter, she was the little monkey I could safely ridicule.

So, no, I don't know that my sister was born with an attitude, but I do know that she was born with a sweet and generous nature, even if I came to recognize this only years later. In our childhood photographs, large ears and all, she looks like a delicate fragile angel, and her sweet demeanor shines through her pale skin and large brown eyes. She looks straight at the camera but rarely smiles, maybe because I'm right next to her, smiling my cocky smile. I had her in my power, or so I believed, when she ran with me in the streets of Jaffa, always silent and always behind—my shadow and in my shadow.

How my parents allowed us to roam the exotic and potentially dangerous streets of Jaffa in the 1950s, I don't know. In many ways, they were laissez-faire parents, perhaps because they both came from very large families where the older child takes charge of the younger ones, while the mother is busy in the kitchen, or gossiping with her neighbors. I don't remember my mother gossiping much with the neighbors, but I do remember her in the kitchen, cooking and baking, bringing to the table delicious meals and desserts, made from scratch. I remember breakfasts in particular, with my mother asking my sister and me what we want, then placing the plates before us; I gobble down my food, while my sister rejects what she has just asked for and demands—and gets—a different dish.

Another vivid and recurring memory is of the two of us, two years or so later, waiting for the bus to our elementary school in Holon. When I saw the bus coming, I told my sister, who was standing on the street, to join me on the sidewalk, which she did, and then, calmly and deliberately, she shoved her breakfast slice of bread in my face, smearing me with butter and jam. She then climbed onto the bus, and I climbed in after her, horrified, humiliated and shocked, mostly because there were people around to witness my shame and bewilderment. One of them gave me a handkerchief to

39

wipe my face and, if I remember correctly, chided my sister for doing such a terrible thing.

And yet, the same sister who pushed me, who smeared my face with her jam sandwich, and who frequently threw tantrums, is also the sister who massaged my mother's feet when she was ailing and dying, the sister who nursed my father when he was ailing and dying. She is the sister who knew how to make my mother laugh, and who makes me laugh when I visit. She was always more blunt and direct than me, sometimes even brutal, not only toward me and my parents, but toward other people as well, so to this day I find it hard to even begin to disentangle the multitude of nerve-endings and make sense of how I feel about her, or what I feel for her, not only as a sister, but as a person. She was an indifferent student, never finished high school, and I know that she is aware that her blunt and often petty, gossipy remarks annoy me. But she doesn't know, I don't think, that her attempts to impress me sometimes with a book she read or a concert she went to, bring back the memory of the sibling who felt, from the very beginning, that she was the lesser member of the family, and this, quite simply, breaks my heart.

It would be easy for me to say that yes, surely, I love her, I've always loved her, but love seems too small a word and imprecise. At bad moments, when I look for ways to torture myself, I imagine her dead or dying, as if preparing for the devastation should something happen to her. Such attempts last only a millisecond, and my terror is so great, I have to stop.

Every piece of writing is a groping into that foggy and confused place where jumbles of thoughts, memories, and feelings agitate. But this particular jumble, the jumble of sisterhood, is the hardest, as it grows more foggy and suspect with the years. A jumble that only a sibling, who was there much of the way, can help me unravel. A sibling who is now the only chronicler and witness of me as a child.

A sibling who remembers me from her own perspective, who watched and saw me from different angles. A sibling I still pit myself against, hoping to get a clearer image of who I was and have become, and often I don't like what I see. I feel especially ashamed when I recall the sibling who willingly served as my appointed and loyal spy when, as an adolescent, I went to dance parties and took her along, so she would spy on the boys and later report to me on who had eyed me or seemed interested in me. As if it were understood that I was the center of attention, and that no one would be interested in her, my little sister.

A few months after the horse episode, my parents packed us up and we moved into a three-room apartment in a new housing complex for immigrants. We left Jaffa behind and forgot about the room overlooking the sea. We now had to go to a special preschool to learn to speak a new language, Hebrew. On the first day, just before we went in, I took my sister by the hand and for the first time as I remember it, treated her the way an older and responsible sister is supposed to treat a younger sibling. I told her that we must forget Yiddish and learn to speak Hebrew; this was something that both she and I would have to endure and overcome. I remember the urgency with which I spoke the words, and perhaps that is why, this time, she didn't rebel but listened, serious and quiet. And then, still hand in hand, we walked in.

Except for periodic eruptions, throughout our childhood and adolescence, I tolerated my sister following me around and joining me and my friends in our games, and, at my parents' urging, I reluctantly helped her with her homework. There was too much tension between us to ever experience true joy together. This tension is still there, but we've learned to be cautious, something our volatile and bewildered parents couldn't teach us. We've learned to tiptoe around our shortcomings and our differences, but in my dreams, usually involving my mother as well, we have ferocious fights, with me raging against my sister's apparent indifference and thoughtlessness.

There is so much to tell, and it is in the nature of memory that bad experiences readily appear in one's psyche where shame and pain are intertwined. When we talk about the past, my sister doesn't recall the incidents about the horse and the jam, nor does she recall the details of more recent confrontations. One of her fondest memories, she says, is the ease with which I studied for my exams, my foot on a chair, the book on the table, and me flipping through the pages. And even though this description amuses and pleases me, I'm annoyed she remains unaware of the times she hurt me and our parents, and maybe that's why I still rage against her, impotently, in my dreams.

My sister and I are middle-aged now and live thousands of miles apart. We talk on the phone, we email. I call her Pieteke, she calls me Sheifale, our father's nicknames for us. She is one of my very few emotional ties to a country I left years ago. She is the flesh and blood link to my dead parents, to a time when the four of us lived in one room and the only luxury we could boast about was the Mediterranean Sea, right outside our window. Through her I'm tethered to something solid and elemental, to a feeling akin to generosity and twin-ness.

Today would have been my mother's 92nd birthday. One of the enduring family myths is that I was my mother's favorite, and my sister, my father's. It was often said that I took after my mother, and that my sister took after my father. With the years, though, my sister and I look more and more alike, and people easily identify us as sisters. Sometimes, I see my father in her, sometimes, my mother, just as I see my parents in myself. Maybe a day will come and I will recognize myself in my sister, a sister who, on the whole, is humble, good-hearted, and well-meaning.

Often, I reach into the jumble and try to realign it; still, the jumble remains intact, as perhaps it must. And as I grasp for reasons and excuses, for definitive answers, I become paralyzed. Anecdotes are not the real or the only story, but anecdotes are what we cling to. I had planned to write a nice fictional account about two sisters, but the little one, the one I begged my father to beat up, wouldn't let me.

SWEET DREAMS

BY Joyce Armor

It's always been a wish of mine
(or should I say a dream)
to scare my sister half to death
and hear her piercing scream.

That's why I squished four bugs until
they all were very dead,
then took them to my sister's room
and put them in her bed.

After we had said goodnight,
my heart began to pound.
I waited and I waited, but
she never made a sound.

And then I got so doggone tired
I couldn't stay awake.
I climbed into my own warm bed
and shrieked—there was a snake!

It wiggled, and I leaped and fell
and bruised my bottom half.
Then I heard an awful sound—
it was my sister's laugh.

DOCKS

BY *Jeanne M. Leiby*

JUST AFTER DAWN the old men wander up the dock alongside our boat, heading out to the end of the pier where they will fish until late morning. They carry plastic buckets, poles, and tin cans of night crawlers. Through the starboard porthole which is my bedroom window, my sister Stel and me count feet—work boots and sneakers and sometimes even bedroom slippers. Twenty-two feet passed by on Tuesday but it was rainy and damp. Thirty-four on Friday and forty-three today, which is Sunday. It is an odd number for counting feet, but One-foot Joe who runs the marina gas pumps doesn't have to work until noon so he goes fishing too. Stel and me barely fit together on my narrow side of the V-bunks, and the porthole is small so we have to take turns looking and counting which is good for Stel who is younger than me. Even though it is summer break and we are not in school, she needs to practice her math. One-foot Joe knows our game, so when he comes lumping by, he knocks our glass with his crutch. It is Stel who is looking and she jumps back, knocks her forehead hard on the upside beam. She covers her mouth with her hand and chokes back crying because it is Sunday early and we do not want to wake our father who is still asleep.

Our father means to take us to church because he promised our mother he would, but Sunday follows close to Saturday night when he plays with his band at the Boat House Bar until it closes, so he will sleep late and we will miss Mass. By the time he wakes up, our growling bellies will be driving Stel and me crazy, and we will be cramped and crooked from the long morning spent peering through my porthole. She, being younger, gets the not-so-good bunk on the side of the boat that faces in toward the bay and the slime and the sludge. Me being older, I let her come and cuddle like we used to do with my mother back when we had a house, a yard, and a dog named Buster. When our father finally wakes, he will make us a big breakfast—sunny-side-up eggs and bacon. He'll knife out chunks of grapefruit and he will let Stel and me dust them with sugar which is a Sunday-only treat because during the week we have to be careful of our teeth. Our father will put the sugar bowl on the table and turn back to the stove where the bacon sizzles. *I don't know anything about what I can't see,* he will say and then wink at the pan, a wink I know Stel and me are supposed to see. Then we'll kid around such that he keeps trying to catch us heaping sugar in our bowls. He doesn't really mean to stop us. Sugar on Sundays is our father's way of making up for the promises he broke to our mother and to God.

Our mother is not dead, just gone away, but our father says *A promise is a promise.* He told Stel and me the last time we went to bingo on a Wednesday night—not a Sunday, but still in church which counts with God—that when he and our mother got married, he had to put his hand on the Bible and swear no matter what, he'd raise his offspring right and proper and Catholic. I should have been confirmed last year and Stel should have made her first communion. But new dresses cost a lot of money and so do new leather shoes. Our father says he wants to wait until he can throw us a big party, rent out the Boat House Bar and invite our mother's family—maybe even some cousins we've never met—because they are likely to give us checks and presents and money for college. They know too that our mother is gone away because Stel and me had to go before a judge and say we wanted to stay on the boat with our father and not go live with our mother's sister who has a big house, a swimming pool, two dogs, no kids, and a swing set she bought on sale at Sears just for Stel and me. The judge was a lady with red hair and she got mad at our father when he punched the table, saying *Dammit they are my kids and you can't have them* and madder still when my mother's sister started to yell, *Living on a boat, they could drown.* Which quieted our father who looked for a minute like he hadn't thought about that. So I said, *You can drown in a swimming pool just as easy.* The judge laughed a little bit but she sounded sad until she made me promise that I would look out for Stel my younger sister, and then told our father that we were his so long as he stayed on his best behavior.

⚜

A promise is a promise and the best way I can think to take care of Stel and me is to keep us safe in this V-bunk until our father wakes up. He tells us time and time again not to run on the deck and never run on the docks where the boards are crooked and it's easy to trip. But Stel is young and she forgets. *Just like your mother,* our father says. *Just like that bitch, your mother.* That word is bad but I tell Stel it means pretty, which our mother was the last time we saw her, sitting in the front seat of a convertible car with her hand around the neck of the guy who mows the marina's grass.

One Sunday not so long ago when our father was still asleep, Stel snuck out of her bunk and went topside on her own to feed stale bread to the gulls. She tripped on the winch bolt and knocked out her front tooth which was okay because it was already loose and wanting to come out. But there was blood from a gash on the inside of her lip. I took quarters from our father's pants pockets which is stealing and wrong, I know. And then I did wrong again by buying us each a popsicle from the machine behind the boathouse which is bad for our teeth. But our father says sometimes when he's roughing up our hair that *Two wrongs do make a right,* and I figured the cold might help cut Stel's pain, maybe stop the blood, and bring down the lump on her bottom lip which it did.

When we are on the docks, our father says, *You girls need to stay right where I can see you* by which he means right where he can see us if he is fishing or napping or sanding the back deck. Or right where One-foot Joe can see us because most days after school it is One-foot Joe who watches after us and gives us M&Ms only if we promise not to tell our father. So after Stel fell and split her lip, I told her that we had to be on our best behavior too because we don't want to go live in our mother's sister's house which smells like fried liver and onions, the thought of which made Stel cry until we started counting feet.

※

When there are no more feet to count and the old men are sitting on their buckets at the end of the pier, we count the fish they catch, adding them up and subtracting the scrub they toss back into the river. One-foot Joe has made a catch and Stel laughs and does her math using her fingers and mine which is fine and not cheating if you aren't taking a test. I let her watch him cast again even though it is my turn at the porthole because she is getting hungry and soon she is going to have to pee which is a hard thing to forget with the sounds of the water moving against the hull. But the head doesn't work right so until our father gets around to getting it fixed, we have to use the johns behind the marina, and that's too long a walk for a Sunday morning when our father is still asleep.

Mrs. Kinseki, my fourth grade teacher, asked me last year if I liked living on the boat and the honest to God answer is sometimes I do and sometimes I don't. It is very damp in the winter and cold in the bones and our towels never dry and my shoes mold and then smell like cabbage when I run and sweat in gym class. In the winter our father worries about the ice because the river and the bay freeze and our boat is wood. After the last of the freighters stopped running in early November, our father and One-foot Joe sank generators next to the boat to keep the water bubbling so as not to freeze us in, which could split the hull and sink us. The gennies run all the time, off and on, day and night. When Stel and me are at school, I worry the gennies will break and we will come home to the boat slipped down beneath the water and the ice, and the worry makes it hard to concentrate on spelling. One-foot Joe promised he'd check our boat every single hour, but I knew this was a lie because he lives above the Boat House Bar which is a long walk with his crutch on the ice. At night, when the gennies are running, they hum and vibrate Stel and me to sleep. When they are not running, I lie awake and think up ways to save Stel my younger sister when the ice comes crunching through the hull.

But like our father says, *It's good to be different* and no other kids in my class live on a boat, so I told Mrs. Kinseki *Yes,* which isn't exactly a lie. Because now it is summer and I do like the boat. I like that we have bunks instead of beds and a galley instead of a kitchen. And even though the head doesn't work, the word "head" sounds a lot better than "toilet."

※

It is Sunday which means that after breakfast, we will take the boat up the river. I am our father's first mate so it is my job to blow out the bilge which is an easy job because it is just a switch to flip but important too because if he starts the engines with gas fumes in the bilge, we will blow ourselves up all the way to Canada. It is also my job to fend off the starboard stern. Stel who is our father's second mate watches portside but unless there is a stranger's boat tied up along the breakwall, which doesn't happen often because of the current, there isn't much for her to do. When we are on the river, it is my job to read the numbers on the buoys so our father can stay in the shipping channel where the water is deep and there are no shoals. Stel and me wear life-jackets and once, when a squall kicked up on the river, our father tied us to the helm which scared Stel and made her cry. But I held her and held on tight so we didn't blow away.

Maybe today we will go to Put-In Bay, drop anchor, and then jump off the swim platform into the deep waters by the old Mama Juda Lighthouse which is good because Stel needs to practice her sidestroke. One-foot Joe told Stel and me that the lighthouse is haunted by the ghost of an old Ojibwa squaw who got hung there for making nasty with the lighthouse keeper's son. *White and red don't mix,* Joe said. *Not then, not now, not ever.* But Stel who gets good grades in art told him no, that red and white mix just fine if you're looking to make a pink. Stel only talks when she knows she is right which isn't very often because she is young and can't quite keep her letters straight, b's and d's and p's and q's being the biggest problem. One-foot Joe laughed at her which made me mad because Stel is shy and laughing hurts her feelings. *I'm talking blood, not paint,* he said which didn't make much sense. When our mother hit our father and made his forehead bleed, it was red, red, red on the white living-room carpet which left a stain as pink as my tongue. Buster tried to lap it up but our mother kicked him in his side and locked him in the basement. Now we have a lazarette instead of a basement, and before she went away, our mother took Buster to the pound. I didn't argue with

One-foot Joe because our father says that arguing with adults is rude and mostly Joe is nice. He plays tambourine with my father's band. Instead I took Stel's hand and said *Good day,* trying hard to sound like Mrs. Kinseki when she is mad at us for talking in the hallways.

Our father says that Catholics believe blood is thicker than water which may be true except for in the back bay where the water doesn't move no matter how strong the wind, so sometimes it is nearly solid with dead fish, seaweed, and zebra mussels.

✳

There is movement in the galley which means our father is awake and I am glad because Stel has been sitting with her knees crossed tight for quite awhile and my neck is sore from crouching. I will take her to the john and hold her hand so she doesn't run on the docks.

But it is not our father who opens the door. It is our mother and her hair is short, dyed black, and her middle is thick so she is going to have another baby. Stel is off the bunk and into our mother's arms in a dive like a gull after breadcrumbs.

Stel, our mother says. *My baby Stel.*

Already I am angry because Stel is young but she is not a baby and our mother should know this. But Stel has got her legs wrapped around our mother's middle and her head is on our mother's shoulder and her thumb is in her mouth which is something she hasn't done since she started 1st grade. Even though my neck is sore and it's hard to move, I look around our mother's body and around the wall, balancing my weight on my hand, and trying to see our father in the galley which is where he must be because the boat already smells like bacon. But it is not our father at the stove. It is the man who mows the lawns and he isn't wearing a shirt, only boxer shorts which is dangerous and stupid because bacon grease can spatter and burn.

Mama, Stel is crying, *I got to pee.* So I hop down off my bunk, my knees feeling weak when my feet hit the wood, and I reach for Stel's elbow so she knows where I am but our mother slaps my hand away and says, *Mind your own business.* And then she turns which is hard because she is fat and the boat is narrow, and she carries Stel to the back of the boat to use the head which she doesn't know is broken. There is a leak in the seal so Stel's pee will drip straight down into the wood and soon it will stink to high heaven back there.

The salon bunk where our father sleeps is empty. I ask the man at the stove for a glass of water, and he says to just wait a minute, can't I see he is busy? And then he says that Stel and me are going to have to eat our eggs scrambled whether we like it or not which I do, but Stel doesn't because she says that scrambled eggs look and feel like snot. On the floor is our mother's red satchel, the one she took with her the day she left and it is open. There is a brown stain on her blue satin nightie, the one me and Stel and our father bought her for Mother's Day. Next to that is a carton of Virginia Slims and the Zippo lighter she got as a gift from her sister who sells them at the flea market. The man who mows the lawns has got his head in the fridge probably looking for the eggs or the butter, and our mother is still with Stel in the head, so I take the lighter which is cold and heavy and slide it into the waistband of my pajama bottoms as something to prove to our father when I find him that our mother is back.

Since I know how not to run, I go up through the hatch topside by myself, thinking maybe our father fell asleep on the deck which he does sometimes when it is hot and if the mosquitoes aren't too bad. Our father is not there but a seagull perched on the windlass looks at me with one black eye like I'm about to snap his neck. Two tugboats are moving close to shore and trawling slow against the current which means there is a freighter making its way up the channel wanting to turn at Hennepin Point which is a slow and steady process. It can be dangerous if the tugs' pilots are young or drunk or scared of ships so big. Last fall, a thousand-foot freighter got stuck on the shoal off Hennepin Point and it took four days and a fierce nor'easter to blow her free and clear. Stel and me watched with One-foot Joe from his upstairs window because our father was at work doing tool and dye, and Joe explained it all to us because he used to be a tug pilot before he lost his foot to the diabetes. Stel fell asleep on the floor because she doesn't much like the water and all of the things that move past on the river, but I listened. So when Mrs. Kinseki made us write a paragraph on what we want to be when we grow up, I wrote Tug Pilot because it is a hard job and very important but you get to spend your time on the water with the wind and the gulls. Mrs. Kinseki laughed and read my paragraph to the class. Then at lunch the girls who sit together on the starboard side of the cafeteria laughed at me and took my books and put them in the trash. They all want to be ballerinas except for the one who wants to be a nurse. Our mother wanted to be a nurse but she is not and she told her older sister who told me that it is my fault because my mother, being Catholic, couldn't use birth control so I got born into this world far too early. When I told this to One-foot Joe, he just laughed and said, *It's good to be a woman ahead of your time,* which is something I don't understand. But he promised me he'd explain on my next birthday when I will get older.

One-foot Joe hobbles up the dock with his bucket and poles, moving slow like he does so his crutch won't catch in the space between the boards. When he sees me shoeless and in my pajamas, he must know something is wrong because our father never lets Stel and me topside unless we are fully dressed and with our hair combed. One-foot Joe shakes his head and mumbles things I cannot understand.

When he gets alongside, he sets down his pail and then balances his poles and his crutch against the starboard side of our boat.

Come on, he says. I lean forward and he lifts me up and over the railing, me swinging my legs to make it easier because the water is high and sometimes One-foot Joe has trouble with his balance. Then he takes his crutch and his poles and leaves his bucket behind which is too heavy for me to carry since it is filled with dead fish that are already starting to stink.

I walk slow and careful because the wood is rough and I don't want a splinter in my foot. I don't know where we are going, but at the end of the dock where the parking lot starts, Joe puts down his poles and then takes my hand, and I walk even slower because the parking lot is gravel and sometimes broken glass which is why our father tells us not to run and why Stel and me never leave the boat without our shoes. Our father's truck is parked next to the river in the shadows of the Boat House Bar and he is asleep, his head bent forward toward the steering wheel.

Joe knocks on the glass and our father jumps, startled by the sound. He starts to roll down the window and then changes his mind and opens the door. Joe lifts me up again and puts me on our father's lap which is uncomfortable and tight because the steering wheel is in the way and the stick shift jabs my side. Our father smells like cigarettes which he only smokes on Saturday nights when he plays guitar with his band and never on the boat because it is wood. And then he is pulling my head to his chest and running his hands through my hair and I think he might be crying which scares me because I have never seen him cry, not even when our mother went away. But he is crying now and tears run down my arm, which is bare because I am still wearing my pajamas. I don't cry even though there is heat and too much spit in the back of my throat because our father says that only babies cry and I am not a baby but neither is he which means he must be very, very sad.

I show him the lighter which is silver and etched with daisies, and he takes it from my hand and throws it in the water which is easy for him even though we are still tight in the front seat because he is left-handed and we're close to the river. I am looking at Joe who is looking at the water where the lighter disappeared, hoping maybe he'll go in and get it, but he doesn't. The ripples are already gone which means the lighter has sunk and will be hard to find. So now I'm mad at One-foot Joe for just standing there, leaning on his crutch. And I am mad at our father because our mother will be angry when she finds the lighter gone, and I will be the one who gets into trouble.

Mack, want me to watch the kid? One-foot Joe says, leaning into the cab and putting his hand on our father's shoulder which is still shaky and warm. *I'm thinking you are going to need to look after business.* I want One-foot Joe to go back to our boat, get Stel dressed and get her shoes on which is easier now that she knows her port from her starboard and because it is summer and we don't need to wear socks. I will comb her hair when she is here in this truck with me and our father.

Our father does not say no to One-foot Joe's offer, but he does not say yes either. He buries his nose into the crook of my shoulder so hard it almost hurts.

The tugboats are waiting which means the freighter is close and setting up to turn which makes it dangerous now to be out on the river in the channel by the point. One-foot Joe says it takes a full eight miles for a freighter to stop, not at all like a car with brakes. One-foot Joe says, *You've got to understand, kid. The water always wins.* The tugboats wait and our father isn't moving.

One-foot Joe stands next to the truck with a hand in his pocket and his eyes nearly closed because the sun is bright. Then he says again, *Mack, you are going to need to make a move.* But my father doesn't move. He holds the back of my head which hurts from the hours in my V-bunk taking care of my younger sister Stel and because I'm try-ing to turn my head to watch the tugs and the river and the huge metal hull which has just now moved into view.

Then there is the sound that I know to be our engines turning over and starting up which is something you should not do unless you've blown the bilge. Our engines are Chryslers and they are brand-new. Our father buying them is what started the fights that ended with our mother going away. *You love this fucking boat more than you do your fucking family* which isn't exactly true. Our father does love the boat and the water and the bar where his band plays on Saturday night, and Stel and me can tell he is happy in the morning with his coffee, throwing bread to the gulls. But he loves us too which is why he pays Joe to watch us after school even though Joe says we are sweet and he'd do it for free. He loves us which is why he doesn't let us run when we could trip and fall and why he got so mad at the judge who wanted to take us away. And I like the boat except in the winter when I'm scared, and I love our father which is why I tell my younger sister Stel that we have got to be on our best behavior even though she doesn't much like the water and, more like our mother, would rather be running barefoot through a sprinkler on the lawn.

I am our father's first mate and I know the sound of our engines and I know too that it is a bad, bad idea to hit the river when a freighter is waiting to turn at Hennepin Point. So I squirm and I fight and I kick free of our father and the cab and the truck.

Stel is on the bow in her pajamas and she is not wearing a life-jacket which is very bad because she doesn't know the sidestroke and that's the stroke that One-foot Joe calls most important because it's how you save your energy. Stel is crying, I can tell, and she's scream-ing something awful but I can't hear exactly what she's saying. Our mother gets the starboard lines and throws them sloppy on the deck which she knows better than to do. Before she went away, she was our father's first mate and he taught her how to coil them right and proper. The man who mows the lawns is at the helm still without a shirt and he is laughing. And I am barefoot on gravel that's cutting hard the soles of my feet.

One-foot Joe is running now as best he can with his stump and his crutch, over the gravel and up the dock where he trips on a board and falls on his face. Our father doesn't move. His chin is on his chest so he doesn't see that Stel is crying and gripping the rail where she should not be when the boat is underway. Our mother waves.

The Lady L used to be the Lady Luck but our father sanded off the u-c-k when our mother moved away—*there are no lucky ladies.* He promised soon he'd paint the transom again, add an i-l-a which is me, his first mate, Lila.

Our father screams and hits the steering wheel hard with his hands and then with his head, and the tugboats move out to the buoy by the point which means the freighter is starting its turn. And One-foot Joe is on his knees, trying for his crutch, which has slipped into the bay. And finally Stel is screaming loud my name, but then our mother comes to the bow with binoculars. They are big and heavy. Stel is trying and she's trying hard, and she is so young and small and fragile. She gets them up to her eyes, but she's got them pointed the wrong way, an easy mistake when you're only the second mate. I'm crying hard and stamping my feet but there's nothing I can do. I know exactly what she sees because before our mother went away, I was a sloppy second mate. My younger sister Stel sees me, her older sister who made her a promise—she sees me, Lila, smaller through the lens, not bigger. Her older sister Lila, far away and getting smaller which is going to make her think that I won't be back.

THE HOUSE SLAVE

BY Rita Dove

The first horn lifts its arm over the dew-lit grass
and in the slave quarters there is a rustling—
children are bundled into aprons, cornbread

and water gourds grabbed, a salt pork breakfast taken.
I watch them driven into the vague before-dawn
while their mistress sleeps like an ivory toothpick

and Massa dreams of asses, rum and slave-funk.
I cannot fall asleep again. At the second horn,
the whip curls across the backs of the laggards—

sometimes my sister's voice, unmistaken, among them.
"Oh! pray," she cries. "Oh! pray!" Those days
I lie on my cot, shivering in the early heat,

and as the fields unfold to whiteness,
and they spill like bees among the fat flowers,
I weep. It is not yet daylight.

REPRIEVE

BY Claire Bateman

The same day the doctor confirmed my mother's pregnancy, he also informed her that she was carrying not one but two children—twins, one a human female, the other a pearl. "They are chemically incompatible," he said. "You must choose in favor of one, who will then absorb the other, or you will surely lose them both." Cruel dilemma for a woman who not only possessed a strong maternal instinct, but loved the beautiful and the mysterious as well! For the proverbial three days and three nights she pondered, unable to make up her mind. Finally, however, as if to register my own opinion, I gave a feeble kick, a gossamer flutter, and that decided her, so dutifully, though with considerable sorrow, she began an intense course of the balancing medicine the doctor gave her, and my sister the pearl gradually weakened, finally dissolving into me. Had she been the one with fishy little legs and arms—in other words, had *she* been human and *I* a pearl—no doubt she'd have done the same thing, and I wouldn't have begrudged her this feeble gesture toward self-preservation, so I'm certain she experienced no rancor as she felt herself begin to come apart.

Surely there are many aspects of my nature that can be explained only by her presence in my bloodstream—for instance, my acute sensitivity to sunlight; any true pearl would sell the very soul she doesn't have for five minutes of shade. There's nothing a pearl detests more than daylight—in fact, she goes into a kind of hysterical coma in sunshine, recovering from her swoon only in the safety of her long, black-velvet-lined box. I myself get migraines from glare, burn easily, and would, if permitted, permanently hibernate indoors. That's why all year round I wear enormous black sunglasses despite the ridicule of passersby. Also, like a pearl, I am mostly a loner, and I tend to surround myself with loners, just as each pearl pierced through by the same golden chain basks in the luminescence of the others even as she secretly believes she's the only one suspended there, and whines, "I'm so lonely."

As for differences between my sister and me—were you surprised when I mentioned that a pearl has no soul? It's true; you can test this for yourself—candle her like an egg, and all you'll find is a cool cloudiness; send X-rays through her with the most state-of-the-art lauegram, and all you'll see is that tell-tale hexagonal pattern of dots designating the crystalline structure; slice her in half, and all you'll discover is layer upon layer of aragonite, no true core at the center, only the original parasite or grain of sand, not a soul but an anomaly, an intrusion, though come to think of it, a human soul does feel to its bearer, that is, to me, not unlike an irritation, so maybe in this aspect too, we are more alike than different.

Very probably, then, I'm a pearl on the inside and a human on the outside, in which case my mother is *not,* as she has assumed all these years, guilty of my sister's death, for in choosing me she saved both of us, and thus, she can unshackle herself from the under-water rock where she has been doing penance all these years, her chin barely above the surface.

FROM MEMOIRS OF A DUTIFUL DAUGHTER

BY Simone de Beauvoir

WE CALLED HER POUPETTE; she was two and a half years younger than me. People said she took after Papa. She was fair-haired, and in the photographs taken during our childhood her blue eyes always appear to be filled with tears. Her birth had been a disappointment, because the whole family had been hoping for a boy; certainly no one ever held it against her for being a girl, but it is perhaps not altogether without significance that her cradle was the centre of regretful comment. Great pains were taken to treat us both with scrupulous fairness; we wore identical clothes, we nearly always went out together; we shared a single existence, though as the elder sister I did in fact enjoy certain advantages. I had my own room, which I shared with Louise, and I slept in a big bed, an imitation antique in carved wood over which hung a reproduction of Murillo's *Assumption of the Blessed Virgin*. A cot was set up for my sister in a narrow corridor. While Papa was undergoing his army training, it was I who accompanied Mama when she went to see him. Relegated to a secondary position, the "little one" felt almost superfluous. I had been a new experience for my parents: my sister found it much more difficult to surprise and astonish them; I had never been compared with anyone: she was always being compared with me. At the Cours Désir the ladies in charge made a habit of holding up the older children as examples to the younger ones; whatever Poupette might do, and however well she might do it, the passing of time and the sublimation of a legend all contributed to the idea that I had done everything much better. No amount of effort and success was sufficient to break through that impenetrable barrier. The victim of some obscure malediction, she was hurt and perplexed by her situation, and often in the evening she would sit crying on her little chair. She was accused of having a sulky disposition; one more inferiority she had to put up with. She might have taken a thorough dislike to me, but paradoxically she only felt sure of herself when she was with me. Comfortably settled in my part of elder sister, I plumed myself only on the superiority accorded to my greater age; I thought Poupette was remarkably bright for her years; I accepted her for what she was—someone like myself, only a little younger; she was grateful for my approval, and responded to it with absolute devotion. She was my liegeman, my *alter ego,* my double; we could not do without one another.

I was sorry for children who had no brother or sister; solitary amusements seemed insipid to me; no better than a means of killing time. But when there were two, hopscotch or a ball game were adventurous undertakings, and bowling hoops an exciting competition. Even when I was just doing transfers or daubing a catalogue with water-colours I felt the need of an associate. Collaborating and vying with one another, we each found a purpose in our work that saved it from all gratuitousness. The games I was fondest of were those in which I assumed another character; and in these I had to have an accomplice. We hadn't many toys; our parents used to lock away the nicest ones—the leaping tiger and the elephant that could stand on his hind legs; they would occasionally bring them out to show to admiring guests. I didn't mind. I was flattered to possess objects which could amuse grown-ups; and I loved them because they were precious: familiarity would have bred contempt. In any case the rest of our playthings—grocer's shop, kitchen utensils, nurse's outfit—gave very little encouragement to the imagination. A partner was absolutely essential to me if I was to bring my imaginary stories to life.

A great number of the anecdotes and situations which we dramatized were, we realized, rather banal; the presence of the grown-ups did not disturb us when we were selling hats or defying the Boche's artillery fire. But other scenarios, the ones we liked best, required to be performed in secret. They were, on the surface, perfectly innocent, but, in sublimating the adventure of our childhood, or anticipating the future, they drew upon something secret and intimate within us which would not bear the searching light of adult gazes. I shall speak later of those games which, from my point of view, were the most significant. In fact, I was always the one who expressed myself through them; I imposed them upon my sister, assigning her the minor roles which she accepted with complete docility. At that evening hour when the stillness, the dark weight, and the tedium of our middle-class domesticity began to invade the hall, I would unleash my fantasms; we would make them materialize with great gestures and copious speeches, and sometimes, spellbound by our play, we succeeded in taking off from the earth and leaving it far behind until an imperious voice suddenly brought us back to reality. Next day we would start all over again. "We'll play *you know what*," we would whisper to each other as we prepared for bed. The day would come when a certain theme, worked over too long, would no longer have the power to inspire us; then we would choose another, to which we would remain faithful for a few hours or even for weeks.

I owe a great debt to my sister for helping me to externalize many of my dreams in play: she also helped me to save my daily life from silence; through her I got into the habit of wanting to communicate with people. When she was not there I hovered between two extremes:

words were either insignificant noises which I made with my mouth, or, whenever I addressed my parents, they became deeds of the utmost gravity; but when Poupette and I talked together, words had a meaning yet did not weigh too heavily upon us. I never knew with her the pleasure of sharing or exchanging things, because we always held everything in common; but as we recounted to one another the day's incidents and emotions, they took on added interest and importance. There was nothing wrong in what we told one another; nevertheless, because of the importance we both attached to our conversations, they created a bond between us which isolated us from the grown-ups; when we were together, we had our own secret garden.

We found this arrangement very useful. The traditions of our family compelled us to take part in a large number of duty visits, especially around the New Year; we had to attend interminable family dinners with aunts and first cousins removed to the hundredth degree, and pay visits to decrepit old ladies. We often found release from boredom by running into the hall and playing at "you know what." In summer, Papa was very keen on organizing expeditions to the woods at Chaville or Meudon; the only means we had of enlivening the boredom of these long walks was our private chatter; we would make plans and recall all the things that had happened to us in the past; Poupette would ask me questions; I would relate episodes from French or Roman history, or stories which I made up myself.

What I appreciated most in our relationship was that I had a real hold over her. The grown-ups had me at their mercy. If I demanded praise from them, it was still up to them to decide whether to praise me or not. Certain aspects of my behaviour seemed to have an immediate effect upon my mother, an effect which had not the slightest connexion with what I had intended. But between my sister and myself things happened naturally. We would disagree, she would cry, I would become cross, and we would hurl the supreme insult at one another: "You *fool!*" and then we'd make it up. Her tears were real, and if she laughed at one of my jokes, I knew she wasn't trying to humour me. She alone endowed me with authority; adults sometimes gave into me: she obeyed me.

One of the most durable bonds that bound us together was that which exists between master and pupil. I loved studying so much that I found teaching enthralling. Playing at school with my dolls did not satisfy me at all: I didn't just want to go through the motions of teaching: I really wanted to pass on the knowledge I had acquired.

Teaching my sister to read, write, and count gave me, from the age of six onwards, a sense of pride in my own efficiency. I liked scrawling phrases or pictures over sheets of paper: but in doing so I was only creating imitation objects. When I started to change ignorance into knowledge, when I started to impress truths upon a virgin mind, I felt I was at last creating something real. I was not just imitating grown-ups; I was on their level, and my success had nothing to do with their good pleasure. It satisfied in me an aspiration that was more than mere vanity. Until then, I had contented myself with responding dutifully to the care that was lavished upon me: but now, for the first time, I, too, was being of service to someone. I was breaking away from the passivity of childhood and entering the great human circle in which everyone is useful to everyone else. Since I had started working seriously time no longer fled away, but left its mark on me: by sharing my knowledge with another, I was fixing time on another's memory, and so making it doubly secure.

※

Thanks to my sister I was asserting my right to personal freedom; she was my accomplice, my subject, my creature. It is plain that I only thought of her as being "the same, but different," which is one way of claiming one's pre-eminence. Without ever formulating it in so many words, I assumed that my parents accepted this hierarchy, and that I was their favourite. My room gave on to the corridor where my sister slept and at the end of which was my father's study; from my bed I could hear my father talking to my mother in the evenings, and this peaceful murmur often lulled me to sleep. But one evening my heart almost stopped beating; in a calm voice which held barely a trace of curiosity, Mama asked: "Which of the two do you like best?" I waited for Papa to say my name, but he hesitated for a moment which seemed to me like an eternity: "Simone is more serious-minded, but Poupette is so affectionate. . . ." They went on weighing the pros and the cons of our case, speaking their inmost thoughts quite freely; finally they agreed that they loved us both equally well: it was just like what you read in books about wise parents whose love is the same for all their children. Nevertheless I felt a certain resent-ment. I could not have borne it if one of them had preferred my sis-ter to myself; if I was resigned to enjoying an equal share of their affection, it was because I felt that it was to my advantage to do so. But I was older, wiser, and more experienced than my sister: if my parents felt an equal affection for us both, then at least I was entitled to more consideration from them; they ought to feel how much closer I was to their maturity than my sister.

IDELLA'S DRESS

BY Beverly Jensen

BAY CHALEUR, NEW BRUNSWICK (JULY 1924)

Idella was the only one around the house. Dalton was in the barn, Dad had gone off somewhere, back into the field probably, and Avis was picking blueberries. The highbushers by the edge of the pasture had ripened in these last few days of July heat, and she had set out this morning to get them before the Doncaster boys found them.

Idella would have liked to have gone too. Just to get out. But she had to stay and scrub Dad's and Dalton's work clothes. They were full of those "goddamned burr things" as Dad called them. "They'd scrape the skin right off a bull's ass," he'd said, throwing them in a pile at her feet. "Here, Della, clean these damned things." Never a please. Never a thank you.

Idella stood now at the stove, boiling up water. It was too hot to be boiling anything, let alone the likes of this. The clothes reeked of manure and mud. She'd had to pick through them, pulling out the spiny prickles and thorns. Her fingers were sore from the sharp points. She had gotten a stick from the edge of the woods out the back of the house, and she lowered the stinking mass of clothing into the big tin wash tub, the one they took their baths in. When the kettle of water was boiling, she lifted it off the stove, wrapping her skirt around the hot wire handle, and held the kettle as high as she could with both her hands. Turning her face away, she poured the water down over the clothes and stirred them with the stick. Steam rose up around her and made her hair all stringy. She kept trying to brush back strands with the top of her shoulder. Her nose itched, and she gagged from the heavy smell of the steaming manure.

There is no end to it, she thought, the things to be done. She was sixteen years old next week and she'd never gotten to be a child, not one day in her life since Mother died. Idella carried the empty kettle over to the water pump and filled it again. "This'll take half the day," she muttered. "They'll put 'em on and go right back out into it."

It was then that she heard the mailman's car come puttering down the road toward the house. Most days he kept on going past the farm, but today he was turning in. She could tell by the nearness of the sound. Maybe there was something for her. Maybe Dad got her something for her birthday. He'd given Bossy to Avis two years ago. Twelve years old and she got a cow for her birthday. Avis was always out there in the barn bothering the poor thing. A cow. That's about the last thing on this earth that Idella needed—something else to take care of.

The Sears catalog might be coming any time now—maybe that was it. Idella could think of no better way to spend an afternoon than looking through its pages and making up orders in her head.

The mailman's car was near the house now. She put down the heavy kettle and ran to the open door. Mr. McPhee, the only mailman she'd ever known, was making a cloud of dust right up to the door with his old roadster. It was one of the few cars around, and everybody knew the sound of the motor.

"Hey there, young lady," he called as he yanked the car to an abrupt stop, leaving the motor running. "You Hillock girls get taller and skinnier every time I see one of you. I've got a package here. It's got 'Idella Hillock' written on it. Should I send it back?"

He made this joke every time he brought something special. It might be clothes from Aunt Francie! He smiled through his open window, purposely making her wait a little. Men thought teasing was so funny.

"Well," he said finally, "if you're sure you want it." He reached to the back seat and lifted up a large brown box. "Something for the lady of the house. I got to open the door here just to get it out."

Idella walked up to the car door, wiping her hands in her skirt. She wanted to reach in and just grab the box. "Here you go, young lady."

It was Aunt Francie's beautiful script across the package, no question. Idella held the box so tightly that the corners pushed at the insides of her elbows.

"Thank you, Mr. McPhee."

"How's your Dad? What's Bill Hillock been up to? No good, I suppose?"

"He's out working the field today."

"Tell him I'll see him tonight." The men played cards on Saturday nights, sitting around the table and drinking. They played at their house because there was no woman to shush them and make them go home. "I'm going to whip the pants off him. Tell him to wear two pair."

"I'll tell him. Bye, Mr. McPhee."

Idella walked right past the stinking tub of work clothes, past the filled kettle of cold water she'd left on the floor. She paid no heed to the stove, its fire pouring heat into the stifling July air. She walked up the stairs and into the bedroom that she shared with Avis, closing the door behind her with a foot. A fly, embedded in the folds of a curtain, buzzed in response to the jolt. Tippie, the Doncaster dog, barked. Idella went to her open window and looked out. No one was coming in from the field or the woods. Dalton was clanging away on something in the barn. He never came into the house anyway unless it was supper.

She sat on her bed and stared at the script. Even her name, "Idella," looked pretty when Aunt Francie wrote it. Her fingers found the edge of the brown paper and pulled it off in shreds.

The box's flaps fell open. She lifted back tissue paper with her fingertips. It was something blue, a deep gray blue. There was a collar, and tiny black buttons. Idella stood and unfurled a dress of the most wonderful material and shape and color. She held it at arm's length. It had velvet on the collar and cuffs. Black velvet! And the waistline was low, below the hips, like Idella had only seen in catalogs. And it was short! It was above the ankle, she could tell just by looking. It was beyond beautiful.

Holding the dress by her fingertips she walked up close to the dresser that had been her mother's and stood before the mirror. She could only see herself from the waist up. A pock in the mirror distorted the line of the shoulder. Avis had done that, made that hole, flinging her shoe off one night. Always fooling around. There'd been a stone in her shoe and it had flown out and pinged the mirror, leaving a small hole in one corner. You could never have anything nice.

"Yoohoo! Della!" Avis. She was coming back from picking. "Della, come help me drag these damn buckets." She was coming across the field, her mouth preceding her as usual.

"Quit your yelling!" Idella called through the open window. Then she laid the dress across her bed and carefully folded it. She placed it under the tissue paper. There was a note lying in the box, a letter from Aunt Francie that she hadn't seen. Idella slipped it into her apron pocket.

"Della! Where are you?" Avis was in the kitchen. "I left a bucket in the field. My arm's about pulled out by its roots."

"Hold your horses!" Idella opened the door enough to call down to her and then closed it again. She slid the box as far back under the bed as she could. Avis was tromping up the stairs.

She opened the door. "What the hell have you been up to?" Avis surveyed the room. She was always so suspicious, afraid she'd get left out of something. But Idella wasn't going to show her the package from Aunt Francie till she was good and ready.

"Come on," Idella said, pushing Avis out of the room with her, "let's go see what the poor little birdie picked."

※

Idella finished stewing the clothes and washed them out, and then she scrubbed the tub they'd been in. When she was finally finished, she walked over to the table where Avis sat sorting through the blueberries. There were more leaves and sticks and bad ones than if Idella had done the picking.

"Wouldn't those damn Doncasters love to've found these," Avis crowed. "They'd have stood like bears on their hind legs and eaten 'em off the branches." Avis kept her head bent over the bucket. She looked up at Idella, with only her eyes moving. "I thought maybe we could make some pies with these berries. It's poker night, and I thought I could make the men some pies. As a surprise." Idella watched as Avis pursed up her lips and started speaking in her baby-doll voice. It was the only way that Avis could ask for help from anyone, by making a joke. "I could make a berry pie if Mama bird would help her poor little baby sister."

"All right." Idella sighed. She sat down next to Avis and started picking out leaves. "I'll help you make the dough. And I'll help you to measure. If I don't, you'll use all my sugar."

"I'll be good, Della. I promise." Avis reached an arm around and stuck a blueberry into Idella's ear. "Thank you, Mama bird."

"Don't call me that. Avis, so help me, if you start acting up, I won't do a thing to help you."

Avis took a handful of berries, stood up, and dropped them down the front of her dress.

"Jesus, Avis," Idella said, "you're not fit to live in a house. We should keep you tied up out in the barn with that cow."

Avis crawled under the table and rounded up the scattered berries. Idella knew that she was excited. Avis loved poker nights. She was a favorite among the men. They were neighbors, other farmers, and Dad showed her off. She'd sit on Dad's lap like the cat who ate the canary, and watch them play by the hour. They teased her and tried to get her to tell Dad's hands, but she had a face that revealed nothing when she didn't want it to, and a mouth on her that would say anything. The men egged her on something terrible, and she was always after them to give her sips of whiskey.

Idella made herself scarce on these evenings. She'd sneak up to the bedroom as soon as she could. The men made her self-conscious. They started out nice. Most of them she'd known all her life. But the later it got, the rowdier they were.

Dad would always embarrass her. "When you going to get some meat on your bones?" he'd say to her, in front of everyone. "I've got me some goddamned stick figures for daughters." Then he'd reach over and slap her on the behind. He laughed when he said it, but it was his mean sort of laugh, his whiskey laugh. It shamed Idella something terrible.

※

All afternoon the two sisters worked on the pies. Idella knew she wouldn't be alone till evening. Dad and Dalton stayed out in the fields. There was much rolling of pins and flicking of aprons, but in the end there were three grand pies and a patchwork tart steaming on the windowsill in the summer heat.

When Dad came in, Idella had supper on the table as usual. He was in a good mood—he always was on poker night. "No dessert tonight," Avis announced before he'd even set down in his chair. "There was no time." It was impossible to ignore the sweet smell of blueberries and cinnamon that hung in the sticky evening air.

Avis had insisted on hiding the pies on the wooden bench behind the stove. She was going to surprise the poker players when they all got seated at the table. She didn't even want Idella to be there, she said, she wanted to do it all herself. That was fine. Idella didn't need to show anyone that she could make pies.

"Damn," Dad said, looking Avis's floury figure up and down, "I'd have sworn you were going out to pick berries. I was hoping for pie."

"Nope," Avis said. "Those damn Doncaster boys must've found 'em. There was nothing there but big footprints. Not one goddamned berry in the whole place."

"Well that's too bad. We'll have to speak to Jim tonight when he comes. Tell him to shoot those boys." He winked at Idella.

Avis laughed. "That'd be good. Then next year I'll pick 'em."

"What's that smell I'm smelling? It smells like horse manure. You smell it Idella?"

"Nope."

"How about you, Dalton? You smell it?"

Dalton kept on eating, barely lifting his head from over his plate. He was fixing to leave as soon as supper was over. He never joined Dad's poker games. "Nope," he said. "Nothing."

"Avis-Mavis puddin' and pie, don't you smell anything?"

"Nope." She started giggling and looked down at her hands. "Just Della's feet." She could barely get the words out for laughing—they came out in a snort.

"Jesus, Avis," Idella said, standing to clear the table. "There's no need to make fun of me."

"You're a fresh one, Avis-Mavis, puddin' and pie." Dad always took to her foolishness, Idella thought. She got away with murder. "You just be sure that tonight you don't kiss the boys and make them cry."

Idella felt like she'd been waiting to be alone for days. "Come on, Avis, help me wash the dishes. They're going to be here soon and I want to go upstairs and read."

※

Idella was alone in the bedroom. She had been standing and sitting in her beautiful blue dress for more than an hour, observing her shadow's silhouette stretch silently across the flowered wallpaper and up to the ceiling. The poker game roared below. She had combed and pinned and parted her hair in different ways. She had watched herself in the mirror and in the reflected lamplight of the bedroom window.

The men had all come. They were settled with their bottles and their glasses around the kitchen table. Avis had uncovered her pies to a roar of applause. The men had teased her mercilessly and praised her nonstop. Avis was in her element. The noise would rise up to the bedroom in walloping bursts and then settle down to the quiet shuffles and flicks of cards being dealt, of glasses being set heavily on the table. Idella could hear Avis's laugh getting louder and rowdier with the rest of them, as the evening wore on.

Idella went to the bottom of her closet and felt for her Sunday shoes. She reached down into the toes till she found the lipstick she'd been hiding since she'd discovered it going through her mother's trunk.

In the yellow light she stood up close to the mirror and uncapped the lipstick. It had a wonderful perfume smell. The rounded end had been worn down by her mother's lips. Idella leaned in to the mirror and applied the lipstick with trembling fingers. It looked dark and uneven but she was afraid to try to fix it. She daubed little streaks on each cheek, like she'd seen Mrs. Doncaster do, and rubbed them in with her palm.

Idella looked startling, even to herself, in the mirror. She wasn't sure if she was pretty, she couldn't say, but she did look different. The straight drop of the dress's loose bodice was broken by the small points of her breasts. She'd never worn anything before that showed them.

"Della!" Dad's voice broke her dreamy solitude. "Della, get the hell down here!" Idella's chest tightened like it had been suddenly bound. "Della! Get down here and slice us another pie. We're all of us pie-eyed!" The men laughed. She could hear Avis cackling.

"Come down here, Della," Dad roared. "We need you to wait on Queen Avis. She can't be cutting her own pies. Get your skinny ass down here."

"I'll be there in a minute!" Idella called through the closed door. It made her so mad—that calling and yelling and loudness. There was no need for it. At the end of poker nights he always got mean. He treated her like she was a belonging, something he owned, like a horse or a cow.

"Della, get your ass down here!" That was Avis calling. That was Avis! Her voice had an edge to it. Whiskey.

"That little bitch," Idella whispered. "I showed her how to make the goddamned pies." She went to the mirror, brushed her hair off her face, and refastened it with the barrette that Mrs. Doncaster had given her. "I won't stoop my shoulders," she said to her reflection.

"Della! Get your ass down here!" That wasn't even Dad. That was one of the men talking to her like that.

The louder they got, the more deliberately she prepared herself. "I'm coming!" she shouted, to stop their yelling. They were down there banging their glasses on the table, the bastards. Idella opened her door and stepped out into the hall. "Quit yelling. I'm coming."

She stopped at the top of the stairs. The cigarette smoke made her eyes water. The room below was hazy with it. She started to come down slowly, keeping her back straight, not sure of where to put her hands. One by one the men saw her. One by one their voices stopped.

"La-dee-da!" a loud voice called when she reached the bottom step. "Will you look at what's come down the steps." Someone whistled. "Bill Hillock, you been holdin' out on us. Look at what you've been hiding." For a moment, there was silence.

"Well, I'll be damned," Dad whispered under his breath. He put his cards face down on the table and pushed Avis off his lap. He stood, his face flushed from whiskey, watching Idella. His voice got soft. "Don't you look pretty, Idella. Don't you look pretty. Avis, look at your pretty sister."

"She turned into a woman, Bill, when you wasn't looking."

Idella thought that was Mr. McPhee's voice. She stood frozen. The lipstick felt strange and waxy. She forced herself to look into the room, to see each face. She looked at Avis last.

"Where'd you get that dress?" Avis was staring hard. Her voice was low and queer. "Where did you get that dress?" Idella averted her eyes. She turned back to Dad's flushed face.

"I got me a princess I been raising," he said. "She's even got titties on her. Will you look at that." Idella felt her cheeks go hot.

One of the men stood up. "Let's drink to the lady," he said. "Let's drink to Bill's Idella."

All the men stood, scraping back their chairs. They raised their glasses. "To Idella," they said.

There was a loud crash. "What the hell?" Dad turned behind him. Avis stood in front of the stove. Dark gobs of pie-filling were spewed across the wooden floor. Avis scooped a glossy handful and rushed at Idella. She smeared it across the front of the blue dress. "Where did you get it? Where did you get that dress?" She was clawing at Idella. "Where did you get it?"

"Damn you!" Idella cried, untangling the clutching fists. "Damn you, Avis. Leave me be!" She got hold of Avis's wrists and squeezed them hard.

"You whore!" Avis screamed. "You're nothing but a whore!" Idella thrust the writhing figure from her. Dad came up behind and pulled Avis away, kicking. "Whore!" Avis screamed.

Idella was shaking. She stood up and looked out into the room of men, her arms covering the smeared dress. Her eyes bored through the smoke to the stunned faces. "Damn you," she said in a low voice. "Damn all of you in this godforsaken place." She turned and ran up the steps into her room. She crouched behind the closed door, jamming her fists over her wretched mouth. Avis's wails, coming now in waves, pierced the floorboards. They matched Idella's own hopeless sobs.

※

A week later, Avis's dress came. Aunt Francie's note had said it would. She'd been waiting on an order of lace. The mailman drove up with the box on the seat next to him. Aunt Francie's writing was unmistakable. Mr. McPhee didn't tease Idella when she came to get it from him. He handed it to her with a sorry smile and said that he hoped she was feeling better.

She walked listlessly back into the house and up the stairs to the bedroom. She put the box on Avis's bed and left. She slammed the door behind her, even though it was still hot and the open door let air move through the house a little.

Avis's dress was forest green with brown tortoise buttons and fancy stitching. The lace was on the collar and at the edge of the cuffs. It was beautiful. But it never got worn, not even once.

FROM THE LIARS' CLUB
BY Mary Karr

WHEN WE HIT PORT ARTHUR, TEXAS, Mother started to sing under her breath. It was an old song she liked to play on our turntable when she was drinking. She had a scratchy recording of Peggy Lee or Della Reese, one of those whiskey-voiced lounge singers:

> *Oh the shark has zippy teeth, dear,*
> *And he shows them pearly white.*
> *Just a jack knife has his teeth, dear,*
> *And he keeps them out of sight...*

Nobody in my family can sing a note. The few times we went to church with the neighbors, Lecia and I had the good sense to lip-synch the hymns so it wouldn't be too noticeable. My mother, too, had a bad voice—wavery and vague. She was a natural alto who'd probably been nagged into the higher ranges by overfeminine choir teachers. So she sang the wrong words in a ragged soprano under her breath that morning, whispery and high. The car seemed to pick up speed as she sang, and the fear that had been nuzzling around my solar plexus all morning started to get real definite when I saw, dead ahead of us, the gray steel girders of the Orange Bridge.

The Orange Bridge at that time was said to be the highest bridge in the country. Your ears popped when you drove over it. The engineers had built it that tall so that even tugs shoving oil platforms with full-sized derricks on them could pass under with room to spare. The Sabine River it ran over wasn't very wide, so the bridge had easily the sharpest incline of any I've ever crossed.

Not surprisingly, this was the scene of a suicide every year or so. Jilted suitors and bankrupt oilmen favored it. Those who jumped from the highest point of the bridge broke every bone in their bodies. I remember Mother reading this fact out loud from the paper one time, then saying that women tended to gas themselves or take sleeping pills—things that didn't mess them up on the outside so much. She liked to quote James Dean about leaving a beautiful corpse.

Anyway, it was this bridge that the car bumped onto with Mother singing the very scariest part of "Mack the Knife." She sang it very whispery, like a lullaby:

> When the shark bites with his teeth, dear,
> Scarlet billows start to spread. . . .

The car tipped way back when we mounted the bridge. It felt sort of like the long climb a roller coaster will start before its deep fall. Mother's singing immediately got drowned out by the steel webbing under the tires that made the whole car shimmy. At the same time— impossibly enough—we seemed to be going faster.

Lecia contends that at this point I started screaming, and that my screaming prompted Mother to wheel around and start grabbing at me, which caused what happened next. (Were Lecia writing this memoir, I would appear in one of only three guises: sobbing hysterically, wetting my pants in a deliberately inconvenient way, or biting somebody, usually her, with no provocation.)

I don't recall that Mother reached around to grab at me at all. And I flatly deny screaming. But despite my old trick of making my stomach into a rock, I did get carsick. The bile started rising in my throat the second we mounted the bridge, which involved the car flying over a metal rise that felt like a ski jump. We landed with a jolt and then fishtailed a little.

I knew right away that I was going to throw up. Still, I tried locking down my belly the way I had on the Tilt-A-Whirl. I squinched my eyes shut. I bore down on myself inside. But the rolling in my stomach wouldn't let me get ahold of it. I wouldn't have opened my window on a dare. And I sure didn't want to ask Mother to pull over mid-bridge. Lecia was in charge of all Mother-negotiations that day anyway, and she had opted for the same tooth-grinding silence we'd all fallen into. Even though she was normally devout about watching the speedometer and nagging Mother to slow down (or, conversely, Daddy to speed up), she kept her lip zipped that morning. Anyway, at the point when I felt the Cheerios start to rise in my throat, I just ducked my head, pulled the neck of my damp T-shirt over my nose and away from my body a little, and barfed down my shirt front. It was very warm sliding down my chest under the wet shirt, and it smelled like sour milk.

Mother responded to this not at all. Neither did Grandma, who had a nose like a bloodhound but had turned into some kind of mannequin. Really, she might have been carved from Ivory soap for all the color she had. Lecia would normally have seized the opportunity to whack me for being so gross. Maybe I even wanted whacking, at that point. Surely I wanted to break the bubble of quiet. But Lecia just tied her red bandanna around her nose like a bank robber and shot me a sideways look. I knew then it was one of Mother's worst days, when my horking down my own shirt didn't warrant a word from anybody. Lecia watched Mother, who watched some bleary semblance of road.

Anyway, that's the last thing I remember before the crash— Lecia's bandanna drawn over her nose.

Then for some reason I still don't understand, the car went into a three-hundred-and-sixty-degree spin. I don't know if this was accidental or deliberate on Mother's part. As I said before, Lecia holds that I was wailing and Mother was turning around to swat at me. I do remember seeing Mother turn the wheel sharply to the left, which forced the car into a spin. After a long time whirling around, I saw the railing on the other side of the bridge rush forward. Then for an instant, we were launched in the air. Our tires just left the bridge altogether. The car jumped the raised pedestrian walkway and flew toward the top rung of the railing. (People never walked over, of course, but workers hung platforms off it for painting and repairs.) I saw the rail flying laterally at us. Then the car crunched to a stop. By this time I was screaming and crying.

Amazingly enough, the crash just crumpled the front fender and took out the right headlight. Nobody seemed that rattled about what happened but me. Mother didn't even get out to inspect the damage. Grandma just hunkered more deeply over her lace. Mother said, "Everybody all right!" but in a cheery voice, like a camp counselor after a long hike. She didn't even turn around when she said it. In the mirror her teeth were showing in a scary smile.

I was really howling by this time. The car got thrown in reverse, and we unpried ourselves from the rail. We bounced off the opposite walkway backward and headed down the slope, gaining speed.

Lecia slid over about this time and laced her fingers with mine, for which kindness I remain grateful. I can't have smelled very good. Plus I was blubbering. Big tusks of snot were hanging out of my nose. Anyway, she just took my big hand in her big hands. (We both have hands perfect only for fieldwork and volleyball.) I always felt safe when she did that. Usually it shut me up, too, but this time I whispered why was Mother trying to kill us and was she really going stark crazy. Lecia just said to pipe down, that we'd be at Auntie's house in twenty minutes and everything would be okay then.

II

SISTER–SISTER

THE EVE OF THE SPIRIT FESTIVAL
BY Lan Samantha Chang

AFTER THE BUDDHIST CEREMONY, when our mother's spirit had been chanted to a safe passage and her body cremated, Emily and I sat silently on our living room carpet. She held me in her arms; her long hair stuck to our wet faces. We sat as stiffly as temple gods except for the angry thump of my sister's heart against my cheek.

Finally she spoke. "It's Baba's fault," she said. "The American doctors would have fixed her."

I was six years old—I only knew that our father and mother had decided against an operation. And I had privately agreed, imagining the doctors tearing a hole in her body. As I thought of this, I felt a sudden sob pass through me.

"Don't cry, Baby," Emily whispered. "You're okay." I felt my tears dry to salt, my throat lock shut.

Then our father walked into the room.

He and Emily had grown close in the past few months. Emily was eleven, old enough to come along on his trips to the hospital. I had often stood in the neighbor's window and watched them leave for visiting hours, Emily's mittened hand tucked into his.

But now my sister refused to acknowledge him. She pushed the back of my head to turn me away from him also.

"First daughter—" he began.

"Go away, Baba," Emily said. Her voice shook. The evening sun glowed garnet red through the dark tent of her hair.

"You told me she would get better," I heard her say. "Now you're burning paper money for her ghost. What good will that do?"

"I am sorry," Baba said.

"I don't care."

Her voice burned. I squirmed beneath her hand, but she wouldn't let me look. It was something between her and Baba. I watched his black wingtip shoes retreat to the door. When he had gone, Emily let go of me. I sat up and looked at her; something had changed. Not in the lovely outlines of her face—our mother's face—but in her eyes, shadow-black, lost in unforgiveness.

※

They say the dead return to us. But we never saw our mother again, though we kept a kind of emptiness waiting in case she might come back. I listened always, seeking her voice, the lost thread of a conversation I'd been too young to have with her. I did not dare mention her to Emily. Since I could remember, my sister had kept her most powerful feelings private, sealed away. She rarely mentioned our mother, and soon my memories faded. I could not picture her. I saw only Emily's angry face, the late sun streaking red through her dark hair.

After the traditional forty-nine day mourning period, Baba did not set foot in the Buddhist temple. It was as if he had listened to Emily: what good did it do? Instead he focused on earthly ambitions, his research at the lab.

At that time he aspired beyond the position of lab instructor to the rank of associate professor, and he often invited his American colleagues over for "drinks." Emily and I were recruited to help with the preparations and serving. As we went about our tasks, we would sometimes catch a glimpse of our father, standing in the corner, watching the American men and studying to become one.

But he couldn't get it right—our parties had an air of cultural confusion. We served potato chips on lacquered trays; Chinese landscapes bumped against watercolors of the Statue of Liberty, the Empire State Building.

Nor were Emily or I capable of helping him. I was still a child, and Emily said she did not care. Since my mother's death, she had rejected anything he held dear. She refused to study chemistry and spoke in American slang. Her rebellion puzzled me, it seemed so vehement and so arbitrary.

Now she stalked through the living room, platform shoes thudding on the carpet. "I hate this," she said, fiercely ripping another rag from a pair of old pajama bottoms. "Entertaining these jerks is a waste of time."

Some chemists from Texas were visiting his department and he had invited them over for cocktails.

"I can finish it," I said. "You just need to do the parts I can't reach."

"It's not the dusting," she said. "It's the way he acts around them. 'Herro, herro! Hi Blad, hi Warry! Let me take your coat! Howsa Giants game?'" she mimicked, in a voice that made me wince, a voice alive with cruelty and pain. "If he were smart he wouldn't invite people over on football afternoons in the first place."

"What do you mean?" I asked, startled. Brad Delmonte was our father's boss. I had noticed Baba reading the sports pages that morning—something he rarely did.

"Oh, forget it," Emily said. I felt as if she and I were utterly separate. Then she smiled. "You've got oil on your glasses, Claudia."

89

Baba walked in carrying two bottles of wine. "They should arrive in half an hour," he said, looking at his watch. "They won't be early. Americans are never early."

Emily looked away. "I'm going to Jodie's house," she said.

Baba frowned and straightened his tie. "I want you to stay while they're here. We might need something from the kitchen."

"Claudia can get it for them."

"She's barely tall enough to reach the cabinets."

Emily stood and clenched her dustcloth. "I don't care," she said. "I hate meeting the people you have over."

"They're successful American scientists. You'd be better off with them instead of running around with your teenage friends, these sloppy kids, these rich white kids who dress like beggars."

"You're nuts, Dad," Emily said—she had begun addressing him the way an American child does. "You're nuts if you think these bosses of yours are ever going to do anything for you or any of us." And she threw her dustcloth, hard, into our New York Giants wastebasket.

"Speak to me with respect."

"You don't deserve it!"

"You are staying in this apartment! That is an order!"

"I wish you'd died instead of Mama!" Emily cried. She darted past our father, her long braid flying behind her. He stared at her, his expression oddly slack, the way it had been in the weeks after the funeral. He stepped toward her, reached hesitantly at her flying braid, but she turned and saw him, cried out as if he had struck her, and ran out of the room. His hands dropped to his sides.

Emily refused to leave our bedroom. Otherwise that party was like so many others. The guests arrived late and left early. They talked about buying new cars and the Dallas Cowboys. I served pretzels and salted nuts.

Baba walked around emptying ashtrays and refilling drinks. I noticed that the other men also wore vests and ties, but that the uniform looked somehow different on my slighter, darker father.

"Cute little daughter you have there," said Baba's boss. He was a large bearded smoker with a sandy voice. He didn't bend down to look at me or the ashtray that I raised toward his big square hand.

I went into our room and found Emily sitting on one of our unmade twin beds. It was dusk. Through the window I could see that the dull winter sun had almost disappeared. I sat next to her on the bed. Until that day, I think, it was Emily who took care of me and not the other way around.

After a minute, she spoke. "I'm going to leave," she said. "As soon as I turn eighteen, I'm going to leave home and never come back!" She burst into tears. I reached for her shoulder but her thin, heaving body frightened me. She seemed too grown up to be comforted. I thought about the breasts swelling beneath her sweater. Her body had become a foreign place.

※

Perhaps Emily had warned me that she would someday leave in order to start me off on my own. I found myself avoiding her, as though her impending desertion would matter less if I deserted her first. I discovered a place to hide while she and my father fought, in the living room behind a painted screen. I would read a novel or look out the window. Sometimes they forgot about me—from the next room I would hear one of them break off an argument and say, "Where did Claudia go?" "I don't know," the other would reply. After a silence, they would start again.

One of these fights stands out in my memory. I must have been ten or eleven years old. It was the fourteenth day of the seventh lunar month: the eve of Guijie, the Chinese Spirit Festival, when the living are required to appease and provide for the ghosts of their ancestors. To the believing, the earth was thick with gathering spirits; it was safest to stay indoors and burn incense.

I seldom thought about the Chinese calendar, but every year on Guijie I wondered about my mother's ghost. Where was it? Would it still recognize me? How would I know when I saw it? I wanted to ask Baba, but I didn't dare. Baba had an odd attitude toward Guijie. On one hand, he had eschewed all Chinese customs since my mother's death. He was a scientist, he said; he scorned the traditional tales of unsatisfied spirits roaming the earth.

But I cannot remember a time when I was not made aware, in some way, of Guijie's fluctuating lunar date. That year the eve of the Spirit Festival fell on a Thursday, usually his night out with the men from his department. Emily and I waited for him to leave but he sat on the couch, calmly reading the *New York Times.*

I finished drying the dishes. Emily began to fidget. She had a date that night and had counted on my father's absence. She spent half an hour washing and combing her hair, trying to make up her mind. Finally she asked me to give her a trim. I knew she'd decided to go out.

"Just a little," she said. "The ends are scraggly." We spread some newspapers on the living room floor. Emily stood in the middle of the papers with her hair combed down her back, thick and glossy, black as ink. It hadn't really been cut since she was born. Since my mother's death I had taken over the task of giving it a periodic touch-up.

I hovered behind her with the shears, searching for the scraggly ends, but there were none.

My father looked up from his newspaper. "What are you doing that for? You can't go out tonight," he said.

"I have a date!"

My father put down his newspaper. I threw the shears onto a chair and fled to my refuge behind the screen.

Through a slit over the hinge I caught a glimpse of Emily near the foyer, slender in her denim jacket, her black hair flooding down her back, her delicate features contorted with anger. My father's hair was disheveled, his hands clenched at his sides. The newspapers had scattered over the floor.

"Dressing up in boys' clothes, with paint on your face—"

"This is nothing! My going out on a few dates is nothing! You don't know what you're talking about!"

"Don't shout." My father shook his finger. "The neighbors will hear you."

"Goddammit, Dad!" Her voice rose to a shriek. She stamped her feet to make the most noise possible.

"What happened to you?" he cried. "You used to be so much like her. Look at you—"

Though I'd covered my ears I could hear my sister's wail echo off the walls. The door slammed, and her footfalls vanished down the stairs.

Things were quiet for a minute. Then I heard my father walk toward my corner. My heart thumped with fear—usually he let me alone. I had to look up when I heard him move the screen away. He knelt down next to me. His hair was streaked with gray, and his glasses needed cleaning.

"What are you doing?" he asked.

I shook my head, nothing.

After a minute I asked him, "Is Guijie why you didn't go play bridge tonight, Baba?"

"No, Claudia," he said. He always called me by my American name. This formality, I thought, was an indication of how distant he felt from me. "I stopped playing bridge last week."

93

"Why?" We both looked toward the window, where beyond our reflections the Hudson River flowed.

"It's not important," he said.

"Okay."

But he didn't leave. "I'm getting old," he said after a moment. "Someone ten years younger was just promoted over me. I'm not going to try to keep up with them anymore."

It was the closest he had ever come to confiding in me. After a few more minutes he stood up and went into the kitchen. The newspapers rustled under his feet. For almost half an hour I heard him fumbling through the kitchen cabinets, looking for something he'd probably put there years ago. Eventually he came out, carrying a small brass urn and some matches. When Emily returned home after midnight, the apartment still smelled of the incense he had burned to protect her while she was gone.

✳

I tried to be a good daughter. I stayed in every night and wore no make-up, I studied hard and got all A's, I did not leave home but went to college at NYU, right down the street. Jealously I guarded my small allotment of praise, clutching it like a pocket of precious stones. Emily snuck out of the apartment late at night; she wore high-heeled sandals with patched blue jeans; she twisted her long hair into graceful, complex loops and braids that belied respectability. She smelled of lipstick and perfume. Nothing I could ever achieve would equal my sister's misbehavior.

When Emily turned eighteen and did leave home, a part of my father disappeared. I wondered sometimes: where did it go? Did she take it with her? What secret charm had she carried with her as she vanished down the tunnel to the jet that would take her to college in

California, steadily and without looking back, while my father and I watched silently from the window at the gate? The apartment afterward became quite still—it was only the two of us, mourning and dreaming through pale-blue winter afternoons and silent evenings.

Emily called me, usually late at night after my father had gone to sleep. She sent me pictures of herself and people I didn't know, smiling on the sunny Berkeley campus. Sometimes after my father and I ate our simple meals or TV dinners I would go into our old room, where I had kept both of our twin beds, and take out Emily's pictures, trying to imagine what she must have been feeling, studying her expression and her swinging hair. But I always stared the longest at a postcard she'd sent me one winter break from northern New Mexico, a professional photo of a powerful, vast blue sky over faraway pink and sandy-beige mesas. The clarity and cleanness fascinated me. In a place like that, I thought, there would be nothing to search for, no reason to hide.

After college she went to work at a bank in San Francisco. I saw her once when she flew to Manhattan on business. She skipped a meeting to have lunch with me. She wore an elegant gray suit and had pinned up her hair.

"How's Dad?" she asked. I looked around, slightly alarmed. We were sitting in a bistro on the East Side, but I somehow thought he might overhear us.

"He's okay," I said. "We don't talk very much. Why don't you come home and see him?"

Emily stared at her water glass. "I don't think so."

"He misses you."

"I know. I don't want to hear about it."

"You hardly even call him."

"There's nothing we can talk about. Don't tell him you saw me, promise?"

"Okay."

During my junior year at NYU, my father suffered a stroke. He was fifty-nine years old, and he was still working as a lab instructor in the chemistry department. One evening in early fall I came home from a class and found him on the floor, near the kitchen telephone. He was wearing his usual vest and tie. I called the hospital and sat down next to him. His wire-rimmed glasses lay on the floor a foot away. One-half of his face was frozen, the other half lined with sudden age and pain.

"They said they'll be right here," I said. "It won't be very long." I couldn't tell how much he understood. I smoothed his vest and straightened his tie. I folded his glasses. I knew he wouldn't like it if the ambulance workers saw him in a state of dishevelment. "I'm sure they'll be here soon," I said.

We waited. Then I noticed he was trying to tell me something. A line of spittle ran from the left side of his mouth. I leaned closer. After a while I made out his words: "Tell Emily," he said.

The ambulance arrived as I picked up the telephone to call California. That evening, at the hospital, what was remaining of my father left the earth.

※

Emily insisted that we not hold a Buddhist cremation ceremony. "I never want to think about that stuff again," she said. "Plus, all his friends are Americans. I don't know who would come, except for us." She had reached New York the morning after his death. Her eyes were vague and her fingernails bitten down.

On the third day we scattered his ashes in the river. Afterward we held a small memorial service for his friends from work. We didn't talk much as we straightened the living room and dusted the furniture. It took almost three hours. The place was a mess. We hadn't had a party in years.

It was a warm cloudy afternoon, and the Hudson looked dull and sluggish from the living room window. I noticed that although she had not wanted a Buddhist ceremony, Emily had dressed in black and white according to Chinese mourning custom. I had asked the department secretary to put up a sign on the bulletin board. Eleven people came; they drank five bottles of wine. Two of his Chinese students stood in the corner, eating cheese and crackers.

Brad Delmonte, paunchy and no longer smoking, attached himself to Emily. "I remember you when you were just a little girl," I heard him say as I walked by with the extra crackers.

"I don't remember you," she said.

"You're still a cute little thing." She bumped his arm, and he spilled his drink.

Afterward we sat on the couch and surveyed the cluttered coffee table. It was past seven but we didn't talk about dinner.

"I'm glad they came," I said.

"I hate them." Emily looked at her fingernails. "I don't know whom I hate more: them, or him—for taking it."

"It doesn't matter anymore," I said.

"I suppose."

We watched the room grow dark.

"Do you know what?" Emily said. "It's the eve of the fifteenth day of the seventh lunar month."

"How do you know?" During college I had grown completely unaware of the lunar calendar.

"One of those chemistry nerds from Taiwan told me this afternoon."

I wanted to laugh, but instead I felt myself make a strange whimpering sound, squeezed out from my tight and hollow chest.

"Remember the time Dad and I had that big fight?" she said. "You know that now, in my grown-up life, I don't fight with anyone? I never had problems with anybody except him."

"No one cared about you as much as he did," I said.

"I don't want to hear about it." She twisted the end of her long braid. "He was a pain, and you know it. He got so strict after Mama died. It wasn't all my fault."

"I'm sorry," I said. But I was so angry with her that I felt my face turn red, my cheeks tingle in the dark. She'd considered our father a nerd as well, had squandered his love with such thoughtlessness that I could scarcely breathe to think about it. It seemed impossibly unfair that she had memories of my mother as well. Carefully I waited for my feelings to go away. Emily, I thought, was all I had.

But as I sat, a vision distilled before my eyes: the soft baked shades, the great blue sky of New Mexico. I realized that after graduation I could go wherever I wanted. A rusty door swung open and filled my mind with sweet freedom, fearful coolness.

"Let's do something," I said.

"What do you mean?"

"I want to do something."

"What did we used to do?" Emily looked down at the lock of hair in her hand. "Wait, I know."

We found newspapers and spread them on the floor. We turned on the lamps and moved the coffee table out of the way, brought the wineglasses to the sink. Emily went to the bathroom, and I searched for the shears a long time before I found them in the kitchen. I glimpsed the incense urn in a cabinet and quickly shut the door. When I returned to the living room it smelled of shampoo. Emily stood in the middle of the papers with her wet hair down her back, staring at herself in the reflection from the window. The lamplight cast circles under her eyes.

"I had a dream last night," she said. "I was walking down the street. I felt a tug. He was trying to reach me, trying to pull my hair."

"Just a trim?" I asked.

"No," she said. "Why don't you cut it."

"What do you mean?" I snipped a two-inch lock off the side.

Emily looked down at the hair on the newspapers. "I'm serious," she said. "Cut my hair. I want to see two feet of hair on the floor."

"Emily, you don't know what you're saying," I said. But a pleasurable, weightless feeling had come over me. I placed the scissors at the nape of her neck. "How about it?" I asked, and my voice sounded low and odd.

"*I don't care.*" An echo of the past. I cut. The shears went *snack*. A long black lock of hair hit the newspapers by my feet.

The Chinese say that our hair and our bodies are given to us from our ancestors, gifts that should not be tampered with. My mother herself had never done this. But after the first few moments I enjoyed myself, pressing the thick black locks through the shears, heavy against my thumb. Emily's hair slipped to the floor around us, rich and beautiful, lying in long graceful arcs over my shoes. She stood perfectly still, staring out the window. The Hudson River flowed behind our reflections, bearing my father's ashes through the night.

When I was finished, the back of her neck gleamed clean and white under a precise shining cap. "You missed your calling," Emily said. "You want me to do yours?"

My hair, browner and scragglier, had never been past my shoulders. I had always kept it short, figuring the ancestors wouldn't be offended by my tampering with a lesser gift. "No," I said. "But you should take a shower. Some of those small bits will probably itch."

"It's already ten o'clock. We should go to sleep soon anyway." Satisfied, she glanced at the mirror in the foyer. "I look like a completely different person," she said. She left to take her shower. I wrapped up her hair in the newspapers and went into the kitchen. I stood next to the sink for a long time before throwing the bundle away.

✻

The past sees through all attempts at disguise. That night I was awakened by my sister's scream. I gasped and stiffened, grabbing a handful of blanket.

"*Claudia,*" Emily cried from the other bed. "Claudia, wake up!"

"What is it?"

"I saw Baba." She hadn't called our father Baba in years. "Over there, by the door. Did you see him?"

"No," I said. "I didn't see anything." My bones felt frozen in place. After a moment I opened my eyes. The full moon shone through the window, bathing our room in silver and shadow. I heard my sister sob and then fall silent. I looked carefully at the door, but I noticed nothing.

Then I understood that his ghost would never visit me. I was, one might say, the lucky daughter. But I lay awake until morning, waiting; part of me is waiting still.

FROM CAROLINE'S WEDDING
BY *Edwidge Danticat*

CAROLINE WAS still awake when I returned to our room. "Is she ever going to get tired of telling that story?" she asked.

"You're talking about a woman who has had soup with cow bones in it for all sixty years of her life. She doesn't get tired of things. What are you going to do about it?"

"She'll come around. She has to," Caroline said.

We sat facing each other in the dark, playing a free-association game that Ma had taught us when we were girls.

"Who are you?" Caroline asked me.

"I am the *lost* child of the night."

"Where do you come from?"

"I come from the inside of the *lost* stone."

"Where are your eyes?"

"I have eyes *lost* behind my head, where they can best protect me."

"Who is your mother?"

"She who is the *lost* mother of all."

"Who is your father?"

"He who is the *lost* father of all."

Sometimes we would play half the night, coming up with end-less possibilities for questions and answers, only repeating the key word in every sentence. Ma too had learned this game when she was a girl. Her mother belonged to a secret women's society in Ville Rose, where the women had to question each other before entering one another's houses. Many nights while her mother was hosting the late-night meetings, Ma would fall asleep listening to the women's voices.

"I just remembered. There is a Mass Sunday at Saint Agnès for a dead refugee woman." Ma was standing in the doorway in her night-gown. "Maybe you two will come with me."

"Nobody sleeps in this house," Caroline said.

I would go, but not her.

※

They all tend to be similar, farewell ceremonies to the dead. The church was nearly empty, with a few middle-aged women scattered in the pews.

I crossed myself as I faced the wooden life-size statue of a dying Christ, looking down on us from high above the altar. The chapel was dim except for a few high chandeliers and the permanent glow of the rich hues of the stained glass windows. Ma kneeled in one of the side pews. She clutched her rosary and recited her Hail Marys with her eyes tightly shut.

For a long time, services at Saint Agnès have been tailored to fit the needs of the Haitian community. A line of altar boys proceeded down the aisle, each carrying a long lit candle. Ma watched them as though she were a spectator at a parade. Behind us, a group of women was carrying on a conversation, criticizing a neighbor's wife who, upon leaving Haiti, had turned from a sweet Haitian wife into a self-willed tyrant.

"In New York, women give their eight hours to the white man," one of the worshipers said in the poor woman's defense. "No one has time to be cradling no other man."

There was a slow drumbeat playing like a death march from the altar. A priest in a black robe entered behind the last altar boy. He walked up to the altar and began to read from a small book.

Ma lowered her head so far down that I could see the dip in the back of her neck, where she had a port-wine mark shaped like Manhattan Island.

"We have come here this far, from the shackles of the old Africans," read the priest in Creole. "At the mercy of the winds, at the mercy of the sea, to the quarters of the New World, we came. Transients. Nomads. I bid you welcome."

We all answered back, "Welcome."

The altar boys stood in an arc around the priest as he recited a list of a hundred twenty-nine names, Haitian refugees who had drowned at sea that week. The list was endless and with each name my heart beat faster, for it seemed as though many of those listed might have been people that I had known at some point in my life.

Some of the names sent a wave of sighs and whispers through the crowd. Occasionally, there was a loud scream.

One woman near the front began to convulse after a man's name was called. It took four people to drag her out of the pew before she hurt herself.

"We make a special call today for a young woman whose name we don't know," the priest said after he had recited all the others. "A young woman who was pregnant when she took a boat from Haiti and then later gave birth to her child on that boat. A few hours after the child was born, its precious life went out, like a candle in a storm, and the mother with her infant in her arms dived into the sea."

There are people in Ville Rose, the village where my mother is from in Haiti, who believe that there are special spots in the sea where lost Africans who jumped off the slave ships still rest, that those who have died at sea have been chosen to make that journey in order to be reunited with their long-lost relations.

During the Mass, Ma tightened a leather belt around her belly, the way some old Haitian women tightened rags around their middles when grieving.

"Think to yourself of the people you have loved and lost," the priest said.

Piercing screams sounded throughout the congregation. Ma got up suddenly and began heading for the aisle. The screams pounded in my head as we left the church.

We walked home through the quiet early morning streets along Avenue D, saying nothing to one another.

※

Caroline was still in bed when we got back.

She wrapped a long black nightgown around her legs as she sat up on a pile of dirty sheets.

There was a stack of cards on a chair by her bed. She picked it up and went through the cards, sorting most of them with one hand and holding the rest in her mouth. She began a game of solitaire using her hand and her lips, flipping the cards back and forth with great agility.

"How was Mass?" she asked.

Often after Mass ended, I would feel as though I had taken a very long walk with the dead.

"Did Ma cry?" she asked.

"We left before she could."

"It's not like she knows these people," Caroline said. Some of the cards slipped from between her lips.

"Ma says all Haitians know each other."

Caroline stacked the cards and dropped them in one of the three large open boxes that were kept lined up behind her bed. She was packing up her things slowly so as to not traumatize Ma.

She and Eric were not going to have a big formal wedding. They were going to have a civil ceremony and then they would take some pictures in the wedding grove at the Brooklyn Botanic Garden. Their honeymoon would be a brief trip to the Bahamas, after which Caroline would move into Eric's apartment.

Ma wanted Eric to officially come and ask her permission to marry her daughter. She wanted him to bring his family to our house and have his father ask her blessing. She wanted Eric to kiss up to her, escort her around, buy her gifts, and shower her with compliments. Ma wanted a full-blown church wedding. She wanted Eric to be Haitian.

"You will never guess what I dreamt last night," Caroline said, dropping her used sheets into one of the moving boxes she was packing. "I dreamt about Papa."

It had been almost ten years since Papa had died of untreated prostate cancer. After he died, Ma made us wear mourning clothes, nothing but black dresses, for eighteen months. Caroline and I were both in high school at the time, and we quickly found ways to make wearing black a fashion statement. Underneath our black clothes we were supposed to wear red panties. In Ma's family, the widows often wore blood-red panties so that their dead husbands would not come back and lie down next to them at night. Daughters who looked a lot like the widowed mother might wear red panties too so that if they were ever mistaken for her, they would be safe.

Ma believed that Caroline and I would be well protected by the red panties. Papa, and all the other dead men who might desire us, would stay away because the sanguine color of blood was something that daunted and terrified the non-living.

For a few months after Papa died, Caroline and I dreamt of him every other night. It was as though he were taking turns visiting us in our sleep. We would each have the same dream: Papa walking in a deserted field while the two of us were running after him. We were never able to catch up with him because there were miles of saw grass and knee-deep mud between us.

We kept this dream to ourselves because we already knew what Ma would say if we told it to her. She would guess that we had not been wearing our red panties and would warn us that the day we caught up with Papa in our dream would be the day that we both would die.

Later the dreams changed into moments replayed from our lives, times when he had told us stories about his youth in Haiti or evenings when he had awakened us at midnight after working a double shift in his taxicab to take us out for Taste the Tropics ice cream, Sicilian pizzas, or Kentucky Fried Chicken.

Slowly, Papa's death became associated with our black clothes. We began carrying our loss like a medal on our chests, answering every time someone asked why such young attractive girls wore such a somber color, "Our mother makes us do it because our father is dead."

Eighteen months after his death, we were allowed to start wearing other colors, but nothing too bright. We could wear white or gray or navy blue but no orange, or red on the outside. The red for the world to see meant that our mourning period had ended, that we were beyond our grief. The red covering our very private parts was to tell our father that he was dead and we no longer wanted anything to do with him.

"How did you dream of Papa?" I asked Caroline now.

"He was at a party," she said, "with all these beautiful people around him, having a good time. I saw him in this really lavish room.

I'm standing in the doorway and he's inside and I'm watching him, and it's like watching someone through a glass window. He doesn't even know I'm there. I call him, but he doesn't answer. I just stand there and watch what he's doing because I realize that he can't see me."

She reached into one of her boxes and pulled out a framed black-and-white picture of Papa, a professional studio photograph taken in the nineteen fifties in Haiti, when Papa was twenty-two. In the photograph, he is wearing a dark suit and tie and has a solemn expression on his face. Caroline looked longingly at the picture, the way war brides look at photographs of their dead husbands. I raised my nightshirt and showed her my black cotton panties, the same type that we had both been wearing since the day our father died. Caroline stuck her pinkie through a tiny hole in the front of my panties. She put Papa's picture back into her box, raised her dress, and showed me her own black panties.

We have *never* worn the red panties that Ma had bought for us over the years to keep our dead father's spirit away. We had always worn our black panties instead, to tell him that he would be welcome to visit us. Even though we no longer wore black outer clothes, we continued to wear black underpants as a sign of lingering grief. Another reason Caroline may have continued to wear hers was her hope that Papa would come to her and say that he approved of her: of her life, of her choices, of her husband.

"With patience, you can see the navel of an ant," I said, recalling one of Papa's favorite Haitian proverbs.

"Rain beats on a dog's skin, but it does not wash out its spots," Caroline responded.

"When the tree is dead, ghosts eat the leaves."

"The dead are always in the wrong."

Beneath the surface of Papa's old proverbs was always some warning.

Our Cuban neighbor, Mrs. Ruiz, was hosting her large extended family in the yard next door after a Sunday christening. They were blasting some rumba music. We could barely hear each other over the crisp staccato pounding of the conga drums and the shrill brass sections blaring from their stereo.

I closed my eyes and tried to imagine their entire clan milling around the yard, a whole exiled family gathering together so far from home. Most of my parents' relatives still lived in Haiti.

Caroline and I walked over to the window to watch the Ruiz clan dance to the rumba.

"Mrs. Ruiz has lost some weight since we saw her last," Caroline said.

"A couple of months ago, Mrs. Ruiz's only son had tried to hijack a plane in Havana to go to Miami. He was shot and killed by the airplane's pilot."

"How do you know such things?" Caroline asked me.

"Ma told me."

When we were younger, Caroline and I would spend all our Sunday mornings in bed wishing that it would be the blessed day that the rest of Caroline's arm would come bursting out of Ma's stomach and float back to her. It would all happen like the brass sections in the Ruizes' best rumbas, a meteoric cartoon explosion, with no blood or pain. After the momentary shock, Caroline would have a whole arm and we would all join Mrs. Ruiz's parties to celebrate. Sometimes Sunday mornings would be so heavy with disappointment that we thought *we* might explode.

Caroline liked to have her stub stroked. This was something that she had never grown out of. Yet it was the only part of her that people were afraid of. They were afraid of offending her, afraid of staring at it, even while they were stealing a glance or two. A large vein throbbed just below the surface, under a thick layer of skin. I ran my pinkie over the vein and felt it, pulsating against my skin.

"If I slice myself there, I could bleed to death," Caroline said. "Remember what Papa used to say, 'Behind a white cloud, a bird looks like an angel.'"

✼

Ma was in the kitchen cooking our Sunday breakfast when we came in. She was making a thick omelet with dried herring, served with boiled plantains. Something to keep you going as if it were your only meal for the day.

"Mass was nice today," Ma said, watching Caroline balance her orange juice between her chin and her stub. "If you had gone, you would have enjoyed it a lot."

"Yes. I hear it was a ball," Caroline said.

"You two have been speaking for a long time already," Ma said. "What were you discussing?"

"This and that," I said.

"I've been jealous," Ma said.

YELLOW DRESSES

BY C.D. Wright

A woman and her sisters would follow
The bees to their tree.
There was no wind or word
From New Orleans. She wore several yards
Of gauze over her clothes,
Long gloves to pull the comb out of the trunk.
The others lay down in the grass,
Cats in the sunlight,
And the smallest sister would lie
In the lap of the oldest
Until she stroked her hair and spoke.
Close to the swarm, the fine vibration
In her voice, spirit of the hive.

SADIE AND MAUD

BY *Gwendolyn Brooks*

Maud went to college.
Sadie stayed home.
Sadie scraped life
With a fine-tooth comb.

She didn't leave a tangle in.
Her comb found every strand.
Sadie was one of the livingest chits
In all the land.

Sadie bore two babies
Under her maiden name.
Maud and Ma and Papa
Nearly died of shame.
Every one but Sadie
Nearly died of shame.

When Sadie said her last so-long
Her girls struck out from home.
(Sadie had left as heritage
Her fine-tooth comb.)

Maud, who went to college,
Is a thin brown mouse.
She is living all alone
In this old house.

TWIN BED

BY Ana Maria Jomolca

MY SISTER, LOURDES MARIA TRAVIESO, was born on January 15th 1962 in Havana, Cuba, and six months later was smuggled into Miami disguised as a heat blanket. Batista had just recently been overthrown and the revolution had everyone distracted. Castro was just settling in and no one thought to question the need for a heat blanket in ninety-degree weather. Her fugitive beginning marked the baptism of a lifetime of irreverence and trailblazing.

The eldest of five, my sister was a natural born leader and recreational dictator. I was born four years and two siblings later than she and was immediately taken under her wing, her pet project. I had no idea this project would span the course of thirty-five years. While my sister has maintained her lead with effortless grace and poise, I have been a frantic mess, barely holding my ground, much less one-upping her in any skill, insight, or fashion savvy. For years I have accepted her discarded apparel and beauty supplies only to discover that I look and feel fabulous *only* while they are still in her ownership and/or worn in her territory. But as soon as she offers them up, hands them over (or down) to me, and the property changes hands and locale, all cargo depreciates. The hair gel goes from accentuating my curls to igniting my frizz. The mascara clumps. The white scarf turns gray and dingy. The wire under the left cup of the Mira-cle Bra mysteriously twists out of shape en route from the Baltimore Travel Plaza to New York's Port Authority. This phenomenon has tormented me throughout most of my adult life.

Lourdes Maria Travieso was the poster girl for sexuality un-leashed. At the age of twelve she was filling out a 34C and clipping articles from *Cosmopolitan*. Even her food choices were mature. She preferred French toast to pancakes, International Coffee's Viennese Cappuccino to Yoo Hoo, and fresh claw crab meat to Salisbury steak. Lourdes dated men, not boys. During her high school years, she refused to acknowledge any of her male classmates as viable escorts. She dated college dropouts who owned their own businesses and any man wearing wing tips and a Fedora. Men with experience or style. Lourdes was a founding member of the South Florida Junior Achievement Club and president of the yearbook committee. She was also the Captain of the cheerleading squad and scoffed at the many quarterbacks and tight ends who assumed that her cheering,

"BE AGGRESSIVE.

"BE BE AGGRESSIVE.

"BEEEEEEEEEE AGGRESSIVE!" was evidence of a longing to be dominated. They took her enthusiastic pony mount, kneeling torch and leaps through the air, legs akimbo, as evidence of the cheerleaders' desire to be tackled by the Gunner.

"I'm a *dancer*, pinhead, not a pom pom monkey," she informed them.

When I was nine I snuck behind the curtain of our living room while my sister was lying on the couch, "watching T.V." with her boyfriend, Rolando, an entrepreneur who sold knock-off Seiko's in the parking lot of Sedano's Supermarket. His hand stroked the inside of her thigh and then dipped between her legs and slid up, cupping her crotch. I could see her head cocked back and her mouth agape, eyes rolling into the back of her head. She looked drunk. Later, alone in my room, I spent hours thinking of my sister, Rolando and his floating hand as I cut the heads and torsos of celebrity hunks and pasted them onto the cover of my slam book: Shaun Cassidy, Scott "Chachi" Baio, Jimmy McNichol, Lance Kerwin, Donnie Osmond, Leif Garrett, and a group shot of K.C. and the Sunshine Band under a coconut tree. Leif was missing a large chunk of forehead and Chachi was chinless. Donnie was one-legged and limping. It was a *Teen Beat* massacre. I ran my finger down their necks and along their hips, dipping below their hips and resting on their groin. I wanted to feel the same drunk I saw in my sister's eyes.

My sister was the first of her class to use tampons, despite *El Himno Sagrado's* claim that tampons were for whores. Decent *jovencitas* use pads. At the age of fourteen I had yet to see any spotting on my underoos and was taken to Doctor Echeverria every two weeks on account of my stunted growth. I stood four feet small and weighed seventy-two pounds. There was concern. I was prescribed six egg yolks a day and many hours of hanging upside down from barbells or tree limbs.

In 1992, my sister fled Miami and the promise of living the Cuban Debutante Dream: a beautiful four bedroom home in Coral Gables, a wealthy Attorney, Doctor or Accountant husband, "His" and "Hers" Range Rovers, and a closet full of pastel blazers. I chased after her eight months later, claiming my own rebellion: my boyfriend had just informed me that I was not the last stop on his highway of lovers. I was more like a service station. Or a drive-by shooting. So I left town before he left me, driving and crying all the way to my sister's house in Maryland. She cleaned out the spare room and shot Michael, her boyfriend, a scathing look, daring him to interfere. "Love me, love my sister," she said, gripping the potato peeler tightly in her hand. Michael made himself scarce, spending his afternoons at Carwash Tom's house drinking Schlitz and smoking weed. My sister bought me all my favorite Johnson & Johnson No More Tears bath products and fed me Little Debbie Swiss Miss Rolls, Count Chocula cereal, and Cheez Whiz on pretzel sticks. She nursed me back to self-righteous blame and a lethal dose of rage.

"Men are dickheads," she explained. "Dicks in their heads. Their heads are dicks." She illustrated by book ending each side of her head with both palms.

Her therapist diagnosed her a Man Eater.

"Yes, dickheads!" I chimed in. And although Jerry, a full time ATARI repairman and bipolar Jew, was the only relationship I'd had lasting more than three weeks, I felt justified in my castrating the entire XY species as a result of his cruelty. Upon full recovery from Jerry, I moved to New York City.

My sister and I talk at least once a week, sometimes more, depending on the crisis at hand or the need to reinforce our balance of power.

※

This morning I call my sister to tell her I have been accepted among hundreds, *thousands* of applicants to the Schermakatchewan Artist Housing in Crown Heights that I applied for thirteen years ago. I tell her it is an elevator building. I tell her I'll have a doorman who will joyfully accept all packages she sends me filled with cleaning products and imperfect bras. I tell her my new abode has a fitness room, business center, community banquet hall, roof terrace and garden, laundry facilities, and a 200-seat theater for the artists and their proposed ensembles. I tell her my apartment overlooks blocks of quaint brownstones and cobblestone roads lined up against the backdrop of a stunning Brooklyn skyline. Just below me, I continue, are blocks and blocks of cozy cafes, boutiques, pastry shops, bookstores, and antique stores. I add that the A train practically drops me off right onto my balcony.

My apartment does not have a balcony. I do not tell her this. I do not tell her the Schermakatchewan Artist Housing Project is not the Schermakatchewan *Artist* Housing Project, but just the Schermakatchewan Housing Project and that while it aims to provide affordable housing for artists, it also targets two other markets: the formerly homeless and the mentally challenged. I do not tell her that the fitness room consists of one StairMaster, two geriatric stationary bicycles, and a weight scale donated by Metropolitan Hospital. I do not tell her the business center is actually called the computer room and is exactly that: *the computer* room. One computer for 230 residents. I do not tell her the doormen are "formerly incarcerated individuals" who failed the Doe Funds *Ready, Willing & Able* drug test and are now seeking a second, third, or twelfth chance. I do not tell my sister that the roof garden is a concrete terrace of gray, sandy cement with four folding chairs and a wicker Jade plant, or that the Community Banquet Hall is the basement space located next to the boiler room and will host Bingo on Mondays, Musical Show Tunes Karaoke on Wednesdays, Budgeting Your Food Stamps workshops on Thursdays, and cooking classes on Fridays.

I do tell her that my studio apartment is quite spacious and then remind her that I am a very small person, 4'11 and a half, 99.5 lbs, and that 240 square feet is a palace for me. I go on to say that the apartment has no closet in the traditional sense. "It's more like a large cupboard, an extension of the kitchen cabinets, if you will." I tell her I am approaching this whole experience as an exercise in minimalism, an exploration of wanting versus needing.

A heavy sigh comes through the telephone line. My cue to proceed. I remind her that I have been on countless writing residencies and artist retreats, both locally and internationally, and have discovered that I can (and do) live without many of the possessions I once swore were non-negotiable.

"I spent two months in New Zealand without shaving my legs," I say. Silence. I tell her that I don't mind the sink *inside* the bathtub, and that upon second thought I find it quite innovative and visionary. Futuristic even. Certainly very green.

"Humph," I hear through the wire.

"Humph," she repeats.

And so, I tell my sister, "I don't even mind the twin bed—"

"Twin bed?" she gasps.

"Yes, twin bed," I repeat, suddenly uncertain whether the bed is a twin, queen, king, or futon.

"Twin?!" she screeches.

"Yes. Twin!" I am now screeching too.

"Twin-size bed." A statement. And then as though confirming the last four digits of my Social Security number or speaking to an overcrowded classroom of Chinese ESL students, she says, "Twiiinnn sssiiizzze bed?" I say nothing. It is a trap. She is wheezing or choking now. "Are you sure?"

"No," I quickly reply and I am not lying. My sister has a way of making me doubt every thing I've done, every word I've spoken and every thought I've entertained throughout the entire course of my career on this earth as a chronically indecisive Libran with a propensity for catastrophizing everything from one unreturned phone call to falling short of the required stock of staples to get me through the next eighteen months. No matter how well I complete a task, there is always a far more efficient and effective way to approach it. *Her* way.

I am always wrong. An *atrasada mental*. A cognitive mishap in constant relapse. I dig one knuckle deep into my eye socket.

※

My sister lives in a restored five-bedroom house, with a two-car garage, glass encased sunroom, two-acre yard replete with mini forest, Japanese garden, and fishpond in a suburb of Maryland known as Croftown. She lives with her husband, his two sons (every other weekend) and my twelve-year-old nephew, who owns his own piano and plays three different versions of Green Day's *Boulevard of Broken Dreams*.

In July 2007 Croftown was named by *Money* magazine as one of "100 Best Places to Live" in the United States. The residential community is enclosed by Croftown Parkway, a scenic 3.5-mile loop that encircles the homes, Town Hall, a community pool, tennis courts and the Croftown Country Club, which houses 7100 yards of putting green supposedly designed by Jack Nicklaus, and hosts the annual Halloween parade, Christmas-tree lighting, Santa's arrival on a fire truck, and a parade down Croftown Parkway to mark the beginning of toddlers' baseball in the spring. The name Croftown was chosen because it "sounds well and implies that this is a pleasant place to live." They boast a growing ethnic population citing "the Hispanic or Latino" jump from 2.48% in 2000 to 2.51% within an unspecified amount of time. My nephew's birth and Lulu, their Latino Jack Russell terrier, probably account for 80% of that increase.

Schermakatchewan... Croftown... *Croftown*... Schermakatchewan. I mouth each carefully, annunciating every syllable but fail to draw any phonetic comparison that might dignify Schermakatchewan. My new residential community sounds like an abandoned railroad. In 1883, the Schermakatchewan line was forced to shut down as a result of infrequent travel in this wretched cropless, barren town.

I decide to refer to the neighborhood (or borough) skirting Schermakatchewan. "Certainly you've heard of Brooklyn Heights?" I ask my sister, "the Historic District?"

"The Heights?" she says, "like that musical?"

"No, no, no. That's *'Da* Heights as in *Washington* Heights. And that's Dominican ghetto," I whisper as though I were in line at Fracatan Check Cashing. "No Dominicans in Brooklyn Heights," I laugh, "like they could afford it." I sneer and roll my eyes so far into the back of my head that I tilt dizzily, my eyeballs like slot machines spinning into white. I am praying she will join me in my diss on the Dominicans, an inside joke among the Cubans, the superior race, unequivocally more educated, cultured, skilled, and groomed than the mixed breeds of Latinos that infiltrated Miami years later, profiting off our hard work.

"Miami would be nothing but gas pumps and fish tackle had it not been for the Cubans," my father often said. Suddenly my need to believe this is not fractionally as important as the need for my sister to believe it *with* me. Bonding through our parents' xenophobia might be just the decoy needed to shift us from rivals to allies.

My sister yawns.

Last summer during one of my biannual visits to her home, I was lectured on the proper way to boil an egg. I was in the garage, looking for Gorilla Glue to repair the baby Jesus head from the Mexican Nativity scene they keep by the doggie door, when I heard my sister scream, "Jesus Christ!" I dropped the box of flathead screws and the cardboard tore open, flinging two-inch spears in every direction.

"Cristina Maria!" my sister screamed, and then to herself, "Where is that little troll?"

I thought to run out the side door and down the street and keep running and running, past Eden Lane, past the country club, past Giants Supermarket, up by I-95, past Delaware and Jersey, swim across the Hudson, and race up Lexington Avenue until I reached my apartment in East Harlem. But it was seventeen degrees out and my nephew was making his theater debut that night as the understudy spoon in *Beauty and the Beast*. I gathered the nails and threw them in the garbage, and walked toward the kitchen, rehearsing my confession, and speedy offer to repair, reimburse, or replace Jesus's cranium and his crew of gawkers. When I entered the kitchen, my redemption was quickly thwarted. My sister held a pot in her hand and thrust it at me.

"Are these your eggs?" she asked. I opened my mouth. "Of course they're your eggs. Who else would leave a pot of boiling eggs on the stove unattended?!" I closed my mouth. "You do not put eggs to boil on HIGH. They crack and spill over and look"—she points to three drops of water by the toaster oven—"you could have short-circuited the whole house, or electrocuted my son."

"But they didn't boil over," I say. She rolls her eyes and huffs her way, pot in hand, to the sink.

"Of course they didn't boil over. Because I walked in—just in time!"

Just in time. My sister always appears *just in time*. She seems to flawlessly arrive on the brink of disaster, the cusp of catastrophe; a figure floating through doors, walls, crowds, performing countless acts of Divine Intervention.

※

"Twin-size bed?!"

"Yes. Twin. Size. Bed," I tell her firmly. And this is when it hits me. The precise moment when I realize that my sister is not mortified by the visual of me falling off the mattress or sleeping with my limbs continually dangling off the sides of the bed, cutting off my circulation. I am moving into an apartment with a twin-size bed. I have not slept in a twin-size bed since I was nine years old. Room for ONE only. What kind of message is *that* sending the Universe? I am sealing the permanence of my solitary confinement between the sheets. My sexual inertia catalogued and embedded. Suddenly I cannot remember the last time someone touched me *deliberately*. I will be sleeping in a twin-size bed. I will die alone and untouched in that twin bed.

"What's the big deal?" I say. "It's just a goddamn bed. I sleep only five hours a night anyhow. That's one fifth of my day, one and a half days out of my week, six days out of my month, seventy-three days out of my year—" I trail off, my rage escalating until there is no speech coming forth, only dry-heaving and hissing like Donald Sutherland in *Invasion of the Body Snatchers*.

This move was supposed to be my breakout role, a testament to my growing up and moving on. I am leaving my best friend and enabler, a gay thirty-year-old male I've been living with for twelve years—a symbolic leap away from the safe and familiar toward the perilous and unknown. Maybe I'm just a fag hag pulling a geographic.

I want to reach through the telephone line and strangle my sister. But most of all, I just want my sister to want something that *I* have. It need not be a physical attribute or personality trait, but perhaps some article, one insignificant item that I own; a scarf, eye pencil, an ashtray. For once I would like to be the one to turn her on to some new gadget, hair accessory, or cleaning product.

"Why can't you want what I have?" I scream through the phone.

"What?"

"Surely there must be something, *one* thing I have that you want. Something that *I* own, something that *I* have done, that you don't own, that you haven't done. You must have some culpable longing, some painful desire, a black hole of unfulfilled hunger? Aren't you sick of being so self-sufficient? It's not healthy. Envy is a basic human need—like fiber! Without it, you'll never know what's missing in your life. Covet *me* dammit!"

And then there is a silence so unbearable I drop to all fours and mouth the words, *Somebody kill me.* Outside my window the jackhammer is pounding as civilians shuffle past newsstands and tamale carts, descend the subway stairs and disappear below ground. If I jump from the fire escape, I think to myself, there is no way of knowing whether I'd be instantly killed or maimed for life.

"Yes," a voice low and slow comes through the phone line.

"Yes?" I repeat. I am entirely unprepared for her response. I hear her breathing, short intervals of inhale, exhale and then—

"Just for one day I'd like to wake up and make coffee for *one,* do laundry for *one,* make dinner for *one,* buy socks, cereal, movie tickets, and colored pencils for *one.* Just for one day I'd like to book a flight to South Africa, New Zealand, and Costa Rica for *one.* Just for one day, I would like to be the cool aunt from New York City." And now we are both silent. "There. Feel better?"

"Yes. Exponentially." I hear Lulu growling and barking violently in the background and then a piercing whine settling into a resigned whimper.

"Gotta go," my sister says, "Lulu's attacking some jogger on the road."

"Probably Dominican," I say. Humph.

"Cuban, more likely," she says and hangs up.

EVERYDAY USE

BY *Alice Walker*

for your grandmama

I WILL WAIT FOR HER in the yard that Maggie and I made so clean and wavy yesterday afternoon. A yard like this is more comfortable than most people know. It is not just a yard. It is like an extended living room. When the hard clay is swept clean as a floor and the fine sand around the edges lined with tiny, irregular grooves, anyone can come and sit and look up into the elm tree and wait for the breezes that never come inside the house.

Maggie will be nervous until after her sister goes: she will stand hopelessly in corners, homely and ashamed of the burn scars down her arms and legs, eyeing her sister with a mixture of envy and awe. She thinks her sister has held life always in the palm of one hand, that "no" is a word the world never learned to say to her.

※

You've no doubt seen those TV shows where the child who has "made it" is confronted, as a surprise, by her own mother and father, tottering in weakly from backstage. (A pleasant surprise, of course: What would they do if parent and child came on the show only to curse out and insult each other?) On TV mother and child embrace and smile into each other's faces. Sometimes the mother and father

123

weep, the child wraps them in her arms and leans across the table to tell how she would not have made it without their help. I have seen these programs.

Sometimes I dream a dream in which Dee and I are suddenly brought together on a TV program of this sort. Out of a dark and soft-seated limousine I am ushered into a bright room filled with many people. There I meet a smiling, gray, sporty man like Johnny Carson who shakes my hand and tells me what a fine girl I have. Then we are on the stage and Dee is embracing me with tears in her eyes. She pins on my dress a large orchid, even though she has told me once that she thinks orchids are tacky flowers.

In real life I am a large, big-boned woman with rough, man-working hands. In the winter I wear flannel nightgowns to bed and overalls during the day. I can kill and clean a hog as mercilessly as a man. My fat keeps me hot in zero weather. I can work outside all day, breaking ice to get water for washing; I can eat pork liver cooked over the open fire minutes after it comes steaming from the hog. One winter I knocked a bull calf straight in the brain between the eyes with a sledge hammer and had the meat hung up to chill before nightfall. But of course all this does not show on television. I am the way my daughter would want me to be: a hundred pounds lighter, my skin like an uncooked barley pancake. My hair glistens in the hot bright lights. Johnny Carson has much to do to keep up with my quick and witty tongue.

But that is a mistake. I know even before I wake up. Who ever knew a Johnson with a quick tongue? Who can even imagine me looking a strange white man in the eye? It seems to me I have talked to them always with one foot raised in flight, with my head turned in whichever way is farthest from them. Dee, though. She would always look anyone in the eye. Hesitation was no part of her nature.

※

"How do I look, Mama?" Maggie says, showing just enough of her thin body enveloped in pink skirt and red blouse for me to know she's there, almost hidden by the door.

"Come out into the yard," I say.

Have you ever seen a lame animal, perhaps a dog run over by some careless person rich enough to own a car, sidle up to someone who is ignorant enough to be kind to him? That is the way my Maggie walks. She has been like this, chin on chest, eyes on ground, feet in shuffle, ever since the fire that burned the other house to the ground.

Dee is lighter than Maggie, with nicer hair and a fuller figure. She's a woman now, though sometimes I forget. How long ago was it that the other house burned? Ten, twelve years? Sometimes I can still hear the flames and feel Maggie's arms sticking to me, her hair smoking and her dress falling off her in little black papery flakes. Her eyes seemed stretched open, blazed open by the flames reflected in them. And Dee. I see her standing off under the sweet gum tree she used to dig gum out of; a look of concentration on her face as she watched the last dingy gray board of the house fall in toward the red-hot brick chimney. Why don't you do a dance around the ashes? I'd wanted to ask her. She had hated the house that much.

I used to think she hated Maggie, too. But that was before we raised the money, the church and me, to send her to Augusta to school. She used to read to us without pity; forcing words, lies, other folks' habits, whole lives upon us two, sitting trapped and ignorant underneath her voice. She washed us in a river of make-believe, burned us with a lot of knowledge we didn't necessarily need to know. Pressed us to her with the serious way she read, to shove us away at just the moment, like dimwits, we seemed about to understand.

Dee wanted nice things. A yellow organdy dress to wear to her graduation from high school; black pumps to match a green suit she'd made from an old suit somebody gave me. She was determined to stare down any disaster in her efforts. Her eyelids would not flicker for minutes at a time. Often I fought off the temptation to shake her. At sixteen she had a style of her own: and knew what style was.

※

I never had an education myself. After second grade the school was closed down. Don't ask me why: in 1927 colored asked fewer questions than they do now. Sometimes Maggie reads to me. She stumbles along good-naturedly but can't see well. She knows she is not bright. Like good looks and money, quickness passed her by. She will marry John Thomas (who has mossy teeth in an earnest face) and then I'll be free to sit here and I guess just sing church songs to myself. Although I never was a good singer. Never could carry a tune. I was always better at a man's job. I used to love to milk till I was hooked in the side in '49. Cows are soothing and slow and don't bother you, unless you try to milk them the wrong way.

I have deliberately turned my back on the house. It is three rooms, just like the one that burned, except the roof is tin; they don't make shingle roofs any more. There are no real windows, just some holes cut in the sides, like the portholes in a ship, but not round and not square, with rawhide holding the shutters up on the outside. This house is in a pasture, too, like the other one. No doubt when Dee sees it she will want to tear it down. She wrote me once that no matter where we "choose" to live, she will manage to come see us. But she will never bring her friends. Maggie and I thought about this and Maggie asked me, "Mama, when did Dee ever *have* any friends?"

She had a few. Furtive boys in pink shirts hanging about on washday after school. Nervous girls who never laughed. Impressed with her they worshiped the well-turned phrase, the cute shape, the scalding humor that erupted like bubbles in lye. She read to them.

When she was courting Jimmy T she didn't have much time to pay to us, but turned all her faultfinding power on him. He *flew* to marry a cheap city girl from a family of ignorant flashy people. She hardly had time to recompose herself.

※

When she comes I will meet—but there they are!

Maggie attempts to make a dash for the house, in her shuffling way, but I stay her with my hand. "Come back here," I say. And she stops and tries to dig a well in the sand with her toe.

It is hard to see them clearly through the strong sun. But even the first glimpse of leg out of the car tells me it is Dee. Her feet were always neat-looking, as if God himself had shaped them with a certain style. From the other side of the car comes a short, stocky man. Hair is all over his head a foot long and hanging from his chin like a kinky mule tail. I hear Maggie suck in her breath. "Uhnnnh," is what it sounds like. Like when you see the wriggling end of a snake just in front of your foot on the road. "Uhnnnh."

Dee next. A dress down to the ground, in this hot weather. A dress so loud it hurts my eyes. There are yellows and oranges enough to throw back the light of the sun. I feel my whole face warming from the heat waves it throws out. Earrings gold, too, and hanging down to her shoulders. Bracelets dangling and making noises when she moves her arm up to shake the folds of the dress out of her armpits. The dress is loose and flows, and as she walks closer, I like it. I hear Maggie go "Uhnnnh" again. It is her sister's hair. It stands straight up like the wool on a sheep. It is black as night and around the edges are two long pigtails that rope about like small lizards disappearing behind her ears.

"Wa-su-zo-Tean-o!" she says, coming on in that gliding way the dress makes her move. The short stocky fellow with the hair to his navel is all grinning and he follows up with "Asalamalakim, my mother and sister!" He moves to hug Maggie but she falls back, right up against the back of my chair. I feel her trembling there and when I look up I see the perspiration falling off her chin.

"Don't get up," says Dee. Since I am stout it takes something of a push. You can see me trying to move a second or two before I make it. She turns, showing white heels through her sandals, and goes back to the car. Out she peeks next with a Polaroid. She stoops down quickly and lines up picture after picture of me sitting there in front of the house with Maggie cowering behind me. She never takes a shot without making sure the house is included. When a cow comes nibbling around the edge of the yard she snaps it and me and Maggie *and* the house. Then she puts the Polaroid in the back seat of the car, and comes up and kisses me on the forehead.

Meanwhile Asalamalakim is going through motions with Maggie's hand. Maggie's hand is as limp as a fish, and probably as cold, despite the sweat, and she keeps trying to pull it back. It looks like Asalamalakim wants to shake hands but wants to do it fancy. Or maybe he don't know how people shake hands. Anyhow, he soon gives up on Maggie.

"Well," I say. "Dee."

"No, Mama," she says. "Not 'Dee,' Wangero Leewanika Kemanjo!"

"What happened to 'Dee'?" I wanted to know.

"She's dead," Wangero said. "I couldn't bear it any longer, being named after the people who oppress me."

"You know as well as me you was named after your aunt Dicie," I said. Dicie is my sister. She named Dee. We called her "Big Dee" after Dee was born.

"But who was *she* named after?" asked Wangero.

"I guess after Grandma Dee," I said.

"And who was she named after?" asked Wangero.

"Her mother," I said, and saw Wangero was getting tired. "That's about as far back as I can trace it," I said. Though, in fact, I probably could have carried it back beyond the Civil War through the branches.

"Well," said Asalamalakim, "there you are."

"Uhnnnh," I heard Maggie say.

"There I was not," I said, "before 'Dicie' cropped up in our family, so why should I try to trace it that far back?"

He just stood there grinning, looking down on me like somebody inspecting a Model A car. Every once in a while he and Wangero sent eye signals over my head.

"How do you pronounce this name?" I asked.

"You don't have to call me by it if you don't want to," said Wangero.

"Why shouldn't I?" I asked. "If that's what you want us to call you, we'll call you."

"I know it might sound awkward at first," said Wangero.

"I'll get used to it," I said. "Ream it out again."

Well, soon we got the name out of the way. Asalamalakim had a name twice as long and three times as hard. After I tripped over it two or three times he told me to just call him Hakim-a-barber. I wanted to ask him was he a barber, but I didn't really think he was, so I didn't ask.

"You must belong to those beef-cattle peoples down the road," I said. They said "Asalamalakim" when they met you, too, but they didn't shake hands. Always too busy: feeding the cattle, fixing the fences, putting up salt-lick shelters, throwing down hay. When the white folks poisoned some of the herd the men stayed up all night with rifles in their hands. I walked a mile and a half just to see the sight.

Hakim-a-barber said, "I accept some of their doctrines, but farming and raising cattle is not my style." (They didn't tell me, and I didn't ask, whether Wangero (Dee) had really gone and married him.)

We sat down to eat and right away he said he didn't eat collards and pork was unclean. Wangero, though, went on through the chitlins and corn bread, the greens and everything else. She talked a blue streak over the sweet potatoes. Everything delighted her. Even the fact that we still used the benches her daddy made for the table when we couldn't afford to buy chairs.

"Oh, Mama!" she cried. Then turned to Hakim-a-barber. "I never knew how lovely these benches are. You can feel the rump prints," she said, running her hands underneath her and along the bench. Then she gave a sigh and her hand closed over Grandma Dee's butter dish. "That's it!" she said. "I knew there was something I wanted to ask you if I could have." She jumped up from the table and went over in the corner where the churn stood, the milk in it clabber by now. She looked at the churn and looked at it.

"This churn top is what I need," she said. "Didn't Uncle Buddy whittle it out of a tree you all used to have?"

"Yes," I said.

"Uh huh," she said happily. "And I want the dasher, too."

"Uncle Buddy whittle that, too?" asked the barber.

Dee (Wangero) looked up at me.

"Aunt Dee's first husband whittled the dash," said Maggie so low you almost couldn't hear her. "His name was Henry, but they called him Stash."

"Maggie's brain is like an elephant's," Wangero said, laughing. "I can use the churn top as a centerpiece for the alcove table," she said, sliding a plate over the churn, "and I'll think of something artistic to do with the dasher."

When she finished wrapping the dasher the handle stuck out. I took it for a moment in my hands. You didn't even have to look close to see where hands pushing the dasher up and down to make butter had left a kind of sink in the wood. In fact, there were a lot of small sinks; you could see where thumbs and fingers had sunk into the wood. It was beautiful light yellow wood, from a tree that grew in the yard where Big Dee and Stash had lived.

After dinner Dee (Wangero) went to the trunk at the foot of my bed and started rifling through it. Maggie hung back in the kitchen over the dishpan. Out came Wangero with two quilts. They had been pieced by Grandma Dee and then Big Dee and me had hung them on the quilt frames on the front porch and quilted them. One was in the Lone Star pattern. The other was Walk Around the Mountain. In both of them were scraps of dresses Grandma Dee had worn fifty and more years ago. Bits and pieces of Grandpa Jarrell's paisley shirts. And one teeny faded blue piece, about the size of a penny matchbox, that was from Great Grandpa Ezra's uniform that he wore in the Civil War.

"Mama," Wangero said sweet as a bird. "Can I have these old quilts?"

I heard something fall in the kitchen, and a minute later the kitchen door slammed.

"Why don't you take one or two of the others?" I asked. "These old things was just done by me and Big Dee from some tops your grandma pieced before she died."

"No," said Wangero. "I don't want those. They are stitched around the borders by machine."

"That'll make them last better," I said.

"That's not the point," said Wangero. "These are all pieces of dresses Grandma used to wear. She did all this stitching by hand. Imagine!" She held the quilts securely in her arms, stroking them.

"Some of the pieces, like those lavender ones, come from old clothes her mother handed down to her," I said, moving up to touch the quilts. Dee (Wangero) moved back just enough so that I couldn't reach the quilts. They already belonged to her.

"Imagine!" she breathed again, clutching them closely to her bosom.

"The truth is," I said, "I promised to give them quilts to Maggie, for when she marries John Thomas."

She gasped like a bee had stung her.

"Maggie can't appreciate these quilts!" she said. "She'd probably be backward enough to put them to everyday use."

"I reckon she would," I said. "God knows I been saving 'em for long enough with nobody using 'em. I hope she will!" I didn't want to bring up how I had offered Dee (Wangero) a quilt when she went away to college. Then she had told me they were old-fashioned, out of style.

"But they're *priceless*!" she was saying now, furiously; for she has a temper. "Maggie would put them on the bed and in five years they'd be in rags. Less than that!"

"She can always make some more," I said. "Maggie knows how to quilt."

Dee (Wangero) looked at me with hatred. "You just will not understand. The point is these quilts, *these* quilts!"

"Well," I said, stumped. "What would *you* do with them?"

"Hang them," she said. As if that was the only thing you *could* do with quilts.

Maggie by now was standing in the door. I could almost hear the sound her feet made as they scraped over each other.

"She can have them, Mama," she said, like somebody used to never winning anything, or having anything reserved for her. "I can 'member Grandma Dee without the quilts."

I looked at her hard. She had filled her bottom lip with checkerberry snuff and it gave her face a kind of dopey, hangdog look. It was Grandma Dee and Big Dee who taught her how to quilt herself. She stood there with her scarred hands hidden in the folds of her skirt. She looked at her sister with something like fear but she wasn't mad at her. This was Maggie's portion. This was the way she knew God to work.

When I looked at her like that something hit me in the top of my head and ran down to the soles of my feet. Just like when I'm in church and the spirit of God touches me and I get happy and shout. I did something I never had done before: hugged Maggie to me, then dragged her on into the room, snatched the quilts out of Miss Wangero's hands and dumped them into Maggie's lap. Maggie just sat there on my bed with her mouth open.

"Take one or two of the others," I said to Dee.

But she turned without a word and went out to Hakim-a-barber.

"You just don't understand," she said, as Maggie and I came out to the car.

"What don't I understand?" I wanted to know.

"Your heritage," she said. And then she turned to Maggie, kissed her, and said, "You ought to try to make something of yourself, too, Maggie. It's really a new day for us. But from the way you and Mama still live you'd never know it."

She put on some sunglasses that hid everything above the tip of her nose and her chin.

Maggie smiled; maybe at the sunglasses. But a real smile, not scared. After we watched the car dust settle I asked Maggie to bring me a dip of snuff. And then the two of us sat there just enjoying, until it was time to go in the house and go to bed.

HANNAH

BY Catherine Chung

THE YEAR THAT HANNAH DISAPPEARED, the first frost came early, killing everything in the garden. It took the cantaloupe and the tomatoes; the leaves of lettuce turned brittle and snapped. Even the kale withered and died. In front, the wine-colored roses froze, powdered gray with the cold, like silk flowers in an attic covered with dust. My father and I stood on the lawn, surveying the ruin, tracking damp patches of green wherever we stepped. He and I had planted the garden over several weekends, and tended it carefully. When I was at school, my mother called me each evening and told me what she had picked and served from it that day. It had overgrown itself, the tomatoes winding themselves up the wall of our house and stretching out to span the distance to the fence.

"We're selling the house," my father said, rubbing frost off a vine. The tendons in his neck were taut. His breath steamed slowly around his face. Everything was inside-out, or at least the cold had turned the insides of things visible. The green tomatoes had turned gray and translucent, their skins puckering at the stems, ready to burst at the bottoms and discard their sagging pulp.

"We want you to find Hannah," my father said.

"Aren't you cold?" I said. "Let's go inside." I hadn't known my parents had made a decision on selling the house. Maybe I'd expected this, but it felt suddenly difficult to breathe in the cold air.

"We're going to have to clean this up," my father said, gesturing at the garden, "if the house is going to sell."

"When are you leaving?" I asked.

"As soon as possible," my father said. "In the next couple weeks."

"I can't find her that quickly," I said. "And I want to go with you."

My father shook his head. He had blamed me after the initial panic, when we discovered that Hannah hadn't been abducted, or killed, or gone crazy, but had simply left without telling us, without leaving us a way to contact her. I was her older sister, living in the same city. He thought I should have seen it coming. My dad was already sick then, but hadn't told us yet. I wonder if Hannah would have been able to pick up and leave like that if she had known.

When I moved back home for the summer, my father couldn't hide his illness anymore. Instead of talking about it, he grilled me about Hannah. He wanted to know everything she'd said to me in the months prior to her departure: what she had looked like, what she had said. What I had noticed: why I hadn't noticed more.

Then we tracked her down through some friends, and my parents tried to call her. When she hung up on them, they asked *me* to establish contact. I didn't want to. They needed to see her, to hear her voice, to know she was safe. I understood: I needed that too. But it wasn't up to me.

※

Inside, we sat at our kitchen table, waiting for my mother to come down. My father's hands relaxed on the table, the fingers eased into a slight curl around his mug. They were old hands, and they looked fragile against the smooth blue of the mug, his veins raised thick and soft. I wanted to take his hands in mine. The impulse irritated me because they had always looked like that, had always betrayed a false vulnerability. Growing up, Hannah and I always worried we'd inherit those veins, huge and tinged blue. My father's body had pulled into itself in the last couple years so that his bones protruded, but this too was a trick. His eyes were still sharp, discerning, and his hands were the same hands that had built this table, the same hands that refused to let anything go.

"I want you to do it," my father said. "I want you to bring her home."

"I can't," I said. "She hangs up every time I call. She doesn't even say hello. She just clicks over and hangs up."

"So go there and talk to her face to face."

"She doesn't want to. I don't want to."

"She's your only sister."

"She's a brat."

We both looked up when we heard my mother's footsteps coming down the stairs: my father tilted his head and called out, "We're in the kitchen!" He leaned forward, took my hand in his. He whispered, "Not a word to your mother, you know how it upsets her."

One word about Hannah was enough to make my mother dissolve into tears for at least an hour. *Dissolve* was not too strong a word. This could happen anywhere, at any time. Even in public. At first I wondered how my mother could sustain such anxiety, how one body could hold it all. Then I realized it was a question of density.

There's a theorem in mathematics that says roughly if you take something the size of an onion and cut it into small enough pieces, you can take those pieces and construct something larger than the sun. We learned to be careful around my mother. We had no past. Everything was off limits. Coming home was entering oblivion—my father was obsessed with my last conversations with Hannah, and my mother resolutely surrounded herself with silence. So when she came padding into the kitchen, a pink robe as old as I could remember hanging raggedly around her, I slapped a smile onto my face, same as my father.

To be honest, I never really understood what Hannah had against my parents. Sure, they'd made mistakes, but nothing we shouldn't be able to get over. They had tried their best. When Hannah left for college in Chicago, I was already in my junior year at the University of Michigan. My dorm was a forty-five minute drive from our house, and I came home every other weekend to visit. The summer before Hannah left for school, she broke curfew nearly every night. At first my parents waited up for her. As the summer wore on, they waited until morning to pound on her door.

How she slept through all that pounding, I'll never know. I woke up after two seconds of it. I'd jump in the shower to drown out the noise. Besides, I knew what came next. After several minutes my father would call, "I'm coming in!" and pick her lock open with a toothpick. Then my parents would stand over Hannah's defiantly sleeping body, scolding and prodding her shoulders to wake her up. And Hannah would turn, scowling, hugging her pillow over her head.

"Let me sleep," she murmured. "Go away."

In the end it was her unwillingness to respond that defeated my parents. Even when she was awake she didn't argue, a polite smile frozen to her face. "I got into college, what more do you want from me?" she asked at breakfast after a late night out.

My mother unleashed a tirade about gratitude, filial duty.

"I guess I just don't agree," Hannah said, as if there were nothing more to say.

✳

When Hannah left for college it was as if she was leaving for good. She took her own beat-up Corolla packed full of clothes and books and music.

"I don't need anything else," she said when my parents insisted on going with her to buy sheets and posters, to help her get settled in. "I'll be fine."

My mother cried the day Hannah left, but Hannah pulled away. "I'll call you when I get there," she mumbled, shaking my father's hand. She got into her car, and pulled the door shut. My parents and I stood on the driveway, watching her silently. She started the car and didn't look back, but she opened the window and waved once. Then her arm relaxed as though all the goodbyes she had to make were taken care of, and she let her arm hang limply out the window as she drove away.

When she got to college we didn't hear from her, except for a curt call to tell us she had arrived. After a few months she started calling me once a week, just to talk about what classes were like and what kind of people she was meeting. But she only called my parents' house when she knew they wouldn't be home.

"You'll never understand," she said the last time we came home together for Thanksgiving. "They were useless as parents—when did they give us what we needed?"

The sleeves of her red shirt were pulled over her hands, her thumbs beginning to wear familiar holes along the seams. "They gave us food," I said. "They gave us water, shelter, life."

"Whatever." Hannah waved those things away. "Big deal."

✳

When Hannah and I were young we spent hours playing the Dead Auntie game. My mother's sister had died when my mother was still a child. Each year, when we followed our parents up the mountains to the graves of our ancestors to offer them food and wine, I wondered why we left my aunt's burial mound unattended. In front of the other graves we shouted out our names.

"Grandfather, we are here! Haejini and Jeehyuni! We are saying hello!"

We bowed to our grandparents, then to their parents, then to the seven generations of ancestors buried on that mountain. The path to my aunt's burial mound was overgrown, and full of snakes and biting insects, and wild berries. We did not bow in front of her grave, or call out our names. My mother quietly trimmed the grass that grew over the mound with her long curved blade, chanting the Buddha's name the entire time.

Once Hannah cried out exuberantly, "Auntie, we've come to visit you!" and my mother knelt in front of my sister and slapped her hard. When Hannah began to cry, my mother turned away, picking up the blade that she had dropped.

After that we were not allowed to visit my auntie's grave, but waited at the edge of the path and played among the trees that shaded the mountain, tapping long sticks on the ground to keep the snakes away. We picked the dark, sweet mountain berries that grew along the path so when my parents came back our hands and mouths were stained a dark, almost purple red.

The adults would never tell us how our Auntie had died. Alone, we pretended I was Auntie, and Hannah was our mother. Sometimes we switched roles so I could play the bad guys who killed her, or the doctor who diagnosed her with the fatal disease. Hannah and I would actually weep as we played this game, imagining my mother's family at the news that our Auntie was dead. I always played her brave, never giving up hope to the very last, never betraying national secrets to the North Korean spies, always standing up for what she believed in and protecting those she loved.

After Hannah went to college we started growing apart. That was the year that I became a math major. It's funny because later I went to grad school in Chicago just to be near her. She never understood my chosen field, and she considered it a betrayal in the deepest sense: a defection to my father's fortress of reason and logic.

"You can't even divide up a bill," she said. "You're horrible with numbers." I tried to tell her about complex and imaginary numbers, primes and transcendentals, numbers with families and personalities, but she rolled her eyes.

"I just don't know how you can think any of that is *important,*" she said. She was a biologist, deep in the gunk of life and committed to saving the earth, and could see no beauty in what I did. I loved math. I had been suckered in by the language, which was rich and full of promise. The classes I took were on chaos, complexity, hyperreality, completeness and incompleteness. And Hannah was right to feel left behind, maybe even betrayed. Because when I started talking shop with my father, something changed between us.

My father had always wanted a son. We women were unreliable creatures, prone to fits of emotion and flights from logic that generally ended with him being at the receiving end of a pointed finger. One day in the summer after my sophomore year of college, as my father and I tried to construct the 17-gon with a straightedge and compass, our talk turned to symmetry groups. My father loved their elegance, their ability to transform all the elements of a mapping while leaving the whole unchanged. As we tried to find automorphisms in our heads for increasingly complex patterns, something in him eased up and fell away. When we talked math, the words flowed, pure and easy. We laughed as we moved the game into hyperbolic space, made nonsensical jokes about our family in mathematical terminology. Here were rules we could both abide by, here was a language that was eloquent, and spoke to us about the world.

Later that summer, my father and I were sitting in our backyard going over what I thought at the time was a particularly complex proof. The smell of my mother's roses drifted over from the edge of the lawn. A beetle flew onto the picnic table and landed on our paper.

"Do you see this beetle?" my father said, pointing at its shiny back with his pencil. "Just think—it's mathematical fact! Even the tiniest insect has as many points on its back as the entire universe."

I was not used to my father paying any attention to an insect, except to kill it, so I was silent, curious.

"Life is like that," my father mused. He tapped his pencil by the beetle several times. "The tiniest insect carries infinity on its back: each life contains as much meaning as all of history."

Then my father leaned forward and blew a quick sharp breath on the beetle, which unfolded tiny transparent wings, lifted into the wind, and flew away.

I called Hannah that night. She was spending the summer in Chicago. I told her, "Dad's becoming human." I felt like a traitor as soon as I said it, but I'd had to put the sarcastic note in to get her to listen.

"Not interested," she said.

※

In the first anxious days after Hannah went missing, we called the police and Hannah's friends, and my mother and I went to her apartment in Chicago. When we arrived, it was clean and already bare. Even the rugs on her hardwood floor had been rolled up and stashed against a corner.

There was a note on the refrigerator in her loopy, crooked handwriting.

"Anything left in the apartment is free to take."

The refrigerator itself was empty. I'm not sure what I expected when I opened the door. A pizza, a half-eaten can of peas, a carton of milk, maybe. It was when I saw the blank insides gleaming out at me that I knew she wasn't planning on coming back. She had even polished the trays.

We ransacked her bedroom for clues of where she'd gone, for any note. We looked behind her bare desk and under her swept-out bed, but I knew there'd be nothing there.

I kept her note. I took it to my own apartment and put it inside my fridge. She'd been so deliberate, so thorough, in leaving us that I stopped worrying she'd had a breakdown, or that someone had forced her to leave. I stopped searching for her then because I was afraid of all the ways in which she would hurt us when we found her.

If I'd found her, what would I have said? My parents wanted me to tell her about my father's illness. They didn't want her to find out some other way. Their protectiveness infuriated me. Part of me wanted to punish her: wanted her to return after his illness had played out to its end. It was a cruel impulse, I knew, cruel to my parents as well as to her. But I wanted her to suffer. I wanted her to miss all of it, and know when she returned that her absence was unforgivable.

※

Hannah called me a couple of days before she disappeared, crying because the baby of a woman she worked with had died the night before.

I'd hit a wall in my dissertation several weeks before, and when Hannah called, I hadn't slept for days, had spent them instead pacing, swiping at a blackboard that I had put up in my living room to make me feel more legitimate, but which I used only to scrawl obscenities upon in large angry script when things weren't going well.

"He's dead," was the first thing Hannah wept into the phone.

"Who's dead?"

"The baby," Hannah sobbed. "The baby's dead."

"What baby?" I asked. Had Hannah been pregnant? Did I know anyone with a baby?

"Marjorie's baby, a woman from work," Hannah said, crying so hard my ear felt clammy.

"For God's sake," I said. "Hannah, are you trying to scare me to death?"

"Listen to me," Hannah said. "Her neighbor's children *threw* her baby out the window while she was at work."

"Well, was anyone watching her baby?" I asked.

"His brother."

"I'm sorry," I said. "How is your friend?"

"How do you think?" And then, "I don't really know her. I tried to find a phone number for her, but she's not listed."

"That's really awful," I said. I wrote "What the fuck?" on my blackboard, quietly so she couldn't hear the chalk.

On cue, Hannah started to cry again.

"They were only twelve years old," she said. "I don't know how to deal with this."

I shrugged at the blackboard. I made a face, outraged somehow that she could take this woman's tragedy and try to make it personal. As though the world hurt her in particular and no one else.

Some people have real problems, I wanted to say. That woman whose baby died, *she* has real problems.

"Hannah, stop," I said. "Don't," but that only made her cry harder. I could think of nothing to say that would help.

�֎

A couple months after Hannah disappeared, the kids who had thrown the baby out the window went on trial. I followed the case out of some perverse loyalty. This is what I learned: it turned out Marjorie wasn't a colleague of Hannah's, but a cleaning lady who worked in her building. She lived not in Hannah's trendy Northside neighborhood but in one of the South Side housing projects.

Her surviving son's name was Kevin. He was ten years old. The neighbor's kids had been giving him trouble for some time before the incident. The lock on Kevin's door had been broken for weeks, and those kids had come to rifle through the things in his house, to eat his mother's food. When they came the boy was sitting on the sofa watching cartoons; his baby brother was in his lap.

Roadrunner was outwitting the Wily Coyote whose Acme mail orders never quite got the job done. Boulders, buildings, pianos hung suspended in air a beat too long. The Roadrunner zoomed fearlessly beneath impending doom, but the Wily Coyote, always too slow, was flattened on the desert landscape.

That day his neighbors asked Kevin for candy. They pulled his baby brother out of his lap and pushed him. Kevin began to cry, but he had no candy. So they held his brother, dangling him by his frail legs, out the window. His brother loved it, gurgled with infant laughter, held seventeen stories above the ground.

Kevin's eyes met the boy's who held his little brother. There was no sound when the boy let go. Through the open window they saw an empty sky.

Kevin turned and ran out the door of his apartment. His feet pounded one hundred separate steps. He didn't know about the laws of gravity or physics. He imagined his brother hung suspended in the air. He thought if he could just make it down in time, his arms could catch his little brother before he hit. He ran down the stairs and out the door: his gaze aimed at the sky, his arms outstretched.

※

After the trial, I couldn't sleep at night. I stayed up thinking how I should have done things differently. When Hannah called, I should have taken a movie over to her place, and some tea, and told her our old jokes until she laughed. At night I should have lain in bed next to her and stuck my feet between her legs and asked if she remembered how mad she used to get when I did that. I should have wrapped my arms around her and talked about places we'd lived and games we had played until she was wrapped up in the comfort of who we used to be. Where was she, I wondered. In those days I lost weight and watched my parents suffer. I should have spent that night with her, I thought. If I could have done it differently I wouldn't, no matter what, have said nothing and let her go.

SISTER—SISTER

BY *Marie Luise Kaschnitz*

You've been dead eight years now, I say to my sister, would you
like to know what's been happening? No, my sister says. Fine,
I say, then I'll tell you. The Vietnam war still isn't over. I
could have predicted that, my sister says. There's still no cure
for cancer, I say. You've got to die of something, my sister
says. There are planes now, I say, which have room for five
hundred passengers and take a few hours to fly between
Europe and America. That doesn't interest me, my sister says.
All bills are figured by computers, I say. They store all the
knowledge in the world, and you can ask them questions.
I don't understand, my sister says. You've studied law, I say.
Perhaps you'll be interested to know that the accused no
longer rises before the judge and that the witnesses litter the
courtroom. I condemn that, my sister says. Perhaps, I say,
you'd also like to know that parents nowadays have great trouble bringing up their children. That the children talk back to
their parents and even hit them. Serves them right, my sister
says. Recently they flew around the moon, I say. They took
pictures from there, and on the pictures the earth is as blue
as a sapphire. I wish I could have seen that, my sister says.

Translated by Lisel Mueller

RED SCARF

BY *Jane Hirshfield*

The red scarf
still hangs over the chairback.
In its folds,
like a perfume
that cannot be quite remembered,
inconceivable *before.*

for L.B. 1950-2004

FROM I SEE YOU EVERYWHERE

BY *Julia Glass*

SWIM TO THE MIDDLE (1980)

I avoid reunions. I'm not a rebel, a recluse, or a sociopath, and I'm too young to qualify as a crank, even if it's true that I just spent the evening of my twenty-fifth birthday not carousing with friends or drinking champagne at a candlelit table for two but resolutely alone and working, glazing a large ovoid porcelain bowl while listening to Ella Fitzgerald sing songs by the Gershwin brothers. (A crank could never love Gershwin.) My one real boyfriend in college, just before we broke up, told me I'm nostalgic to a fault. He professed contempt for what he called "the delusional sound track to our parents' deluded lives." He informed me that you can't be nostalgic for things that had their heyday before you were so much as born. Just about any member of my family would have laughed him out the door and down the garden path.

Family reunions are the worst—all that competition disguised as fellowship—and they're also the hardest to avoid. But when my father's Great-Aunt Lucy died last summer, there was an inheritance at stake, a collection of antique jewelry. Not the glossy priceless stuff—no diamonds, tiaras, or niagaras of pearls. Not things you'd sell but things so deliciously old-fashioned and stylish that to wear them makes you feel like a character from a Jane Austen novel or a Chekhov play. The one piece I remembered most vividly was a cameo, two inches square, ivory on steel-blue Pacific coral, a woman's face inclined toward her hand, in her slender fingers an iris. Aunt Lucy had worn that cameo day and night, winter and summer, on lace and wool. Maybe she'd left us a charm bracelet, maybe earrings of garnet or Mexican silver, but mostly I wondered about that cameo. And wanted it. I'd wanted it since I was a little girl. One of my earliest memories is of sitting on Lucy's lap, squirming to find a comfortable spot on her bony thighs yet happy to feel her kind honeyed voice in my hair as she talked with the other grown-ups gathered on her porch. She did not object to my poking and fingering the cameo, probing its fragile details: the woman's eyelids and earlobes, the cuticles of her nails, the harmoniously wandering tendrils of her hair. She let me borrow it once, for a family dinner at a country inn.

Because Lucy never had children, not even a husband, my father long ago became the one who kept an eye on her in the last decades of her very long life. Geographically, he was the closest family member by far; out of a large, tenaciously Confederate clan, they were the only two living anywhere you can count on snow. Once Dad decided to stay north, after earning two degrees at Harvard, the family lumped him together with Lucy: "How are the defectas faring up yonda?" a cousin might ask Dad at a wedding in Memphis or Charleston. Happily, their proximity blossomed into genuine affection.

So Dad was the executor of Lucy's will, which emerged from her bureau drawer along with a letter to my father that she'd written a year before she died. It began, *To my splendid grandnephew Beauchance: Before I take my irreversible leave (which I suppose I will now have taken, strange to think), I am seizing this lucid moment to write down a few matters pertaining to the house and my ragbag possessions therein. I have little doubt that I shall have left the house in a rather sorry state, for which I apologize. Be charitable, if you can, to any bats or raccoons which may have colonized the attic or basement (though none to my knowledge have done so), and please take Sonny's word on any tasks for which he claims I still owe him payment; our mutual accounting has grown slack if not capricious. . . .*

Over the phone, Dad read me the letter in its crisp yet meandering entirety, stopping now and then to chuckle. I heard no tears in his voice until the end, where she wrote, *Whatever modest adornments pass for jewelry, I leave to your daughters, Louisa and Clement. I did not become as intimately acquainted with them as I would have liked, but I did know the satisfaction, one summer to the next, of seeing how they grew; as I wish I had seen you evolve in your youth. I wish I had known much sooner, Beau, that you would become the facsimile of a perfect son, a gift whose pleasures I wish I had been blessed to know firsthand.*

His voice cracked on the word *gift*, as if he didn't deserve such gratitude, my father who will do just about anything for anyone, driving my mother crazy with all the favors he does for everyone else (including, as she likes to say, any random citizen of Outer Slobovia and its most godforsaken suburbs).

I decided to fly across the entire country because I couldn't bear the thought that if I didn't show up in person, my sister might inherit everything—including that cameo—by default. On the plane, I tried to decide which of two equally vulgar motives, materialism or spite, had compelled me to buy a ticket I couldn't afford to a place where I'd see no one I wanted to see. My life was not, as people like to say, in a good place—though, ironically, the place where I lived at the time happened to be Santa Barbara. So I made excuses and timed my visit to avoid the masses of cousins, aunts, and uncles who would descend on Lucy's house to grope the heirlooms by day and drink too much bourbon by night. I may share their Huguenot blood, but not their bad taste in booze and their glutinous drawl. I will never forget how, when our grandmother died two years ago, the family marauded her New Orleans house with no more respect than the Union soldiers who stripped us all bare a century back. You'd think, with all our costly educations, the reconstructed Jardines would avoid civil wars. Well, ha. There was an ugly brawl, which featured weeping and a smashed lamp, over the Steinway grand. Someone with Solomonic intentions actually went so far as to crank up a chainsaw. I could not deal with that type of gathering all over again. Whether I could deal with Clem remained to be seen.

My sister had been living with Aunt Lucy for what proved to be her final summer. After Lucy's death, Clem stayed on while the relatives passed through, finishing up her summer jobs before heading back to college for her junior year. During the days, Clem worked in a bike shop and volunteered at a sanctuary for recovering raptors: birds, she'd explained when I called, that had been shot, struck by small planes, tortured by teenage boys. In the evenings, she kept an eye on Lucy—until her sudden death at the beginning of August. Not that our aunt was infirm, incontinent, or witless, but for the last several months of her life she was afflicted with an obstinate restlessness that sent her out after dark on urgent eccentric missions. Winooski, Vermont, is a snug, friendly place, so she wasn't likely to be mugged or abducted. Nevertheless, reasoned Dad, who could say she wouldn't do something drastic like sell her last shares of Monsanto and Kodak, head for the airport, and unintentionally vanish?

I'd hardly spoken to Clem since moving out west two years before. After college, in pursuit of a man I'd prefer to jettison from memory, I hauled my pottery wheel, my heart, and my disastrously poor judgment from Providence to California. It was completely unlike me to do anything so rash; maybe, subconsciously, I was trying to get back at Clem by pretending to *be* Clem, to annoy her by stealing her role as devil-may-care adventuress. Whatever the reason for my tempestuous act, it backfired. Three weeks after I signed a lease and bought a second-hand kiln, the boyfriend shed me like a stifling, scratchy-collared coat. To keep up with the rent I'd fooled myself into thinking he would share, I gave up my car. After that, I sold a pitcher here, a platter there, but to stave off eviction I wrote articles for a magazine that told workaholic doctors what to do with their leisure time. In college, I'd been just as good with words as I was with clay, and one of my Brit-lit classmates had started this odd publication. People had laughed, but subscriptions to *Doc's Holiday* sold like deodorant soap.

Thus did I hold starvation at bay, but I also felt like the work kept me stuck in a place where I ought to love living but didn't. Everything out there unnerved me: the punk shadows of palm trees slashing the lawns, the sun setting—not rising—over the ocean, the solitude of the sidewalks as I rushed everywhere on foot, carless and stared at. My inner compass refused to budge. *North!* it kept urging me. *East!* I'd just come to the conclusion that I didn't belong there and never would, and I was feeling uncomfortable in my work, both kinds, but I had no intention of letting Clem in on my angst. My plan was never to trust her again, never to fall for her charms the way everyone else, especially men, seemed to do so fervently. And to snare that cameo. Maybe a string of pearls. Oh, Glenn Miller. I love him, too. What's life without a little delusion?

※

If you're to hear Louisa's version of what went on last summer, you will also be hearing mine. Louisa's worst side is the one I call the Judge. À la Salem witchcraft trials. There's this look she gets on her face that tells the world and everyone in it how completely unworthy it and they are to contain or witness her presence. *Beware!* says that look. *The Spanish Inquisition was Entenmann's Danish!*

Her new life in Santa Ladeedabra did not seem to have mellowed her out one iota, because when I pulled up at the airport, that's the look she was wearing, firm as a church hat, beaming her world-weary scorn clear across the state of Vermont. I was late, okay, which didn't help. It didn't help either, I know, that it was me picking her up.

I wonder sometimes what kind of sisters we'll be when we're ancient (if we ever are). Olivia de Havilland and Joan Fontaine: before that visit, you'd have bet the hacienda we'd end up like them. Cold? Suspicious? Resentful? Ever notice how sisters, when they aren't best friends, make particularly vicious enemies? Like, they could be enemies from the time they lay their beady little eyes on each other, maybe because their mother makes them rivals or maybe because there's not enough love to go around and—not out of greed but from the gut, like two hawks zeroing in on a wren—they have no choice but to race for it. (Laws of nature, pure and simple. Be vigilant and survive. Altruism? A myth. Share? Oh please. Whatever it is that feeds the hunger, dive-bomb first, philosophize later.) Or maybe they grow apart in a more conscious way, maybe because their marriages clash: the guys they choose see each other as losers or sellouts; the women are helplessly loyal. But that's not our story. No husbands yet, not even a hint of husband.

I've always been the favorite—our mother's, at least. Partly, it's the animal thing: Mom grew up on a storybook farm where animals ruled life more strictly than clocks. And I happen to be the one who set my sights that way. Saving animals is all I've ever wanted to do. In fourth grade, I asked Mom to give me all her shoe boxes. A hospital: that was the plan. I cut windows in the ends of the boxes and stacked them in the bottom of my closet like high-rise condos. My first baby bird got the penthouse. Next day, he was dead. They almost always die, I'd learn. But that didn't stop me. "You're my daughter, all right," said Mom when she saw what I'd built (though her tone made me wonder if the likeness was such a good thing).

Louisa thinks this makes my life easy—being the favorite. She doesn't realize that once you're the disappointment, or once you've chosen a path seen as odd or unchoosable, your struggle is over, right? On the other side of the fence—mine—every expectation you fulfill (or look like you might, on purpose or not) puts you one step higher and closer to that Grand Canyon rim from which you could one day rule the world—or plummet in very grand style.

In the car, I let Clem do the talking. She was late to pick me up, and I was glad: it gave me a reason to sulk until I could get my bearings. I was glad to be back in New England, but I was cross-eyed with fatigue. I cannot sleep on planes. So Clem filled me in on the reading of the will and what she called the Great Divide: relatives clutching lists, drawing lots, swarming the house like fire ants. But this time there were no dogfights; everyone, said Clem, remembered the piano brawl.

I hadn't seen the place in five years, and when we arrived, I just stood on the walk and stared. It's a Victorian, more aspiring than grand, and it had always looked a little anemic, but now it was a wreck. The sallow paint, formerly white, hung off the clapboards in broad curling tongues, and the blue porch ceiling bore the crusty look of a cave complete with stalactites. The flagstones were fringed with moss. The front steps sagged. That the lawn had just been mowed made the house look even more derelict. "How could Dad let her live this way?" I asked.

With the edge of a sneaker, Clem swiped cut grass from the steps. "She insisted. She felt safer this way. No one busts in if they figure you can't afford a paint job." She shrugged. "Makes sense to me."

"But I remember this caretaker guy...."

"Sonny?" Clem laughed. "Lou, do you know how old *he* is now?"

I walked ahead of her into the house. I braced myself for cob-webbed sofas, curtains spattered with mildew, but I was shocked again. The antique tables were polished, the upholstery taut and preened, the glass over the samplers and watercolor seascapes shimmering with leafy reflections. The floor, once oak plank covered with dark orientals, was now a bright field of linoleum, great black and white squares, stretching from parlor to kitchen. I dropped my bag. "What the hell happened here?"

"She told me she always wanted to live inside a Vermeer." My sister watched me for a moment. "I mean, you're the artist, you can relate."

"Vermeer? This is Captain Kangaroo."

"It was an experiment," said Clem. "Don't be so uptight."

I walked on through the dining room. The same old salt-pocked captain's table and the five-foot brass candlesticks supported by tur-baned Moors now resembled pieces on a chessboard. But the kitchen had become the most eccentric room of all, a time warp. The cabi-nets were the ones I remembered, their rumpled glass panes fram-ing porcelain platters, ranks of translucent teacups, curvaceous tureens (of which, I now realized, I would have liked to claim a few). In the center of the room, like a relic of Pompeii, the same claw-foot bathtub held court: no faucets, a rusted gas-jet heater below. When I was little and we stayed here, Dad would haul water from an out-door pump and turn on the gas. After turning it off, he'd press a towel or two against the bottom so Clem and I could bathe without scalding our bottoms. Beyond the pump was an outhouse shrouded in lilacs. When Dad insisted on plumbing, Aunt Lucy balked. The compromise was one toilet, a washing machine, and a kitchen sink; after that, to fill the tub, she'd hitch a garden hose to the tap in the big soapstone sink. "Luxe de luxe! Just splendid! My dears, you haven't a clue what modern *feels* like," she'd say. "To you, it's the air you breathe. To me, it's a foreign country, an Oriental language."

But the long wooden counter, with its century of scars, now stopped at a double-door frost-free Amana, imposing as a glacier. Lined up along the back of the counter, cheek to cheek, were several brand-new culinary contraptions. A Cuisinart, a coffee grinder, and a microwave, followed by a small turquoise missile whose function I deduced only from its name: Juice King. At the very end, a circular machine with a plastic dome. When I peered inside it, Clem said "It makes bread," and opened the freezer door. Stacked inside were dozens of foil-wrapped cubes. "She sort of stopped sleeping at night, so sometimes I'd stay up, too, and we'd, like, improvise. She never settled for plain white or wheat, no plain *anything*. I'd be a wreck at work the next day, while she'd sleep away the morning. But we had a blast."

Side by side, we examined the contents of the freezer, its chilly white mist scorching our skin. Each loaf was labeled in Lucy's Christina Rossetti cursive on first-aid tape: ZUCCHINI-BIRDSEED, BANANA-MAPLE RYE, ZUCCHINI-CHOCOLATE, PRUNE-PECAN-CASSIS. "Harvey's Bristol sourdough wheat?" I read aloud.

Clem reached past me and took it out. "Awesome with cream cheese. We'll have it for breakfast." She closed the door, leaned against it, and folded her arms. Standing there, she looked for just a minute like our mother, sure of her place in a world where she'd landed almost by accident. I laughed.

"Oh good," said Clem.

"What?"

"You didn't leave it behind after all."

"What?" I said again.

Clem walked toward me and pretended to pull something out of my breast pocket. She held it up, the invisible thing, and shook it in front of my face. "Your sense of humor." She put it back, giving my pocket a tender pat.

I felt the air shift between us, as if we were finally together somehow. This wasn't what I wanted. I walked across the room and looked out the window at the backyard. I counted four bird feeders, all filled. My sister, Saint Francis of Assisi.

"The cousins missed you," said Clem. "Too bad about your deadline. Couldn't you just have brought your typewriter out on the plane?"

I sat on the edge of the tub. I could tell her that I didn't work well away from home, but it would have been a lie, and it might have started a real conversation, which I was doing my best to avoid. "How come the place isn't looted?"

Clem pointed to the kitchen table and chairs. I noticed then that everything wore a claim: a tag or strip of tape marked RACINE, JACKIE J., GAIA, BEAU, and so on. The shippers would pack it all up the following week, after Clem left for school. My father would return, to hire painters and talk to real estate agents.

Clem hadn't taken her eyes off me. She'd spotted my resistance, and I could tell she was contemplating the challenge. "So, you buying me dinner tonight?"

"If you're buying tomorrow. I don't remember owing you any favors," I said.

Her smile opened wide. I've always envied her those perfect teeth: small and square, lined up straight as rails in a banister. "Deal," she said.

A LESSON IN MANNERS
BY *Misty Urban*

ONE DAY SHE NOTICES IT: about the size of a fortune cookie, a hard lump in her side underneath the skin. Best not to think about it, all those squishy organs in there with their unaccountable functions. Let it drift around her innards, float away. One week it begins to send out faint signals of its presence, like blinkers on the brain waves. She doesn't mention it until it's got her flat on her back in the bed. Her hair is longer now. You haven't seen her in three months.

Where do these things begin? Take a mental picture of her in the Austrian bed, the Alps in her window, a tennis ball in her side underneath her hand. Motrin. Tylenol. Mother's Day. Her skin is smooth now the way it never was at home, all the whole milk and red meat of a semester abroad filling her out to a buttery softness, hair like the ferns on the Austrian hills. *Don't*, she says when you go to touch the place that hurts her. So you don't. Who are you? You cannot heal by the laying on of hands. You are the sister, visiting for a week. She is the sister visiting you for nineteen years, who has hidden your favorite blue T-shirt underneath her mattress so you won't find it and take it back home with you.

No one knows why. Only the when. A year ago she rowed on the crew team, her biceps tough as a cornstalk, her skin like almond silk;

she came home drunk from college parties and got her navel pierced. At thirteen when Rusty Stedman took her back behind the middle school to smoke her first bitter cigarette you didn't recognize the smell of tobacco on the flannel shirt she borrowed from Dad's closet. She's five, maybe, when one cell loses its blueprint and its self-respect, becomes reckless in propagation, teeming slowly into a malignant life. Not that either? Take it further back, then, to that one rung in the step-ladder spiral of the DNA, in your father's body, or your mother's, to the place where we are all rogue proteins being carried around like a secret in the bodies of our ancestors, waiting for enough people to have enough sex so our two cells can meet and we can be born.

Maybe sometimes two cells meet again in almost exactly the same way and the next one born is almost exactly you again, only your sister, so in a way she uniquely belongs to you. Look at the picture of you as babies, wearing the same denim overalls and the same red flowered shirts, sitting against a backdrop time will fade to a speckled bronze. You are three years old, she is two, grinning through fat cheeks as she sits buttoned on your lap, so close to your heart. All of your adult lives are already in your faces, if you but knew. But you don't know and so you reach out your hand and she says *don't*, as in don't touch it it hurts stupid and in the many opaque silences that will follow you will wish you had said *I just want to make it go away*. But you don't.

Leave her in Austria with over-the-counter pain relief and the last of your money, maybe twenty dollars. Fly home crowded in steerage with strangers, one of whom drools on your shoulder. You are not blessed with knowing. Perhaps it has no beginning ever, merely springs into being like Athena from the forehead of Zeus, like Venus rising from the sea, there it is, this thing in her side, this characteristic feat of rebellion, these mysterious insides growing mysteriously out of control. These things happen.

✳

So while there are helium balloons for homecomings and helium balloons for hospitals, there are no holiday balloons for homecomings spent in hospitals. Yet here you all are, assembled in this utility-white room after a few phone calls, a scan through a big cold metallic tube, a doctor who can't decide. Heads it's an abscess, tails it's a tumor. He wants backup. He wants to consult a panel of experts. This is not the kindly family doctor who taped fingers and stitched knees throughout your childhood and hers; this is a cool tall made-for-TV doctor who would be too handsome except for the scar on his chin, who would never pat a little girl on the head and give her candy if she cried. The problem is there is no backup. This is a small town, this is a big seeping mass of a kidney that has begun to bully the other organs out of its way.

Show up in the dress pants and blouse you wore to work. Don't stop home to change; instead, unpremeditated, pull into the parking lot of the movie theater. Aaron, the man you long for absolutely, is standing below the marquee with the long flimsy stick shuttling blocky black letters back and forth. This is not a reasoned maneuver. This is your very last chance at a normal life. Yet there is only one way the conversation could go and it is this:

Him: I am very happy with Sarah and I am going to make her my wife and you and I have always been very good friends.

You: Yes, well thank you, I am on my way to the hospital now as my sister is having her kidney removed. Cheers.

When you tell the story you will leave this part out. In narrative terms, it doesn't fit. Perhaps it could be used to develop character but as that is always a painful process you would rather avoid it.

✳

The evening unfolds in varying tempos. This is the *allegretto*, the high drama when your sister's belly-button ring has been discovered. She insists on keeping it. She clung to it despite infection, inflammation, all the stinky pus that demanded swabbing with alcohol and prevented her from sleeping on her stomach. Your mother is vocalizing all the objections that made your sister warn you not to tell her in the first place.

Where are you in all this? You will forget later if you were standing near the head of the bed being useful or standing at the back of the room hovering, an awkward shadow, poked about by the sharp corners with no hint of dust, the sterile white. You will always remember that the chairs are orange. Memory can flush and reorganize everything except the color, that burnt-umber orange and the arrogant white. The lines of this room are askew; the planes of the ceiling slope inward, the walls are distant, the bed in the middle of the room seems enormous with your sister atop it in pale skin and a blue-sprigged hospital gown, like a grand French lady of the 18th century conducting business in her boudoir.

The intern, flanked by a rolling cart of needles and syringes, pokes her arm for the seventh or eighth time, still trying to start an IV. Let me get that, the nurse says with scrubbed and well-practiced efficiency, and the grateful intern diminishes with embarrassment. The nurse takes your sister's wrist and turns her arm out, flicks her middle finger twice against the inside crook of her elbow, picks a new needle off the cart, rips the package open with one hand. Your sister doesn't bat an eyelash as the pin sinks into her vein. The metallic taste at the back of your throat has been there since you left the movie theater. Is this where it begins? Is this it?

Enter the doctor, on cue, with a lean white coat and three different colors of pen in his pocket. The room is suddenly crowded with assurance, expertise. He is wearing white sneakers. He is tall enough to graze his head on the TV bolted to the ceiling. Undoubtedly he played sports in high school; he has an athlete's grace. He is sportsmanlike about his talent, the power to stick knives and needles into people, to juggle organs like balls. Bad kidney, into the bucket with it. He begins to explain procedures, surgery times, recovery times, biopsies, consults, all things that sound organized and terribly normal. At the side of your sister's bed the nurse attaches a small bluecapped vial to the IV and begins to fill it with blood. With slow thoughtfulness the rich dark liquid seeps into the glass container. Think as you watch how simple it is, really, how fragile, that barrier of skin. So easily what is inside can come out.

Your mother looks a little dazed. She has not even seen the pictures from Europe yet and now she is looking at X-ray films, a weedy mass of shadows. The doctor, using his finger as a marker, draws the incision line across your sister's paper-thin bed gown. He starts just shy of the navel, bumps over the rib cage, ends somewhere beneath the left shoulder blade. The line he traces is at least twelve inches long.

In the next twelve hours she is allowed to eat nothing. The jewelry must be removed. Earrings and necklace unclasp; the bellybutton ring does not. Alcohol, infection, or greedy time has fused the slender wire into one hard-bitten circle. The doctor sends the nurse for wire cutters. Your father offers to go home and get his. He has them in three different sizes and he, too, would like to be useful. He can build a house and dismantle a car, pour cement and name all the planets. Right before he met your mother, his own mother died in long agony when the cells of her spine forgot how to be bone cells and turned into something else. It made him the kind of man who does not want to be cremated; better to have the body preserved and safely locked away underground just in case he is wrong and there is a God and a Last Judgment.

Perhaps you are sitting in one of those orange chairs. Perhaps you are holding the slim plastic baggie full of your sister's jewelry. This much you can do. This small thing. Your mother cringes as the doctor wrestles with the navel ring, this tiny, harmless, inorganic piece of metal. At last he snaps the wire. Presto—beads spatter like tiny bullets onto the tiled floor.

✵

Adagio. There is little left to do except wait. Your father goes home to feed the dog. Your mother goes down the hall to make phone calls she doesn't want your sister to overhear. You sit in one of the burnt-orange chairs, taking mental notes, hoping someone will ask you to give blood. Imagine your presence is soothing. Hope someone will ask you for your kidney, to give to her.

Your sister kicks you out when the nurse comes to perform the enema.

Time passes. Night falls. Your mother goes home. You stay; it doesn't occur to you to leave. That is your sister on that bed. All those nights in Austria, alone in a dark room with this thing in her belly; what would have gone through her mind? The nurse simply shrugs. You suppose she must have daughters. She must have watched them brush each other's hair and argue about who got which side of the bed before falling asleep cupped together like spoons.

When the two of you are finally alone, and all the nurses have pattered softly away, move the chair closer to the bed. There is something that can be said here, surely, to ease the awkwardness of these moments, to push the walls gently back into place and let in some air. You do not know what that something is. Begin to reminisce about Austria. She looks at you with eyes dark and huge, as though there is no light in the room. Remind her of when you first met her host brother and how you prattled on at him in English before she gently pointed out that he didn't understand a word past "hello." She laughs: a small triumph. Tell her how the two of you walked along the river in Salzburg one evening singing and listening to the bells of the dozens of churches. That night in the café you ordered a bottle of California wine and the waiter gave you his cigarettes, sliding a cool gaze first over you, then over your sister, eyes flickering back and forth before deciding to leave you alone, the two American tourists, not ugly ones. On the train back to her university she took a picture of you sleeping on the bench with your mouth open. You took a picture of her in the cloudy rain, standing at the gate of the palace gardens in her purple windbreaker, hood pulled over her head, looking up.

Say to her that you will go to Paris. It is a promise, defiant of recovery times or of fate. She hates Paris. A man there lied to her about her departure time so he could invite her back to his flat to pass the five hours until the next train. Venice, she says. A week in Venice. Imagine the two of you floating along a steamy canal, the buildings dripping secrets, the Italian sun.

What else can you give her? Your hand. Your blue shirt. Ask her if she's scared and watch the tears begin to slide down the clear canvas of her face. She has not cried before you since your car accident, since she came home from a friend's house to find you stiffening in your father's armchair, the bump on your head turning into a Technicolor bruise. At the sight of you she burst into tears, the scrapes on your neck, the welt on your forehead. When she comes home two months from now from a different hospital you will know what it is to break into tears at the sight of her, at her graceful thinness, at the way she walks as though preserving some fragile inward space. At her bald head vulnerable and beautiful with a beauty too pure for words.

If only there were tokens you could offer, the gesture that would mean grace. Words, after all, can do so much. Say *I do* and you have bound someone to you in marriage. Say *I love you* and you have bound someone to you for life. Say *my side hurts* and something like a kidney may come out of it. Remain silent and you may be saying *I love you not* or simply, *I don't know.*

You are not yet fluent in tears. You will be.

✳

In the darkness, in the utter absence of light, you can hear each tick of the clock, brassy and distinct. You can hear her breathe. The light is out there, trying to get in beneath the door, but the door is closed. Lie stiffly on the second bed, clothes scratching your skin. This would be the time to pray. This would not be the time to think of Aaron, his steady face, his swift hands.

The door opens. The silhouette backlit in white is your mother. Go home, the silhouette says. I'll stay with her.

Thus ends your vigil. One person watching sleepless through the night is touching and effective; two are redundant. Even now the room is too small. Take your resentment, take your car keys. Put your trust in the holy mission of mothers, who bestow kisses and cough drops, vitamins and formula, who are the pillars who hold up the world. Slide out the door like a ghost.

✳

According to certain theories of astral projection and quantum mechanics, one particle can be in two places at one time. So here you are driving home in your car, and here you are still at the hospital. In a wet midnight the city is sinister, a waiting animal with a half-moon eye. The trees lean inward. Buildings gleam blackly like ore.

Your father sits in his armchair in the living room in a circle of sanity and pale electric light, a *National Geographic* on his lap, a perfectly reasonable behavior, and yet perfectly not. Who are the keepers here? Who are the watchers through this night? You carry a memory of your father that surfaces sometimes, like now. One long-past summer afternoon you and your sister found a small toad on the pool deck and screamed loudly at the sight of it, perhaps more with the joy of screaming than with actual fear. Dad, fixing the lawn mover in the shed, came to deal with the reptile invasion, as dads must. He picked it up and carried it in cupped hands to the edge of the field, where in the tall grass he let it go. Then he went into the house. Remember the red of those small discs of blood that you saw on the sun-washed planks. Remember how you followed him inside and found him bandaging a deep cut in his hand made by the lawnmower blade. In your lifetime your father has shot and killed snakes, birds, gophers, squirrels, deer, rabbits, dogs, and chickens, so it astounds you still that he would carry this toad as gently as a gift in his bleeding hands.

Mom's at the hospital, you tell him, to explain why you are not.

She never can sleep when one of you kids is sick, he says without looking up.

On the opposite wall of your bedroom is a cologne advertisement with a photograph of a beautiful man, taken from a European magazine your sister purchased when she was dreaming of Austria. Next to the bed opposite yours is her baggage, unzipped, only half unpacked. On the wall near the door, Scotch-taped to the trim, is her months-old packing list. She crossed things off as they made their way into her luggage. Wool jacket, leather boots. Years later that list will still be taped there. All the things she could not do without.

✳

You meant not to sleep and you did, deeply. Sleeping or awake, the day will come, and here it is. Your father is leaving for the hospital. He is freshly-shaven and smells of Old Spice. It is his birthday today, but no one has remembered this, perhaps not even him.

※

The hospital room is vacant when you arrive, missing one bed and its occupant, the IV, the trays, everything. The two chairs sit staring into the empty space. She was cracking jokes when they wheeled her out, your mom says. This does not absolve you. A white sun burns through the window. The room is sixteen paces long. Fourteen. Thirty-two. You've lost count; you forgot to count. Decide you will wait here, circling like a shark, until she gets back. It seems fittingly dramatic. You are only the older sister; you are not the one who has been chosen. There is no strong shoulder to circle your wound like a wall.

Your mother, hovering at the door, is not nearly as large in person as she seemed last night. Flowers, she tells you. You are being dispatched; the drama, understand, is being controlled. Flowers, toothpaste, fresh underwear from home. Regulate the small things and the big things will follow the rules.

※

The flower shop overflows with an abundance of exactly three types of flowers, none of which are suitable for this occasion. You might have known from the assortment of flowerpots that the gardener's tastes are not, shall we say, compatible with yours. There is every color of carnation, and you dislike carnations; they're cheap, something on sale at a high school dance, a flower pretending too hard to be something it isn't. There is a whole wall of roses, which are too flagrant, too demonstrative, too open and emotionally needy; I am full of passion, the roses say, I am full of grief. You want something quiet and tasteful—tulips would be lovely—not in season, but lovely for your sister. You imagine she herself would choose something wild and dramatic: orchids, or bird of paradise, the big flower that looks like a trumpeting swan. But it seems hardly suitable to order a flower that would not arrive until the next day or even, knowing your town, two weeks from now. Fume silently to yourself, imagining you project an important look, here as you are on a mission of mercy. Cast your gaze about as though the world has failed you, has failed to appropriately set your scene. The right gesture, after all, is important. The right flowers and skin knits faster, organs resume their accustomed functions. The right word might have made Aaron look at you, if only once.

Near the front counter, in a small and unassuming basket, is your flower, soft and tendril-like, a purple-white tiger lily with indigo at the heart and petals shaped like a tear. These are the ones you will take. These, the flowers that are your kind of flower and not hers, in a vase that is of your own choosing, a thin metal canister with a faux old-country label that says "Peaches." Who but yourself do you have to please, really? Who is noticing you as you racket around town as though it is too hot in your own skin?

※

Discover that the peaches can was never meant to hold water. You have mistaken the decorative for the functional. At least in this narrow hospital bathroom, at this narrow sink, there is no one to witness your blunder. Here you added flower food so carefully, and there it all goes, washing down the drain, not stopping for your fingers or your fear. That sound you hear is your heart beating. If the small things do not obey a natural symmetry—if the small things do not follow the rules—what then?

At home, going through her bag for fresh panties, you feel sneaky, like you are stealing something. On the wall the cologne man stares haughtily into the distance, skin smooth as marble, a promise of what is possible.

Return to the hospital with a vase, with the toothpaste. Deliver the flowers like Pandora's winged hope. It's your story—you get to tell it. The part about the leaking canister you can just leave out.

※

That quickly four hours have gone by. That is her anesthesiologist on the stairs. He is wearing his green scrubs but no gloves or mask. There is not a spot of blood on him. Be grateful for this.

Greet him with the cheer of an old friend: Hi, how is she?

She's doing fine. The surgery went well. She's in the recovery room and you'll be able to go see her. Notice he does not look you in the eye as he speaks. Perhaps he is shy. Run up the rest of the stairs and burst into the waiting room, your arms blooming purple. In your mind, it's over. You think the worst is over. Deliver your news to your waiting parents, exuberance as open as breath.

This is where the narrative takes a vicious turn, where plot snakes into the unforeseen, the unimagined. Your father stands tightly in pinched skin. Your mother's eyes have a cherry redness. Mom, she's fine, say again, as though you can make it so, as though the whole mess will slide right down the drain without even leaving a smear.

The doctor, however, has already been to see your parents. It is not an abscess. It is something else, something the opposite of benign, something that has squatted maliciously over the kidney and sent scouts to the lymph nodes and lungs. The doctor must be equivocal. He does not want to unduly scare anybody. People wearing pajamas come into the waiting room, speak of tissue samples, research centers, tests. Your father's eyes glaze; he is remembering your grandmother, thinking how things skip generations, how we carry our destinies in our blood. Your mother reaches out and puts her arms around you, flowers and all.

Having said their piece, the people in pajamas withdraw to go punish someone else. How unfair of them, you think, to hit you in the face first, then leave you to reel down the hallway to the recovery room. This might be their plan, to blow up the defenses of the family so they can get at the body and snatch it away. Leave you shaken and bruised to face her with this knowledge which you now have and she does not when she, not just shaken, not just bruised, has been lacerated, relieved of a kidney and half a rib, given a twelve-inch scar closed with industrial staples over hairless skin.

Float down the hallway behind your parents in a light too bright for shadows, everything a hollow and unholy white, which seems to come from some hidden place in the walls. If someone asked you later how to find the recovery room, you would not be able to tell them. If someone asked how long it took, you could not say. Later all you will remember are the double doors that open to the large room, the two figures inside it, the nurse and the patient stretched out on the bed.

A blue cotton blanket is heaped over her chest. Her head is turned to the wall, away from you, so you cannot see her face, only the fall of hair behind her ear. The nurse stands with one hand on her bare arm lightly stroking the abandoned skin. The needle in her arm now circulates saline and antibiotics. A small clear tube extends into her mouth, down her trachea, and the respirator pushes air, gently, into her lungs.

Someone has broken your sister. Someone has dropped her here, a limp doll with limbs askew; someone has checked the spirit out of her and put this tube in her body to keep the body alive until the spirit comes back from wherever it is right now, back from surgery, back from Austria, back from wherever spirits go to avoid enduring the unendurable. Everything else stripped away, here you have it, this thinness, this blind absence, this dumb flailing like a fish exposed to light. No wonder you are pinned to the wall. There is nothing you can do. This moment has dropped out of the sky like a boulder, crushing your bones.

Somebody needs to give you a tube for your chest. Somebody needs to give you a tissue. So often choices are as simple as this: breathe or cry. Cry, or leave.

Follow, minutes or hours later, when your mother makes a move toward the door. That step is so much easier than the one that would take you to her side in the tender bravery of the nurse, to stroke her arm, to hold vigil until the wandering spirit decides to return. You know she would hate to see herself like this, exposed and defenseless, depending on this machine. She should not wake to your incoherent tears. You would stand there and hold her body together with your hands if you could, if it would matter, but you are afraid this will require a skill which you will turn out not to possess. You might be the one to break her, to inflict a damage that can never be healed. Leave the room in obedient silence while the wide doors swoosh open and then swoosh closed, shutting her in there with the nurse and the blanket, shutting you out.

In your memory, you went back in there. You stood at her side instead of the nurse; you touched that smooth senseless arm over and over praying that whatever had taken her would forgive her and bring her back, or forgive you. But you never did.

✳

In the waiting room, you are doing what the sign says, waiting. You read a book about Cassandra and the fall of Troy. You watch a brown-haired man on daytime TV break the heart of a made-for-TV woman. The aides will wheel your sister's bed back up to her room, where for a long time she will look at last like she is only sleeping, where she will later open her eyes in a morphine haze and your mother will try to make her look at those stupid flowers. After sleeping hours more she will be the first to say, her voice a hoarse whisper, happy birthday, Dad.

They will tell you many things: pediatric cancer, adult kidney cancer, found most commonly in five-year-old children or forty-year-old males. They will say smoking, no, hereditary. Your mother will endlessly repeat these explanations in search of an explanation. Your father will stretch his memory back to other hospitals, steel rails on beds, his mother with a failing voice introducing him as her baby. Believe none of it; believe what you will; believe it all. Think of Cassandra, who saw her doom coming. Think of the people of Troy, who did not listen to her, and doom came upon them anyway.

Your father does not kill needlessly. Neither, you hope, does God.

When your cousin drove his car and three friends into a tree and disappeared in a spectacular set of pyrotechnics you at least could circle the site, examine the empty space, contemplate the sudden violence, the absence with its sharp edges. Your sister is being stolen in pieces, kidney first. She will be worn down before your eyes into a bright gold thread which becomes too fine to see. Keep to your silence, if you will. Cling to your ignorance. Perhaps you think it is brave of you; perhaps you will be the one who believes, through it all, that there is no danger. Perhaps you can save her by blind faith. Or perhaps, by saying nothing, you will simply lose her into that silence. Let her drift too far away from you and you will never get her back. This is a fire that will fall from the sky in slow drops like rain and it will burn for a long time, leaving in the end only witnesses, which are not the same as survivors.

THE SEAL WOMAN
BY *Cynthia Hogue*

There was a moment when
I thought I would go too.
I'd lived so long with my sisters
crooning to men on shore,
sometimes nuzzling those few
found afloat in our sea
back to motionless land.

At sunset, people would gather
to watch us lifting ourselves up on rocks,
our coats shivered with fire.
Then we'd dip back in,
draw as near as we dared,
and bob in the shallows
watching them too.

But this night I am alone.
I have seen how the strange calls of men
put limbs like their own
on my sisters, stripped their fur
to freezing white skin.
I've seen my two sisters
crawl out of the water

and look back at me with alien faces.
I tried to follow but they said,
in voices already altered,
they gave you no name;
you must stay there.
I waited to be named a long time.
Now I wait for my sisters.

Their hair is white
as their wrinkled hide.
They come down to the water to keen
for their lost skin
and for the one whose name
escapes them. But I've caught
their gaze and—dry so long—

their eyes fill with the sea.

WITHOUT GLOVES

BY *Martha Rhodes*

My sister and I are fighting as always
in dreams, our faces an inch apart.
On the counter: carving knives and platters
(perhaps Mother's)
(perhaps Mother's dead in the cabinet).

What should we do?
Don't pick up the knives.
Don't touch them without gloves.

"I hate your husband," she tells me.
"He hates you," I answer.
"He stares at my breasts."
"Wear a blouse," I tell her.

She tries to touch me as always
in dreams and I call a dog,
the biggest on the block
but a rat answers my whistle,
and attaches to my wrist.

Always rats in dreams with us
or other little rodents.
Little punctures, little nibbles,
my gnawed off little hand
and I'm unable to save it.

FROM GIRL MEETS BOY
BY *Ali Smith*

(OH MY GOD my sister is A GAY.)

(I am not upset. I am not upset. I am not upset. I am not upset.)

I am putting on my Stella McCartney Adidas tracksuit bottoms. I am lacing up my Nike runners. I am zipping up my Stella McCartney Adidas tracksuit top. I am going out the front door like I am a (normal) person just going out of a (normal) front door on a (normal) early summer day in the month of May and I am going for a run which is the kind of (normal) thing (normal) people do all the time.

There. I'm running. That feels better. I can feel the road be-neath my feet. There. There. There.

(It is our mother's fault for splitting up with our father.)

(But if that's true then I might also be a gay.)

(Well obviously that's not true then, that's not true at all.)

(I am definitely, definitely not a gay.)

(I definitely like men.)

(But so does she. So did she. She had that boyfriend, Dave, that she went out with for ages. She had that other boyfriend, Stuart. She had that one called Andrew and that weird English boyfriend, Miles or Giles who lived on Mull, and that boy Sammy, and there was one

177

called Tony, and Nicholas, because she always had boyfriends, she had boyfriends from about the age of twelve, long before I did.)

I am crossing at the lights. I am going to run as far as I can. I am going to run along the river, through the Islands, round by the sports tracks, past the cemetery and up towards the canal

(is that the right way to say it, a gay? Is there a correct word for it?)

(How do you know if you are it?)

(Does our mother know about Anthea being it?)

(Does our father know?)

(It is completely natural to be a gay or a homosexual or whatever. It is totally okay in this day and age.)

(Gay people are just the same as heterosexual people, except for the being gay, of course.)

(They were holding hands at the front door.)

(I should have known. She always was weird. She always was different. She always was contrary. She always did what she knew she shouldn't.)

(It is the fault of the Spice Girls.)

(She chose the video of *Spiceworld* with Sporty Spice on the limited edition tin.)

(She was always a bit too feminist.)

(She was always playing that George Michael CD.)

(She always votes for the girls on *Big Brother* and she voted for that transsexual the year he was on, or she, or whatever it is you're supposed to say.)

(She liked the Eurovision Song Contest.)

(She still likes the Eurovision Song Contest.)

(She liked *Buffy the Vampire Slayer*.)

(But so did I. I liked it too. And it had those girls in it who were both   female homosexuals   and they were portrayed as very sweet, and it was okay because it was Willow, and she was clever, and we knew to like her and everything, and her friend Tara was very sweet, and I remember one episode where they kissed and their feet came off the ground and they levitated because of the kiss, and I remember that the thing to do when we talked about it at school the next day was to make sick noises.)

Four texts on my phone. Dominic.

WOT U UP 2?

COMIN 2 PUB?

GET HERE NOW.

U R REQD HERE.

(I hate text language. It is so demeaning.)

(I will text him when I get back from my run. I will say I left my mobile at home and didn't get the message till later.)

I am down to just over seven stone.

I am doing well.

We are really revolutionising the bottled water market in Scotland.

Eau Caledonia. They love it as a tag. I got a raise.

I get paid thirty-five thousand before tax.

I can't believe I'm earning that much money. Me!

I am clearly doing the right thing. There is good money in water.

(She is still insisting on calling them shaveys or whatever, and it is unfair of her to lump them all together. It is just fashion. Boys are worse followers of fashion than girls. I mean, men than women. She is wrong to do that. She is wrong)

(they were holding hands at the front door, where any neighbour could see, and then I saw Robin Goodman lean my sister gently into the hedge, back against the branches of it, she was so gentle, and)

(and kiss her.)

(I should have known when she always liked songs that had I and you in them, instead of he and I, or he and she, we always knew, we

used to say at college that that was the giveaway, when people preferred those songs that had the word you instead of a man or a
woman, like that classic old Tracy Chapman album our mother left
behind her that she was always playing before she went.)

(I will never leave my children when I have fallen in love and am
married and have had them. I will have them young, not when I am
old, like the selfish generation. I would rather give up any career
than not have them. I would rather give myself up. I would rather
give up everything including any stupid political principle than leave
children that belonged to me. Look how it ends. Thank God that
feministy time of selfishness is over and we now have everything we
will ever need, including a much more responsible set of values.)

It is a lovely day to go for a run. It is not raining. It doesn't even
look like it will rain later.

(My sister is a gay.)

(I am not upset.) (I am fine.)

(It'd be okay, I mean I wouldn't mind so much, if it was someone else's sister.)

(It is okay. Lots of people are it. Just none that I have known personally, that's all.)

I am running along the riverside. I am so lucky to live here at this
time in history, in the Capital of the Highlands, which is exception-
ally buoyant right now, the fastest-developing city in the whole of the
UK at the moment thanks to tourism and retirement, and soon also
thanks to the growing water economy, of which I am a central part,
and which will make history.

We speak the purest English here in the whole country. It is because
of the vowel sounds and what happened to them when Gaelic speakers
were made to speak English after the 1745 rebellion and the 1746 de-
feat when Gaelic was stamped out and punishable by death, and then
all the local girls married the incoming English-speaking soldiers.

If I can remember the exact, correct words to all the songs on that awful Tracy Chapman album, which I can't have heard for years, it must be at least ten years, I'll be able to run for at least three more miles.

It is good to be goal-orientated. It makes all the other things go out of your mind.

I could go via the canal and past the locks and up over towards the Beauly road and then round by

(but dear God my sister has been hanging around for weeks with a person who is a criminal and against whom the company I work for is pressing charges, and not just that but a person whom I remember from school, and a person, I also remember, we all always called that word behind her back at school, and now this person has turned my sister into one of them, I mean One of Them. And I mean, how did we know to call Robin Goodman that word at school? Adolescent instinct? Well, I didn't know, I never really knew. I thought it was because she had a boy's name instead of a girl's name. That's what I used to think, or maybe because she came in on the bus from Beauly, with the Beauly kids, from somewhere else, and because she had a boy's name, that's what I thought. And because she was a bit different, and didn't people used to say that her mother was black, Robin Goodman, and her father was white, or was it the other way round, and was that even true? I don't remember there being any black people living in Beauly, we'd surely have known, we'd all have known, if there was.)

(I can't bring myself to say the word.)

(Dear God. It is worse than the word cancer.)

(My little sister is going to grow up into a dissatisfied older predatory totally dried-up abnormal woman like Judi Dench in that film *Notes on a Scandal*.)

(Judi Dench plays that sort of person so well, is what I thought when I saw it, but that was when I didn't think my sister was going to maybe be one of them and have such a terrible life with no real love in it.)

(My little sister is going to have a terrible sad life.)

(But I saw Robin Goodman lean my sister into the hedge with such gentleness, there is no other word for it, and kiss her, and then I saw, not so gently, Robin Goodman shift one of her own legs in between my sister's legs while she kissed her, and I saw my sister, it wasn't just one-sided, she was kissing Robin Goodman back, and then they were both laughing.)

(They were laughing with outrageous happiness.)

(Neighbours must have seen. It was broad daylight.)

(I might have to move house.)

(Well, that's all right. That's all right. If I have to move house I have enough money to.)

Thirty-five thousand, very good money for my age, and for me being a girl, our dad says, which is a bit sexist of him, because gender is nothing to do with whether you are good at a job or not. It is nothing to do with me being a woman or not, the fact that I am the only woman on the Highland Pure Creative board of ten of us—it is because I am good at what I do.

Actually, I think Keith might ask me to go to the States, maybe for training with the in-house Creatives at Base Camp. I think Base Camp is in L.A.!

He seems very pleased with the Eau Caledonia tag.

He thinks it will corner not just the English-speaking market but a good chunk of the French market, which is crucial, the French market being so water-sales-established worldwide. Scottish, yet French. Well done, he said. They'd like you at Base Camp. You'd like it there.

Me! Los Angeles!

He seemed to be intimating it. He intimated it last Tuesday. He said I'd like it there, that's what he said last week, that I'd like it, that they'd like me.

I told Anthea he had intimated it. She said: Keith intubated you? Like on *ER*?

I said: you're being ridiculous, Anthea.

(There is also that gay woman doctor character on *ER* whose lovers always die in fires and so on.)

(Gay people are always dying all the time.)

Anthea is being ridiculous. I got her a good position and now she is at home doing nothing. She is really clever. She is wasting herself.

(I was sitting at home trying to think of a tag, I'd thought of Mac-Aqua, but McDonald's would sue, I'd thought of Scotteau, I'd been saying the word Eau out loud, and Anthea walked past the table as I said it, and she added Caledonia, we're such a good team, we'd be a good team, we'd have been a good team, oh my God my sister is a)

Well, it is bloody lucky Keith intimates anything to me at all after they did me that favour at Pure about Anthea. She is so naïve, she has no idea what an unusually good salary level she was started at, it is really lucky nobody has associated me with how rude she was that day and that thing happening to the Pure sign

(which is clearly where they met. Maybe I saw the oh so romantic moment they met, last month, I was watching out the window, and the weirdo vandal came down the ladder and she and Anthea were talking, before Security took her away to wait for the police. I saw the name on the forms Security made her fill out. I recognised it. I knew it, the name, from when we were girls. It's a small town. What else can you do, in a small town?)

(Unless they were in cahoots before that and had decided on it as a dual attack on Pure, which is possible, I mean, anything under the sun is possible now.)

(Everything has changed.)

(Nothing is the same.)

I've stopped. I'm not running. I'm just standing.

(I don't want to run anywhere. I can't think where to run to.)

(I better make it look like there is a reason for me to be just standing. I'll go and stand by the pedestrian crossing.)

That word *intimated* is maybe something to do with the word intimate, since the word intimate is so much a part of, almost the whole of, the word intimated.

I am standing at the pedestrian crossing like a (normal) person waiting to cross the road. A bus goes past. It is full of (normal-looking) people.

(My sister is now one of the reasons the man who owns Stagecoach buses had that million-pound poster campaign all over Scotland where they had pictures of people saying things like "I'm not a bigot but I don't want my children taught to be gay at school," that kind of thing.)

(They were laughing. Like they were actually happy. Or like being gay is okay, or really funny, or really good fun, or something.)

I am running on the spot so as not to lose momentum.

(It is the putting of that leg in between the other legs that I can't get out of my head. It is really kind of unforgettable.)

(It is so . . .

intimate.)

I stop running on the spot. I stand at the pedestrian crossing and look one way, then the other. Nothing is coming. The road is totally clear.

But I just stand.

(I don't know what's the matter with me. I can't get myself to cross from one side to the other.)

(My sister would be banned in schools if she was a book.)

(No, because the parliament lifted that legislation, didn't it?)

(Did it?)

(I can't remember. I can't remember either way. I didn't ever think that particular law was anything I'd ever have to remember, or consider.)

(Have I ever noticed or considered anything about it? Should I have?)

(I did. I have. I remember reading in the paper about how people all across the world, and not just people but governments, in Poland and in Russia, but also in Spain, and Italy, are getting more and more tough on people being it. I mean, you'd expect that in Russia and in Poland. But in Italy? In Spain? Those are places that are supposed to be like here.)

(It said in the paper this morning that teenagers who are it are six times more likely to commit suicide than teenagers who aren't it.)

(I don't know what to do with myself.)

I stand at the crossing with no cars coming in either direction and I still don't move to cross the road. I feel a little dizzy. I feel a little faint.

(Anyone looking at me will think I'm really weird.)

SISTERS

BY *Lucille Clifton*

for elaine philip on her birthday

me and you be sisters.
we be the same.
me and you
coming from the same place.
me and you
be greasing our legs
touching up our edges.
me and you
be scared of rats
be stepping on roaches.
me and you
come running high down purdy street one time
and mama laugh and shake her head at
me and you.
me and you
got babies
got thirty-five
got black
let our hair go back
be loving ourselves
be loving ourselves
be sisters.
only where you sing
i poet.

FROM HANGING UP

BY *Delia Ephron*

THE NEXT DAY, while I was writing a press release about higher entrance fees to the Central Park ice-skating rink, Madeline called from Los Angeles.

"I have to talk fast because I'm broke."

"Do you want me to call you?"

"No, I charged this to a fake number, but you usually only get caught if you talk a long time."

"Maddy, that's illegal."

"Oh, Evie, don't be so uptight. What's new?"

"Dad may be moving to New York."

"This is my lucky day," sang Maddy. "Ruby Tuesday, this neat store in Venice, took thirteen sets of my bead earrings on consignment. Presto's friends with the manager, but he really liked them. He would have taken them anyway. I had to call the minute I left the store."

"That's great, Maddy."

"And now Dad's moving to you. Ha, ha-ha, ha-ha."

"It's not for sure. Besides, it's not as if you ever see him."

"But I know he's in L.A., and that's practically the same thing. Who put him in the hospital when he took all those pills?"

"That was two years ago. And you didn't put him in, you just called an ambulance." This last remark is good-natured only on the surface. I change the subject. "So, are you going to college?"

"God, do you and Georgia make plots?"

"Excuse me?"

"That's all she asks about too. She never asks about Presto or my earrings. Eve, would you do me a favor?"

"What?"

"Would you ask Georgia if she'll put my earrings in the magazine? If she'll use them in a fashion spread?"

Georgia was now the associate fashion editor of *Harper's Bazaar*. When she had landed the job, she had called. "Do you realize that I'm only twenty-six? This is big."

Then my father had phoned me. "Your sister's going to be president."

"Of what?"

"Hearst. The country. Who knows?"

I answered Madeline. "Why don't you ask Georgia yourself? Why should I have to ask her?"

"My phone's disconnected, okay? Anyway, she never takes my calls. Sometimes she doesn't call me back for a whole day. I don't ask you for things. I hardly ask you for anything. I never ask anyone for anything."

"Fine, I'll do it."

Maddy brightened immediately. "Thanks, Eve. This really means a lot to me. I'd better get off, before I end up in San Quentin."

✳

I sat in The Hare and the Tortoise pretending to make notes in my Women's Liberation Appointment Calendar, which Adrienne had given me for Christmas, and glancing up every few seconds to check for Georgia.

188

Finally she appeared, bestowing on the hostess her half-smile, the one in which her lips stayed together but the corners of her mouth turned up. She was dressed in a very long sweater—it was a turtleneck that continued past her hips to become a dress, and it was cinched with a wide leather belt, reminding me that she had a better waist than I did.

I was always making the calculations: How do we compare? Being a sister, especially a middle sister, I could understand myself only in comparison with someone, and usually that meant with Georgia.

I suppose I fixated on her because she came first, was there when I arrived. We both shared our parents' dark hair and dark eyes, so the obvious physical distinctions between us were few. And Georgia was so definite, not just now but always, in what she thought, in all her choices. Faced with her certainty, I had trouble fathoming where she stopped and I began.

If Georgia proclaimed an affection for anything—say, macadamia nuts—I couldn't prefer cashews without feeling I'd betrayed her. I never admired her straight and narrow aristocratic nose without remembering that mine turned up slightly, giving me the eager look of a kid while she had the serious appearance of a woman. Today I saw that her waist was not just ideally small and round, but smaller and rounder than mine, which was an oval leading not to broad, but to broader, hips. Madeline was so much another person—five years behind me, much taller, willowy even—a kind of free, not freer, spirit, who swung her arms loosely when she walked. Georgia acted as if she owned the street, Maddy strode along oblivious to it. I tended to watch where I stepped, trying to make my way without causing anyone else too much discomfort.

As I observed Georgia weaving her way over, quickly sizing up the food on tables she passed, I noticed that, around her shoulders, on top of this sweater dress, she had tied another sweater, a matching sweater. I had never seen anyone who was not on a playground walk around with her sweater tied around her, but seeing this style on Georgia made me want to tie everything I owned around my shoulders.

Which reminded me of my father's call several weeks before. "They pay your sister to wear clothes," he had said. This particular call had come when I was doing that humiliating thing known as "waiting for the phone to ring."

I'd met an architect while handing out press releases at the opening of an adventure playground in Central Park. Philip hadn't designed the playground, his boss had. Philip had done the specifications for the jungle gym. He'd asked for my number.

The phone had been sitting next to me on the couch while Adrienne and I watched the evening news, all about Rose Mary Woods and how she had accidentally erased eighteen and a half minutes of a White House tape. I waited two rings, not to appear eager, then answered.

"They pay your sister to wear clothes. Bet you never heard of that before."

"Big deal."

"You said it." He hung up. The phone rang again. Again I waited two rings. "Hello."

"Get a load of this. They pay Georgia to wear clothes."

"Dad, you just called me."

"I thought I dialed Maddy. Don't be mad."

"I'm not," I lied, barely disguising it.

"You know your old man. He gets carried away." He hung up again.

Georgia sat down and blew a kiss across the table. "Hello, darling." Adrienne was right, it was hard to tell what age Georgia was. This kissing bit she had done for a year now, but the "darling" was new. Even though it was an affectation, she knew it was, you could tell by how she said it. "Darling." I liked the sound of it. It was comforting. I leaned closer across the table, a tree leaning to the sun.

"Have a menu." I handed mine over. I saw her eyes whip down it; then she laid it neatly next to her napkin. "I snacked all morning at the office. You eat. I'll just have a tomato juice. Could you have the waiter bring a tomato juice with a slice of lime on the side?" she asked the hostess.

"Dad says they pay you to wear those clothes."

"They don't pay me. They just give me free clothes." She cupped her hand coyly along the side of her mouth, as if someone might overhear. "They normally do this only with the fashion editor. This is the first time they've done it with the associate fashion editor." She returned her hand to her lap. "This dress is Halston."

"Is that a material, like cashmere?"

Georgia smiled. "God, the things you don't know. Halston is a very famous designer. You know, Eve"—this was the first time I'd heard her voice drop a level and sound vaguely as if she'd been brought up in Europe—"if you don't know something, it's usually a good idea to wait awhile and see how the conversation goes, because sometimes you can figure it out for yourself." Then she added, in her normal tone, "That was a really good piece of advice."

"I know all about Halston," I bluffed. "I was just kidding around." I changed the subject. "You know Madeline's earrings?"

"You mean the reason she's not going to college. Because she's becoming an earring factory."

"I know it's completely dumb." We both started laughing. "Does she actually think she can live off this?"

"Who knows?" Georgia squeezed the lime into her tomato juice.

"She asked me to ask you if you would put them in the magazine. In a fashion spread. Actually, she practically started crying, she begged me to ask you, but don't tell her I said that."

Georgia seasoned the tomato juice with salt and pepper. "She should go to college."

"She doesn't want to."

"Here, taste this. Isn't it delicious?"

I took a sip. "Yeah."

"She'll never meet men if she doesn't go to college."

"That's not too liberated, Georgia."

"Is that one of Adrienne's opinions? Adrienne probably doesn't shave under her arms. I'm as liberated as she is. I'm simply being practical."

"Well, you don't have to worry about Madeline and men. She meets guys just waiting for a green light."

"Sure, those kind of guys." Georgia raised her eyes to acknowledge the waiter. "I'm only having tomato juice."

"I'll have the chef's salad."

"Does her chef's salad come in a big wooden bowl?" Georgia asked.

"I'll check." He disappeared.

"He doesn't even know how the chef's salad comes? What kind of a restaurant is this?"

"The food's good. Philip and I eat here. It's near his office."

The waiter returned. "Yes, it does."

"Then you don't want it," said Georgia. "It's too much. You'll get tired just looking at it. Have the crab bisque. I saw one go by."

"Crab bisque, please. So will you use Maddy's earrings?"

"I'll look at them, but they're probably not avenue enough."

I didn't ask what that meant. I figured it would become clear, but it didn't.

"Tell her to send them to me," Georgia said.

"If Dad moves here, will we have to spend Thanksgiving with him?"

Georgia assumed a pose. She put her elbow on the table. Her arm and hand were straight up and her chin was balanced on the tips of her fingers. She narrowed her eyes and thought. "Yes."

III

HAVING OUR SAY

NOT ENOUGH

BY M.F.K. Fisher

PERHAPS THE MAIN DIFFERENCE between Norah and me is that while we are friends (by now), she still thinks of me as her older sister, and I think of her mostly as a friend.

Or in other words, I ask for and accept many things from her that she has never asked from me. I have often called on her for help, and she has without hesitation changed all her complicated plans and come as fast as possible, and I have never doubted her love or her familial devotion. But she is a prouder person than I am, and as yet she has seldom admitted to purely human weaknesses, although lately she does creak audibly when the going is rough.

Once, though, when she asked me for immediate loving help, I stood her off. I think now and then of this strange happening, with self-disgust, or at least an uncomfortable kind of self-doubt.

One Sunday at the Ranch, in perhaps 1950, I asked Nan and Chuck Newton and their little boy Chas to come for lunch, mostly to perk up Rex a little but also because I enjoyed them very much and my girls loved Chas. Rex ambled out in his Sunday velvet house jacket, plainly old and grumpy and not well, and when Chuck came they went off in a corner and Nan came out to help me get lunch, and the children were in the side porch on the floor, playing something.

Norah telephoned from Los Angeles, I think, and she said that she was up there from Sunset Beach where she was living while she and John got a divorce, and that she had a badly infected thumb or finger and that John would drive her and the three children out to the Ranch instead of her going back down to the beach. I said OK, fine indeed. And sorry about the hand. And she said they'd be there in an hour.

So Nan and I held off lunch, and we told Rex that we were going to wait for Norah and the boys. And he suddenly became almost hysterical and was very bitter about John Barr: he's never to set foot on the Ranch again, by God, and so on. I was a treacherous female to let him weasel back in this way, etc., etc.

Chuck took care of him, and Nan and I half fed the three little kids and then we waited around, and finally the car drove in, and Rex got very upset again and Chuck calmed him again, and Nan and I went into the kitchen to welcome the poor lost roaming Barrs.

The two older boys, very small and quick, dashed in and at once settled themselves onto the floor with Chas and my girls, and I think John brought Matt to the door, the back porch door.

Norah came last, looking very gaunt and wan, with one heavily bandaged hand held up as she'd been told to do, after minor but nasty surgery to lance an infection. She was shot full of whatever one was given in those far days—penicillin? She sailed in, and Nan came out to get Matt, and I said to John that Rex was on a tear and would not let him come in.

It was a bad moment.

I think John trusted me as much as he could any of us in those hard days, and he unloaded some stuff from Norah's car so that she could stay overnight with the three boys instead of going down to the beach—the doctors had prescribed several days of rest, but how can a single woman with three small children tackle that?—and then he got into my car and we drove almost silently up to the bus station. We gave each other a good friendly hug, and I did not see him again for several years, which was all right.

When I got back, Norah was standing in the dining room, beautiful and disdainful. Behind her through the three wide-open French doors sat the five little children, aware of tensions and thunder but playing on the floor, something about cards and dice. Nan and Chuck sat having a drink with Rex in the dim living room.

Norah suddenly put both arms around me as if to hold me with passion, a most unfamiliar gesture in our overly decorous family. She was vibrating the way a good arrow vibrates or thrums or shivers after it has been shot out and has then plunged into its target.

But instead of bending to her need for aid and succor, I did what still haunts me (thank God, rarely), and I stiffened and gently undid her long loving needing arms from my shoulders.

She was whimpering. I looked down over her high shoulder and saw the worried eyes of five little children looking with pain and puzzlement up at our sadness, and I said, as I pulled off her beseeching arms, "The children are looking. Stop this!"

I do not know how I said this short cruel thing, but I believe that I was trying to protect them all, no matter how foolishly, from something I myself feared—our futures, maybe.

Norah stiffened and withdrew, and I knew that I had lost a moment of need and comfort that would never happen again. She looked down at the five little mice peering up at us and said with so strong a scorn that it was almost shocking, "To hell with them."

It was a flat statement. The children paled with shock, and then as I withdrew from Norah's desperate embrace, their faces calmed and they went on with whatever it was they were playing—cards, bones...

We went into the living room and behaved properly and then went back to the dining room and behaved properly, and after a long good winey lunch, Nan and I tended to the kitchen stuff and Norah, who was saggy-dizzy with past pain and present medical stress, sat on a tuffet while Chuck played old Fats Waller records in a dim corner of the living room. Rex sat at the other end, smoking.

Nobody seemed to know but me and perhaps Norah—who may by now have forgotten it, if she ever realized it—that I had rejected her that day. Why did I say "the children"? She was right, in the long run, to say, "To hell with them." She needed *me* then, and I was not ready to forget the demands of my current world and give her the true warm love I shall always feel for her.

—*Glen Ellen, California, 1978*

LETTER TO
HELEN ROTHSCHILD DROSTE*

BY *Dorothy Parker*

VILLA AMERICA
Cap D'Antibes, France
September 1929

Dear Mrs. Drots, it's been such a long time now that I am ashamed to write, only I can't go on and face another night's dark without having written. Please don't be sore, although there is no reason on earth why you shouldn't be. You know how it is about writing letters. In fact, if you will pardon my pointing, you are no Madame de Sevigne yourself.

This is a little dear to write, on account of there is heaps to say, but absolutely no news. I'd better begin at the beginning, and if you get too bored, just tear it up as you go. I hope Seward has been letting you know where I am, and when. I asked him to, but he is a fool. Also, I haven't heard from him now for about twenty years, so maybe he has at last decided to stop his stalling, and be dead lying down, instead of sitting at his desk in the Bookman office.

Well, so first I went to London with the Saalburgs for a week, and was that a dull excursion! Then we came to Paris, and they took an apartment, and I spent six weeks as a fascinating divorcee alone in

* Dorothy Parker's married sister

Paris, the home of dancing and light wines, in being so rotten sick I couldn't move out of my hotel room. And a dainty complaint, too,—something the matter with my liver. Oh, my God how sick that makes you feel! And conducting an illness in the French language, of which I know possibly fifty words by heart, is fascinating. I couldn't work or anything; all I did was see Ernest and Pauline Hemingway, who were something swell to me, and stagger dizzily out once or twice to get some of the most ill-advised clothes ever assembled. They were just what somebody with an afflicted liver WOULD have picked out.

Oh, and by the way, Muriel Saalburg is coming home next month, and bringing you four chemises and pants, two slips with pants to match, and four nightgowns. If you want anything else, will you please cable me either here—or which is much cheaper—just Banktrust, Paris, and they forward it right away. I'm bleating about cabling instead of writing because they have to be made, and the French can't hurry.

Well, and so then Mr. Benchley arrived with wife and get—at least, a man called Benchley arrived, but it wasn't the Robert Benchley we used to know. He simply can't speak, in the presence of his bride—and who could? Oh my God, what a woman, oh, my God, WHAT a woman! So they were coming here, to inhabit the Murphys'* farm-house for the Summer, and I was coming here to visit the Murphys, and I motored here from Paris with them—a four-day jaunt, given over to providing educational advantages to the children, and shall we draw a veil over that experience?

So the minute I got here, I was all right. You know what I think of the Murphys, and this villa is, I should think, the loveliest place in the world. It is a great, square, honest house, with the only good modern decors I have ever seen, set high and back, overlooking a

---

*Parker was a guest of Sara and Gerald Murphy's, a legendary expatriate couple who lived in France during the 1920s.

great bay of the Mediterranean, with the island where they kept the Man in the Iron Mask imprisoned, in it. I had their little guest house, which is a little Normandy farm-house, only with plumbing and electricity, exquisitely furnished, and set in the midst of fig trees all full of purple fruit—except I hate figs in any form.—I got to be able to work like a fool, and also to be able to swim two kilometers a day—as Gerald said, striking out for Corsica with a Bailey's Beach stroke, as in knitting. It was just simply swell to be here.

Antibes—in fact, the whole Riviera—was terrible. Every tripe was here, including Peggy Joyce, Rosie Dolly, and Jack Gilbert and bride. There's a pretty romance; the lady entertained a dinner of thirty-eight British nobility by saying she must have been crazy when she, a great artist, married that ignorant ham, and concluded her discourse by throwing a glass at him. But we went out scarcely at all, and didn't see anybody. Only once did I step out with Mr. B., who was in swell shape, for he had just seen Carol—she was in Cannes on a holiday with her beau—and she cut him dead. So we got absolutely blotto, and went out for the night, and I sailed right into trouble. The lucky man was Laddie Sandford, and we wouldn't know each other even if we ever did see each other again. And I don't even feel embarrassed about it, because I can't tell you how little sex means to me now. Or at least I can't tell you how little I think sex means to me now. And polo players wouldn't count, anyway.

And then came the pretty day when I found that I had in the world exactly one thousand francs, or, if the wind is in the right direction, forty dollars. You see, I have been working on that damn book, and not doing things to get paid for. (The book has already been torn up four times, and fun is no word for it.) And then I got a cable that Harold Guinzburg would be in Paris, so I took my thousand francs for carfare—it wasn't quite enough—and went up to Paris with Mr. Benchley, who was sailing. Ah, poor Mr. Benchley! You know, Adele Lovett came over here to the Riviera, and staid Four Days, and then sailed home. It was just to see him, which she did not accomplish. And Betty Starbuck apparently never took pen from paper while he was gone; great wads of letters would be piled on his shoulders, every time a boat came in. He dreaded so to go back to New York and I just had a cable from him, saying, pitifully, "No fun here," which is somehow so much more pitiful than "Frantic with misery."

Well, so there I was in Paris, with no money, and Mr. Benchley gone. The Saalburgs lent me their apartment, because they were going away, and is that a good, gloomy hovel! And the Guinzburgs came, and Harold didn't say one word about a further advance, and I got one of my pretties where I couldn't utter the word money, and everything was just corking. And just as I was looking thoughtfully at the Seine, the Murphys telegraphed me, exactly as if they had been hearing my thoughts, "This is all nonsense you must come right back here." And then in came Harold, dressed, to my dazed eyes, in the uniform of the United States Marines, and gave me a complete set of money, to stay over and finish the book. And so, in three words, here I am.

It is so lovely to be back here. I can't tell you how swell the Murphys are to me. And I honestly don't feel as if I were over-staying, because there is the guest-house, and there are nine servants, and I am alone in my room for a big part of the day, working. There were lots of plans to go to Vienna later on, and then they have been lent an apartment in Moscow, where I should rather go than any place in the world, although it is a far cry from snow-clad Russia to my fur coat which is in your closet. But then their smallest boy, Patrick, got taken very ill, with a bad spot on his lungs, and has to be at a higher altitude. So Sara is away, at the moment, in the mountains with him, and Gerald, two children, nine servants, five dogs and I are living here in no sin whatever. So all plans are contingent on his health—if he improves, up there, Sara will leave him with a nurse, and come back here, and then see if he is well enough to travel. And if he doesn't improve—then I don't know what the hell.

You see, Mrs. Droste, I didn't want to come back to New York just yet. I miss you horribly, and I would give an eye to see you, but I am terrified of coming back. I simply can't face the dingy, sordid life I led there. And about the Garrett thing—I hate to talk about it because it is so rotten ugly, but—Well, you see, when I sailed, he said he was coming over, and would I meet him for a week together somewhere in France, and I must cable him my addresses, so he could keep in touch with me. So I did cable him, because I believe everybody, and I had never a word from him—and cables don't go astray. Then I had a letter—there was a day!—from that charming Mrs. Curtis in Westchester, you know, the one he was sleeping with concurrently. She said, God damn her, "John is sailing next week—but of course he has written you about that. Isn't it too bad Mrs. Fair is already over there." And I never heard from him, and I saw in the paper that he had landed, and I nearly went crazy. And never a word, and I kept brooding, and finally, about three weeks ago, I sent him a cable from here, because I couldn't stand it any longer, saying, in part, "Can't we be friends?" And he answered "Delighted wire always"—three ambiguous words—AND AT DEFERRED RATES! which is about the depth of something. And then—I'm ashamed to tell you this—when I was in Paris this last time, swell and gloomy and alone in the Saalburgs' flat, I wrote him a letter—oh, just the most awful thing I could have done, just spilling my guts out, saying I wanted to come back, and wouldn't he please see me sometimes, and, oh, just as bad as it could be. Oh, I wish anything had happened before I wrote it. And yesterday I got a cable—of course, at deferred rates—saying, "Loved letter dear so happy you are well." Of all the stupid, rotten, misunderstanding, callous, ignorant things. Again I feel cheap and helpless and undignified and dirty. Oh, if you knew what I said in that unfortunate letter—about how I was no better about him and what should I do—oh, I can't tell you. God what a louse he is! Yet if I were within fifty blocks of him, I should be telephoning him tearfully again—and should be being answered by Mrs. Fair. And I don't dare face it. It's a slow process, but it does, sooner or later, do something over here for you. You can't help having the centuries seep in through your pores, and soothe you. And I am at peace and the Murphys make me feel of value and I can work. And every time I think of New York and that drinking I did and all those horrible people in the afternoons and please-send-up-the-bottles-of-White-Rock-and-some-ice—I just can't do it yet. I'd better stay here as long as I can.

Oh, God, that's enough of that. I'm all sweating, just talking about it.

Look, will you please tell Lel something for me? Will you tell her I have a dog? I don't dare tell you, even with the extenuating circumstances of his being a Godsend to me while I was alone and sick in Paris, and I don't know what I should have done without him. So please tell Lel he is a Dandie Dinmont, got in London, and his name, I regret to say, is Timothy—he was named when I got him—and he has taken two prizes, although only fourteen months old, and he is the second sweetest dog in the world, only he fights like hell. And I will get Gerald to take some pictures of him, and send them to her. The Murphys have two Sealyhams, Judy and Johnny, and they had seven puppies, only they had to give them away because the tender little mother tried to kill them all. They also have two Pekineses, but they don't count.

I can't begin to ask you the questions I want to and probably you wouldn't get around to answering them anyhow, you big stiff. But they are mostly about what was your Summer, and how are you, and how are Bill and Lel and Victor, and what is the news, and what else?

I can't tell you how I want to see you—this part of being over here is pretty awful. I get bad waves of homesickness about you. But I just don't dare come back yet.

I am disgustingly well and strong, but unfortunately pretty heavy, despite the long distance swims. (It is only fair to say that they are due less to my athletic prowess than to the fact that you really can't sink, in the Mediterranean.) And I should be very much better off for a letter from you. If this address is a nuisance, Bankers' Trust, Paris, is so easy and always reaches me.

Much, much, much love—Dot.

Thank you so much for the birthday cable. You are an angel.

BORDERLINE

BY Robin Becker

in memory of Jill Wendy Becker, 1953–1986

Brink, brow, verge, brim. I grew
adjacent and then away—leaving you, sister,

on the margin of error, your uncultivated strip,
staring at coastlines where others converged.

Not for you the adaptation, the going along, the realistic
expectation, the rules regarding performance

in work or the timbre of friendship. Not for you
a rowboat with oars and oarlocks from which to paddle

to mudflats and there encounter the stargazer
that buries itself in the muddy sand

or the common shipworm that opens wood
and confounds the shipwright's carpentry.

Oh, the co-housing arrangements of bivalves!
How they drill and devour each other,

like us on the biochemical ledges
where your doctor knew no drug or medication

to help fifteen years ago. You lived between
diagnoses, your illness nonspecific, placeless,

and occupied your indeterminacy
not as protective coloration but condition,

today characterized by some as trauma
in early development affecting brain function

or an intrauterine factor
to which you were genetically predisposed.

Certain patterns, some studies show,
of overinvolvement between parent and child

may be causative factors. You tenanted
an invalidating space where sandbars rose

and disappeared overnight, where organisms
are fragile and prone to rapid deterioration;

thus, mind and place co-create each other
over time, and in you, magical thinker, impulsive

brooder, both remained lawless,
mutable, labile. Neither barrier beach

nor tide pool nor undersea meadow
could nourish you, as the rank estuary sustains

the bottom-dwelling searobin
that learns to walk on wing-shaped fins.

LETTER TO A SISTER WHO LIVES IN A DISTANT COUNTRY

BY Daisy Zamora

> *...And I was sent South of the village of Wei*
> *—carpeted by laurel groves—*
> *and you North of Roku-hoku,*
> *until all we had in common were thoughts and memories.*
> —"Exile's Letter," Li Po

I still remember our first games:
the paper dolls and the parades.
And Teresa, the doll we could not stand:
"Teresa-pone-la-mesa."*

Life doesn't go backwards and I want to know you.
To recognize you.
That is, to get to know you again.
Nevertheless, there must be things about yourself you still
preserve.
I'm interested in learning about the places you are,
your friends, so different from mine
who speak another language and search for other paths.

---

* *"Teresa-pone-la-mesa"*: A children's nonsense rhyme, mocking the doll.

Danbury, Hamden and Middletown,
Hartford and Meriden. All places
so familiar to you and your memories.
Through our shared blood I've lived two lives,
multiple lives.

The coconuts are ripe for picking in the garden
and summer has turned the gentians at the fence deep red.
The days are blue and beautiful,
clear and fresh.
My beloved places are the same as yours.
My words touch you across thousands of kilometers
like a bird I see right now perched on a coconut.

It's been a long time, and the distance great.
But one of these bright days
    (the rose bushes are full of buds)
or on some far away winter day
    (laurel trees are blooming along all the roads,
      and so are the cashews, the mangos, the yellow trumpet trees)
with the last sunshine or in the first downpour
we'll reap the fruits
of our waiting.

Translated by George Evans

FROM THE POISONWOOD BIBLE

BY Barbara Kingsolver

RACHEL PRICE, "THE EQUATORIAL 1984"
This was the first and the absolute last time I am going to participate within a reunion of my sisters. I've just returned from a rendezvous with Leah and Adah that was simply a sensational failure.

Leah was the brainchild of the whole trip. She said the last month of waiting for her husband to get out of prison was going to kill her if she didn't get out of there and do something. The last time he was getting let out, I guess they ended up making him stay another year at the last minute, which would be a disappointment, I'm sure. But really, if you commit a crime you have to pay the piper, what did she expect? Personally, I've had a few husbands that maybe weren't the top of the line, but a criminal, I just can't see. Well, each to his own, like they say. She's extra lonely now since her two older boys are trying out school in Atlanta so they won't get arrested, too, and the younger one is also staying there with Mother for the summer so Leah could be free to mastermind this trip. Which, to tell you the truth, she mostly just arranged for the sole purpose of getting a Land Rover from America to Kinshasa, where she and Anatole have the crackpot scheme of setting up a farm commune in the southern part and then going over to the Angola side as soon as it's safe, which from what I hear is going to be no time this century. Besides, Angola is an extremely Communistic nation if you ask me. But does Mother care about this? Her own daughter planning to move to a communistic nation where the roads are practically made of wall-to-wall land mines? Why no! She and her friends raised the money and bought a good Land Rover with a rebuilt engine in Atlanta. Which, by the way, Mother's group has never raised one red cent for me, to help put in upstairs plumbing at the Equatorial, for example. But who's complaining?

I only went because a friend of mine had recently died of his long illness and I was feeling at loose odds and ends. Geoffrey definitely was talking marriage, before he got so ill. He was just the nicest gentleman and very well to do. Geoffrey ran a touristic safari business in Kenya, which was how we met, in a very romantic way. But he caught something very bad over there in Nairobi, plus he was not all that young. Still, it shouldn't have happened to a better man. Not to mention me turning forty last year, which was no picnic, but people always guess me not a day over thirty so who's counting? Anyway I figured Leah and I could tell each other our troubles, since misery loves company, even though she has a husband that is still alive at least, which is more than I can say.

The game plan was for Adah to ride over on the boat to Spain with the Land Rover, and drive to West Africa. Adah driving, I just couldn't picture. I still kept picturing her all crippled up, even though Mother had written me that no, Adah has truly had a miracle recovery. So we were all to meet up there in Senegal and travel around for a few weeks seeing the sights. Then Adah would fly home, and Leah and I would drive as far as Brazzaville together for safety's sake, although if you ask me two women traveling alone are twice as much trouble as one. Especially my sister and me! We ended up not speaking through the whole entirety of Cameroon and most of Gabon. Anatole, fresh from out of the hoosegow, met us in Brazzaville and they drove straight back home to Kinshasa. Boy, did she throw her arms around him at the ferry station, kissing right out in front of everybody, for a lot longer than you'd care to think. Then off they went holding hands like a pair of teenagers, yakety-yak, talking to each other in something Congolese. They did it expressly to exclude me from the conversation, I think. Which is not easy for someone who speaks three languages, as I do.

Good-bye and none too soon, is what I say. Leah was like a house on fire for the last hundred miles of the trip. She'd made a long-distance call from Libreville to make sure he was getting let out the next day *for sure,* and boy, did she make a beeline after that. She couldn't even bother herself to come up and see the Equatorial—even though we were only half a day's drive away! And me a bereaved widow, practically. I can't forgive that in my own sister. She said she would only go if we went on down to Brazzaville *first,* and then brought Anatole with us. Well, I just couldn't say yes or no to that right away, I had to think. It's simply a far more delicate matter than she understands. We have a strict policy about who is allowed upstairs, and if you change it for one person then where does it end? I *might* have made an exception. But when I told her I had to think about it, Leah right away said, "Oh, no, don't bother. You have your standards of white supremacy to uphold, don't you?" and then climbed up on her high horse and stepped on the gas. So we just stopped talking, period. Believe me, we had a very long time to listen to the four-wheel-drive transmission and every bump in the road for the full length of two entire countries.

When it was finally over I was so happy to get back to my own home-sweet-home I had a double vodka tonic, kicked off my shoes, turned up the tape player and danced the Pony right in the middle of the restaurant. We had a whole group of cotton buyers from Paris, if I remember correctly. I declared to my guests: "Friends, there is nothing like your own family to make you appreciate strangers!" Then I kissed them all on their bald heads and gave them a round on the house.

The trouble with my family is that since we hardly ever see each other, we have plenty of time to forget how much personality conflict we all have when it comes right down to it. Leah and Adah and I started bickering practically the minute we met up in Senegal. We could never even agree on where to go or stay or what to eat. Whenever we found any place that was just the teeniest step above horrid, Leah felt it was too expensive. She and Anatole evidently have chosen to live like paupers. And Adah, helpful as always, would chime in with the list of what disease organisms were likely to be present. We argued about positively everything: even communism! Which you would think there was nothing to argue about. I merely gave Leah the very sensible advice that she should think twice about going to Angola because the Marxists are taking it over.

"The Mbundu and the Kongo tribes have a long-standing civil war there, Rachel. Agostinho Neto led the Mbundu to victory, because he had the most popular support."

"Well, for your information, Dr. Henry Kissinger himself says that Neto and them are followers of Karl Marx, and the other ones are pro-United States."

"Imagine that," Leah said. "The Mbundu and Kongo people have been at war with each other for the last six hundred years, and Dr. Henry Kissinger has at long last discovered the cause: the Kongo are pro-United States, and the Mbundu are followers of Karl Marx."

"Hah!" Adah said. Her first actual unrehearsed syllable of the day. She talks now, but she still doesn't exactly throw words away.

Adah was in the back, and Leah and me up front. I was doing most of the driving, since I'm used to it. I had to slow way down for a stop sign because the drivers in West Africa were turning out to be as bad as the ones in Brazzaville. It was very hard to concentrate while my sisters were giving me a pop quiz on world democracy.

"You two can just go ahead and laugh," I said. "But I read the papers. Ronald Reagan is keeping us safe from the socialistic dictators, and you should be grateful for it."

"Socialistic dictators such as?"

"I don't know. Karl Marx! Isn't he still in charge of Russia?"

Adah was laughing so hard in the backseat I thought she was going to pee on herself.

"Oh, Rachel, Rachel," Leah said. "Let me give you a teeny little lesson in political science. Democracy and dictatorship are *political* systems; they have to do with who participates in the leadership. Socialism and capitalism are *economic* systems. It has to do with who owns the wealth of your nation, and who gets to eat. Can you grasp that?"

"I never said I was the expert. I just said I read the papers."

"Okay, let's take Patrice Lumumba, for example. Former Prime Minister of the Congo, his party elected by popular vote. He was a socialist who believed in democracy. Then he was murdered, and the CIA replaced him with Mobutu, a capitalist who believes in dictatorship. In the Punch and Judy program of American history, that's a happy ending."

"Leah, for your information I am proud to be an American."

Adah just snorted again, but Leah smacked her forehead. "How can you possibly say that? You haven't set foot there for half your life!"

"I have retained my citizenship. I still put up the American flag in the bar and celebrate every single Fourth of July."

"Impressive," Adah said.

We were driving along the main dirt road that followed the coast toward Togo. There were long stretches of beach, with palm trees waving and little naked dark children against the white sand. It was like a picture postcard. I wished we could quit talking about ridiculous things and just enjoy ourselves. I don't know why Leah has to nag and nag.

"For your information, Leah," I informed her, just to kind of close things off, "your precious Lumumba would have taken over and been just as bad a dictator as any of them. If the CIA and them got rid of him, they did it for democracy. Everybody alive says that."

"Everybody alive," Adah said. "What did the dead ones say?"

"Now, look, Rachel," Leah said. "You can get this. In a *democracy*, Lumumba should have been allowed to live longer than two months as head of state. The Congolese people would have gotten to see how they liked him, and if not, replaced him."

Well, I just blew up at that. "These people here can't decide *anything* for themselves! I swear, my kitchen help still can't remember to use the omelet pan for an omelet! For God's sakes, Leah, you should know as well as I do how they are."

"Yes, Rachel, I believe I married one of them."

I kept forgetting that. "Well, shut my mouth wide open."

"As usual," Adah said.

For the entire trip I think the three of us were all on speaking terms for only one complete afternoon. We'd got as far as Benin without killing each other, and Adah wanted to see the famous villages on stilts. But, wouldn't you know, the road to that was washed out. Leah and I tried to explain to her how in Africa the roads are here today, gone tomorrow. You are constantly seeing signs such as, "If this sign is under water the road is impassable," and so forth. *That* much we could agree on.

So we ended up going to the ancient palace at Abomey, instead, which was the only tourist attraction for hundreds of miles around. We followed our map to Abomey, and luckily the road to it was still there. We parked in the center of town, which had big jacaranda trees and was very quaint. It was a cinch to find the ancient palace because it was surrounded by huge red mud walls and had a very grand entryway. Snoozing on a bench in the entrance we found an English-speaking guide who agreed to wake up and take us through on a tour. He explained how in former centuries, before the arrival of the French, the Abomey kings had enormous palaces and very nice clothes. They recorded their history in fabulous tapestries that hung on the palace walls, and had skillful knives and swords and such, which they used to conquer the neighboring tribes and enslave them. Oh, they just killed people right and left, he claimed, and then they'd put the skulls of their favorite enemies into their household decor. It's true! We saw every one of these things—the tapestries depicting violent acts and the swords and knives and even a throne with human skulls attached to the bottoms of all four legs, plated with bronze like keepsake baby shoes!

"Why, that's just what I need for my lobby in the Equatorial," I joked, although the idea of those things being the former actual heads of living people was a bit much for three o'clock in the afternoon.

This was no fairy-tale kingdom, let me tell you. They forced women into slave marriage with the King for the purpose of reproducing their babies at a high rate. One King would have, oh, fifty or a hundred wives, easy. More, if he was anything special. Or so the guide told us, maybe to impress us. To celebrate their occasions, he said, they'd just haul off and kill a bunch of their slaves, grind up all the blood and bones, and mix it up with mud for making more walls for their temples! And what's worse, whenever a King died, forty of his wives would have to be killed and buried with him!

I had to stop the guide right there and ask him, "Now, would they be his favorite wives they'd bury with him, or the meanest ones, or what?"

The guide said he thought probably it would have been the prettiest ones. Well, I can just imagine that! The King gets sick, all the wives would be letting their hair go and eating sweets day and night to wreck their figures.

Even though Leah and I had been crabbing at each other all week, that afternoon in the palace at Abomey for some reason we all got quiet as dead bats. Now, I have been around: the racial rioting in South Africa, hosting embassy parties in Brazzaville, shopping in Paris and Brussels, the game animals in Kenya, I have seen it all. But that palace was something else. It gave me the heebie-jeebies. We walked through the narrow passages, admiring the artworks and shivering to see chunks of bone sticking out of the walls. Whatever we'd been fighting about seemed to fade for the moment with those dead remains all around us. I shook from head to toe, even though the day was quite warm.

Leah and Adah happened to be walking in front of me, probably to get away from the guide, because they like to have their own explanations for everything, and as I looked at them I was shocked to see how alike they were. They'd both bought wild-colored wax-cloth shirts in the Senegal market, Adah to wear over her jeans and Leah to go with her long skirts (I personally see no need to go native, thanks very much, and will stick to my cotton knit), and Adah really doesn't limp a bit anymore, like Mother said. Plus she *talks,* which just goes to show you her childhood was not entirely on the up-and-up. She's exactly as tall as Leah now, too, which is simply unexplanatory. They hadn't seen each other for years, and here they even showed up wearing the same hairstyle! Shoulder-length, pulled back, which is not even a regular fashion.

Suddenly I realized they were talking about Father.

"No, I'm sure it's true," Leah said. "I believe it was him. I think he really is dead."

Well! This was news to me. I walked quickly to catch up, though I was still more or less of a third wheel. "You mean Father?" I asked. "Why didn't you say something, for heaven's sake."

"I guess I've been waiting for the right time, when we could talk," Leah said.

Well, what did she think we'd been doing for the last five days but *talk*. "No time like the present," I said.

She seemed to mill it over, and then stated it all as a matter of fact. "He's been up around Lusambo for the last five years, in one village and another. This past summer I ran into an agricultural agent who's been working up there, and he said he very definitely knew of Father. And that he's passed away."

"Gosh, I didn't even know he'd moved," I said. "I figured he was still hanging around our old village all this time."

"No, he's made his way up the Kasai River over the years, not making too many friends from what I hear. He hasn't been back to Kilanga, that much I know. We still have a lot of contact with Kilanga. Some of the people we knew are still there. An awful lot have died, too."

"What do you mean? Who did we know?" I honestly couldn't think of a soul. We left, Axelroot left. The Underdowns went all the way back to Belgium, and they weren't even really *there*.

"Why don't we talk about this later?" Leah said. "This place is already full of dead people."

Well, I couldn't argue with that. So we spent the rest of our paid-for tour in silence, walking through the ancient crumbling halls, trying not to look at the hunks of cream-colored bones in the walls.

"Those are pearls that were his eyes," Adah said at one point, which is just the kind of thing she would say.

"Full fathom five thy father lies," Leah said back to her.

What the heck that was about I just had to wonder. I sure didn't see any pearls. Those two were always connected in their own weird, special way. Even when they can't stand each other, they still always know what the other one's talking about when nobody else does. But I didn't let it bother me. I am certainly old enough to hold up my head and have my own personal adventures in life. I dreamed I toured the Ancient Palace of Abomey in my Maidenform Bra!

Maybe once upon a time I was a little jealous of Leah and Adah, being twins. But no matter how much they might get to looking and sounding alike, as grown-ups, I could see they were still as different on the inside as night and day. And I am different too, not night or day either one but something else altogether, like the Fourth of July. So there we were: night, day, and the Fourth of July, and just for a moment there was a peace treaty.

A QUARRELING PAIR

BY *Jane Bowles*

THE TWO PUPPETS ARE SISTERS in their early fifties. The puppet stage should have a rod or string dividing it down the middle to indicate two rooms. One puppet is seated on each side of the dividing line. If it is not possible to seat them they will have to stand. Harriet, the older puppet, is stronger-looking and wears brighter colors.

HARRIET   (*The stronger puppet*) I hope you are beginning to think about our milk.

RHODA   (*After a pause*) Well, I'm not.

HARRIET   Now what's the matter with you? You're not going to have a visitation from our dead, are you?

RHODA   I don't have visitations this winter because I'm too tired to love even our dead. Anyway, I'm disgusted with the world.

HARRIET   Just mind your business. I mind mine and I *am* thinking about our milk.

RHODA   I'm so tired of being sad. I'd like to change.

HARRIET   You don't get enough enjoyment out of your room. Why don't you?

RHODA   Oh, because the world and its sufferers are always on my mind.

HARRIET   That's not normal. You're not smart enough to be of any use to the outside, anyway.

RHODA   If I were young I'd succor the sick. I wouldn't care about culture, even, if I were young.

HARRIET   You don't have any knack for making a home. There's blessed satisfaction in that, at any rate.

RHODA   My heart's too big to make a home.

HARRIET   No. It's because you have no self-sufficiency. If I wasn't around, you wouldn't have the leisure to worry. You're a lost soul, when I'm not around. You don't even have the pep to worry about the outside when I'm not around. Not that the outside loses by that! (*She sniffs with scorn.*)

RHODA   You're right. But I swear that my heart is big.

HARRIET   I've come to believe that what is inside of people is not so very interesting. You can breed considerable discontent around you with a big heart, and considerable harmony with a small one. Compare your living quarters to mine. And my heart is small like Papa's was.

RHODA   You chill me to the marrow when you tell me that your heart is small. You do love me, though, don't you?

HARRIET   You're my sister, aren't you?

RHODA   Sisterly love is one of the few boons in this life.

HARRIET   Now, that's enough exaggerating. I could enumerate other things.

RHODA   I suppose it's wicked to squeeze love from a small heart. I suppose it's a sin. I suppose God meant for small hearts to be busy with other things.

HARRIET   Possibly. Let's have our milk in my room. It's so much more agreeable to sit in here. Partly because I'm a neater woman than you are.

RHODA   Even though you have a small heart, I wish there were no one but you and me in the world. Then I would never feel that I had to go among the others.

HARRIET   Well, I wish I could hand you my gift for contentment in a box. It would be so lovely if you were like me. Then we could have our milk in *either* room. One day in your room and the next day in mine.

RHODA   I'm sure that's the sort of thing that never happens.

HARRIET   It happens in a million homes, seven days a week. I'm the type that's in the majority.

RHODA   Never, never, never...

HARRIET   (*Very firmly*) It happens in a million homes.

RHODA   *Never, never, never!*

HARRIET   (*Rising*) Are you going to listen to me when I tell you that it happens in a million homes, or must I lose my temper?

RHODA   You have already lost it. (HARRIET *exits rapidly in a rage.* RHODA *goes to the chimes and sings.*)

My horse was frozen like a stone
A long, long time ago.
Frozen near the flower bed
In the wintry sun.
Or maybe in the night time
Or maybe not at all.

My horse runs across the fields
On many afternoons.
Black as dirt and filled with blood
I glimpse him fleeing toward the woods
And then not at all.

HARRIET   (*Offstage*) I'm coming with your milk, and I hope the excitement is over for today. (*Enters, carrying two small white glasses*) Oh, why do I bring milk to a person who is dead-set on making my life a real hell?

RHODA   (*Clasping her hands with feeling*) Yes. Why? Why? Why? Why? Oh, what a hideous riddle!

HARRIET   You love to pretend that everything is a riddle. You think that's the way to be intellectual. There is no riddle. I am simply keeping up my end of the bargain.

RHODA   Oh, bargains, bargains, bargains!

HARRIET   Will you let me finish, you excitable thing? I'm trying to explain that I'm behaving the way I was molded to behave. I happen to be appreciative of the mold I was cast in, and neither heaven, nor earth is going to make me damage it. Your high-strung emotions are not going to affect me. Here's your milk.

(*She enters* RHODA's *side of the stage and hands her the milk, but* RHODA *punches the bottom of the glass with her closed fist and sends it flying out of* HARRIET's *hand.* HARRIET *deals* RHODA *a terrific blow on the face and scurries back to her own room. There is silence for a moment. Then* HARRIET *buries her face in her hands and weeps.* RHODA *exits and* HARRIET *goes to the chimes and sings.*)

HARRIET   (*Singing*)

> I dreamed I climbed upon a cliff,
> My sister's hand in mine.
> Then searched the valley for my house
> But only sunny fields could see
> And the church spire shining.
> I searched until my heart was cold
> But only sunny fields could see
> And the church spire shining.
> A girl ran down the mountainside
> With bluebells in her hat.
> I asked the valley for her name
> But only wind and rain could hear
> And the church bell tolling.
> I asked until my lips were cold
> But wakened not yet knowing
> If the name she bore was my sister's name
> Or if it was my own.

HARRIET   Rhoda?

RHODA   What do you want?

HARRIET   Go away if you like.

RHODA   The moment hasn't come yet, and it won't come today because the day is finished and the evening is here. Thank God!

HARRIET   I know I should get some terrible disease and die if I thought I did not live in the right. It would break my heart.

RHODA   You do live in the right, sweetie, so don't think about it. (*Pause*) I'll go and get your milk.

HARRIET   I'll go too. But let's drink it in here because it really *is* much pleasanter in here, isn't it? (*They rise.*) Oh, I'm so glad the evening has come! I'm nervously exhausted. (*They exit.*)

RECOLLECTIONS OF A 79-YEAR-OLD SISTER

BY *Clare Coss*

You are my daughter but
you look just like that sister of mine
just like your aunt Mae
we used to be close close
now she's a skunk
she knew mama and Nenaine needed her
she stayed out there in Albuquerque
Dan said she finked us out,
She never came down.

WHEN MRS. HEBERT WAS FITTING us for our confirmation dresses she said, "Mae is going to have more lace on her dress because you're taller than she is." That wasn't fair. Do you think that was fair? Just because I was a year older?

My mother had plenty of milk for Mae. Mae would say, "Mama ti down. Mama ti-ti." But she didn't have any milk for me. Mama said she was exhausted from my crying and I was exhausted from starving. She said she'd go over to Lizbear's to get away from my crying—they were part black, part white, part Indian. But with Mae, it was "Mama ti down" till she was three. She had milk that long.

When I was a little older I remember having to go back to grand-mother's on Sunday nights after spending the weekend with my parents. I'd hear poppa upstairs singing Mae to sleep. He had such a good voice, poppa. "After the ball is over—" that was one of his favorites. And I didn't want to go but Nenaine, she was like a mother to me—she might have been mama's sister, but she was like a mother to me—Nenaine pulled me by the arm and I didn't dare say a word or she'd get in trouble with Grandmere who wore the pants and was strict strict with all of us—mama included.

Your aunt Mae was always full of secrets. I'd try to set her up with dates but she was picky. She hid in the closet when company came on Saturday nights so they wouldn't see her sitting home with mama and poppa while I was out with some boy, dancing. Boys liked her but she found something wrong with every one of them. Until she got to be an old maid and married Tom. He was a friend of your father's—a divorced man with a son who was killed flying over Italy in World War II. And Mae said, "Claudine, don't tell one living soul on earth that Tom was ever married before. I don't want anyone to know." She was always like that. Full of secrets. She didn't want anyone to know she wasn't as good a Catholic as she looked because she married a divorced man.

We had our good times together. We used to mask on Mardi Gras and go to the parades and friends' houses and they'd give us the favors. I dressed up in a blue silk Japanese kimono and wore a lotus in my hair. Mae dressed as Little Bo Peep.

In later years there was Christmas and Thanksgiving. We'd go to Waterville to her house and Mrs. Warner, your uncle Tom's mother, and I would cook and cook. Mae never liked the kitchen. Mae had an aversion to the kitchen. But she'd put the extra leaves in the table and spread the cloth that mama crocheted and set out the best dishes and silverware and order pies from her neighbor, Mrs. Olson. We'd all pitch in and you children played outside with their dog, Joyful. Mae and I were close. I don't know what happened.

When your father and I were first married, Mae would come along on summer trips with us to Yosemite Park and once to Montreal. Dan came, too, our baby boy spoiled by his big sisters. And the year I was so sick and in the hospital, Mae took you kids in and was so good to each one of you. You know all about that. You always wanted your aunt Mae after that.

I named you after her—you look just like her. On the street, people always stopped you in the street and asked—"Are you Mae Robbins' little girl?" I taught you to say, "No,—but thanks for the compliment." I did that.

But when mama and poppa were old and living with Dan—she finked out. That's what Dan said. She didn't come down when we needed her. She's a skunk. She looked more like my aunt Nenaine and I looked more like mama. But Nenaine was sweet and your aunt Mae looked the other way when mama and Nenaine needed help. She's a skunk out there in Albuquerque having fun now while I'm cooped up in this place and can't even cook for myself anymore.

She said she'd keep in touch with me through your brother. I'm going to write and tell her she can go to blazes.

And I don't want you spending your time writing to her or talking to her long distance. If you have free time, you spend it on me, not on my skunk of a sister. I don't want to hear one word about your perfect aunt Mae.

God help me. You look just like her.

A FAMILY RESEMBLANCE

BY *Audre Lorde*

My sister has my hair my mouth my eyes
and I presume her trustless.
When she was young and open to any fever
wearing gold like a veil of fortune on her face
she waited through each rain a dream of light.
But the sun came up
burning our eyes like crystal
bleaching the sky of promise and
my sister stood
Black, unblessed and unbelieving
shivering in the first cold show of love.

I saw her gold become an arch
where nightmare hunted
down the porches of restless night.
Now through echoes of denial
she walks a bleached side of reason.
Secret now
my sister never waits
nor mourns the gold that wandered from her bed.

My sister has my tongue
and all my flesh
unanswered
and I presume her trustless
as a stone.

CLOSE TO THE END

BY *Barbara L. Greenberg*

"And they cried and they cried
and they lay down and died."

Close to the end she cautioned me not to cry
as if I might, as if one had such choices,
as if she were the stoic sister and I the cry-baby
scared of our own two shadows and of shadows generally
at ages six and three again, hands intertwining,
reciting "Babes in the Wood" in Grandma's parlor
then lying down to die, our uncles applauding;
or forty and thirty-seven again, looking to all
the world like twins again, climbing the high tower
where, in a stiff wind coming off the ocean
each told the other the story of her life
until *she* with her arms flung out and laughing violently
turned on me, transposing me and our mother.
"How come you never taught me to fly?" she said.

BASQUE GUIDE

BY Myra Shapiro

for Raina

When I ask why these houses are blue,
Sylvie says, "You cannot stop on the sky
so the flies will never come to them." I buy
blue socks to keep death at bay. In St. Jean-de Luz

I've Dickinson's fly in my head, its buzz
when she died. Sylvie says, "Death is out
of the question." In southern France
my sister and I hike steep, ancient hills

to arrive at old age in new harmony. We say
once a year let's go see beauty together. *"Colchique,"*
Sylvie says, as we *ooh* over blooms
underfoot, blue crocus growing wild

through red ferns I'll press next to dreams
in my book. Sylvie says, "The day I met my man,
we finished the night together." Wild nights.
My dreams still play with men

but I'm finishing days without them.
Singing *Bat bit ru lau,* I count, beating time
to adamant sounds. "Excellent!" Sylvie says.
The narrow pass, the sea below, my agile sister climbing.

PAGANS

BY *Ruth Prawer Jhabvala*

BRIGITTE: CALM, LARGE-LIMBED and golden as a pagan goddess, she loved to lie spread-eagled on the beach or by her swimming pool, in communication with the sun. Los Angeles had been good to her. When she was young, at the time of her marriage, she had been a successful model. Her husband, Louis Morgenstern, was a small wizened shrewd little man, 30 years older than herself but a studio head, a powerful producer, a very rich man. It had been a relief for her to give up her career. She preferred to swim, to sunbathe, to give dinner parties for Louis (studded with stars but as dull, in their different way, as those her sister Frances gave in New York for her banker husband); also to travel in Europe and occasionally take lovers—wry intellectuals who taught her what to read and confirmed her contempt for the sort of films made by the studios, including her husband's.

Her sister Frances had been very skeptical about the marriage to Louis. She was wrong. In spite of the lovers—kept secret, discreet—it lasted almost 30 years and so did Brigitte's respect and liking for her husband. While Frances had married conventionally within their own circle settled in the U.S. for several generations, Louis was the first in his family to be born here and still had a grandmother who spoke no English. Frances and her husband Marshall were ashamed

233

of what they considered their sister's misalliance. They felt themselves to tower over Louis and his family—socially of course, culturally, and physically too, as was clear at the wedding when tiny Morgensterns scurried among the lofty trees of bankers and real-estate developers. Afterward Marshall joked about the ill-matched couple and how Brigitte would be crushing Louis on their wedding night between her mighty thighs.

Brigitte was in her 50s when Louis died, and Frances, for whom Los Angeles was a wasteland, said, "Now perhaps you'll come back to civilization." Brigitte sold her house—the Hollywood mansion of indoor and outdoor pools, patios, and screening rooms—while Frances searched for a suitable apartment in New York for her. Meanwhile Brigitte moved into a suite in a hotel, and although Frances found one Upper East-side apartment and then another, all close to herself and Marshall, Brigitte kept making excuses not to move into them. She liked Los Angeles; unlike New York, it was lightweight and undemanding. From one hotel window, she could see pretty houses frail as plywood scattered over the wooded hillside. From another, she had a view over the city of Los Angeles spread flat as far as the horizon; at night it was transformed into a field of shimmering flickering glow-worms fenced by the cut-out silhouettes of high-rise buildings. And the trees—the tall straight palm trees with their sparse foliage brushing a sky that was sometimes Renaissance blue and sometimes silver with pollution but all day held the sun to pour down on the ocean, the golden beach, and Brigitte herself, past menopause but still golden and firm in her designer swimsuit, and pads on her large smooth lids luxuriantly shut.

Frances was getting impatient. "I suppose she has a new lover out there," she thought to herself; and she said it to Brigitte over the phone: "Who is it now, another of those foreigners filling your head with clever rubbish."

234

Brigitte laughed; she had always laughed at Frances's disapproval, whether it was of Louis, of her lovers, or of her indolence. Brigitte still had male friends—she needed them to tell her what to read—but she had long since reached a stage where she could admit that sex was boring for her. With Louis, she had enjoyed sitting beside him while he explained their stocks and shares and other holdings to her. By the time he died, he had been ill for some years but was only semi-retired, for his successors at the studio continued to need his experience and his financial clout. Twice a year he and Brigitte still gave their dinner parties where the agents and the money men mixed with the stars. Louis had little respect for most of the stars; he mocked their pretensions and perversions, their physical beauty, which he said was the work of plastic surgeons and monkey glands. After each dinner party and the departure of the famous guests, he kissed Brigitte in gratitude for what she was: full-figured and naturally tanned, almost Nordic, God knew how and it was not only the hairdresser and the beautician. Louis had grown-up children from a previous marriage, and when it turned out that Brigitte couldn't have any, he was glad, wanting to keep her perfect, unmarred. Actually, Brigitte was not sorry either; she didn't think she had time for children. Frances said anyway she was too slothful and untidy ever to be able to bring them up. Frances had untold trouble with her own now grown-up son and daughter, who had gone the unstable way of the young and too rich.

✻

Two years after selling her house, Brigitte was still in Los Angeles. By this time she had met Shoki, a young Indian, and an interesting relationship had developed. It may have appeared a classic case of older woman with impoverished young immigrant, but that was not the way it was at all. It was true that he was young, very young; it was also true that he was poor, insofar as he had no money, but the word impoverished was inapplicable. He had the refinement of someone born rich—not so much in money as inherited culture. This expressed itself in him physically, in fine features and limbs; culturally in his manners, his almost feminine courtesy; and spiritually— so Brigitte liked to think—in his eyes, as of a soul that yearned for higher being. These eyes were often downcast, the lashes brushing his cheeks, for he was shy—out of modesty not lack of confidence. As far as confidence was concerned, he reposed as on a rock of ancestral privilege, so that it never mattered to him that he had to take all kinds of lowly jobs to keep himself going. Brigitte had met him while he was doing valet parking at her hotel; he had been filling in for another boy and left after a few weeks to work in a restaurant, again filling in for someone else. There were always these jobs available in a shifting population of unemployed or temporarily unemployed actors and other aspirants to film and television careers.

He himself wanted to become a writer-director, which was why he was here so far from home. He informed Brigitte that film was the medium of expression for his generation—he said it as though it were an idea completely original to himself. He carried a very bulky manuscript from agent to agent, or rather to their secretaries, and was always ready to read from it. Encouraged by Brigitte, he sat in her suite and read to her, while she watched rather than listened to him. Maybe it was all nonsense; but maybe it wasn't, or no more than the films on which Louis had grown so immensely rich; and she wanted him to be successful, so that he wouldn't go away, or wouldn't sink along with the other young people for whom he filled in on an endless round of temporary jobs.

She introduced him to Ralph, who had started off as a producer and now had his own talent agency. He had often been among her and Louis's guests, the powerful locals who had been their friends or had considered themselves so. Actually, some of them had made a pass at her—as who did not, even when she had been beyond the age when any woman could have expected it. Usually she laughed at them, and the one she had laughed at the most had been Ralph: "Come on, you don't mean it." Finally he had to admit that he did not. His excuse was that she was irresistible—"At 55?" she asked. He was the only person ever to explain to her in what way, and of course it was easier for him, with his lack of taste for women, to be impersonal. He said that her attraction was her indifference—the fact that she just *was,* the way a pagan goddess is, Pallas or Athene or someone, ready to accept worship but unconcerned whether it is given or not.

The introduction to Ralph was a success: Shoki came back enthusiastic about Ralph's kindness to him. When Brigitte phoned Ralph to thank him, Ralph said it was one's duty to help young talent. He sounded guarded; there was a silence, then she said, "So what did you think?"

"About the screenplay? It's interesting. Different."

"Yes isn't it."

Brigitte had hoped that Ralph would have had a more explicit opinion. She knew for herself that the work was different and also difficult. The characters spoke in a poetic prose that was not easy to understand, but it sounded beautiful when Shoki read it to her, and every time he looked up for her appreciation, she had no difficulty giving it. Then he continued, satisfied—though really he did not need approval, he had the same confidence in his work as he did in himself.

When there was another crisis in his living arrangement, Brigitte solved it by taking a room for him in the hotel. He was concerned about the expense, but when she reassured him that it wasn't a suite just a single room, he moved in with his small baggage. He liked it very much. It was on the second floor and overlooked the hotel garden with its cypress trees and silver fountain. It was also decided around this time that it was really not necessary for Shoki to take any more jobs when he could do so many helpful things for Brigitte.

Frances found the perfect New York apartment for her sister and Brigitte agreed to take it, pay a deposit, sign papers—"Oh please Frankie whatever." Frances was not satisfied, she knew she was being got rid of and asked herself, "What's going on?" Unfortunately she had no one with whom to share her doubts. Although she and her husband Marshall were known and seen everywhere as an indivisible couple—large and rich—the communication between them was not intimate. Whenever she tried to confide some deeper concerns to him, he answered her with an indifferent grunt or by rattling his newspaper at her in irritation.

"What's the matter with you?" she reproached Brigitte over the telephone. "What's wrong? I thought you wanted to come." Then she said, "Do you have someone out there? . . . A relationship?"

"Oh absolutely. He's sitting right here." Brigitte smiled across the room at Shoki who looked up inquiringly and smiled back.

"It's not a joke. And if you knew how I've been running around trying to find the right apartment for you and at last I have."

"Bless you," Brigitte thanked her, but Frances remained dissatisfied.

A few days later, after a particularly annoying telephone conversation with Brigitte, Frances decided that it would be best if she went herself to Los Angeles. She proposed this idea to Marshall who said at once, "Impossible." They were about to go out to someone's anniversary dinner—she had laid out his evening clothes and was putting on her jewelry.

"Only for a few days," she said.

"Oh yes? And what about the hospital ball, the library, the God-knows-for-what fundraiser." He was looking at himself in the mirror, adjusting his suspenders over his dress shirt. He was a big broad man carrying a load of stomach in front, but it gave him pleasure to dress up and see himself. She, on the other hand, inserted her earrings as though she were undergoing a disagreeable ritual.

"Why?" he said. As if he didn't know that her reason for going to Los Angeles could only be her sister. But she wasn't going to spell anything out for him: If Brigitte was to be mentioned, he would have to do it. "You hate flying," he said, holding out a sleeve for her to insert the cuff link. "You sit there as if the pilot's one ambition is to crash the plane with you in it. You spoil every trip you take with me before it's even started . . . I thought you told me she was moving to New York."

Frances was now concentrating on tying his black tie, something he had had no cause to learn since she did it so expertly.

"Well is she or isn't she?"

"I don't know."

"You don't know. That's your sister all over: playing mystery, making everyone dance to her tune."

But later inside their chauffeured limousine, where they took up the entire back seat as they sat side by side in their party clothes: "Call the office to book your seat; or remind me tomorrow, I'll tell them."

✻

Frances was querulous. The flight had been as horrible as she had expected, she already hated her room, and it was all Brigitte's fault for making her come here. "Yes you did—I knew something was up, and who else is there to care except me."

"Darling," Brigitte acknowledged. She looked around the room: "But it's charming, what's wrong with it?"

"It's cheap and gaudy, like a film set. And the light is giving me a headache."

"I'll draw the curtain"—but Brigitte regretted having to exclude the sun, the bright view.

"Marshall thinks you have a lover, that's why you're sticking on here."

"Did Marshall say that?"

"I'm sure it's what he's thinking."

"I have a friend," Brigitte said.

"A man?"

"God, Frances. What are you thinking."

"Who knows, nowadays." Frances was sad, thinking of her own children, about whose lives she could only speculate. "How old is he?"

"Young. Very young, Frankie."

Her sister was the only person left in the world to call her Frankie, and Frances's mood softened. She said, "I suppose it happens, especially in this place. You'd be far better off in New York."

"There are no young men there?"

"*I'm* there. We'd be together again, after so many years...We don't have to be lonely."

With her cool lips, Brigitte kissed her sister's cheek. "You must be dropping. I'll let you rest."

Frances agreed meekly. She really was tired—certainly too tired to call Marshall and tell him she had arrived safely. Anyway, he would only say that, if she hadn't, he would have heard about it soon enough.

But it was he who called her. He even asked about her flight; he also asked about her return booking, and would she and Brigitte be arriving together? She told him she was worried about the New York apartment for which she was negotiating—it was very desirable and others might preempt it—and in reply he did what she had hoped, asked for details, so she knew that he would be following them up and far more efficiently than she could. There was no reason after that not to hang up, but at the last moment he said, "What's she tell you?"

"About what?"

"About being a crazy woman and getting herself in a mess back there."

※

Brigitte was woken up by a phone call from Ralph, asking her if she knew where Shoki was. He was trying not to sound agitated: "He's not in his room so I thought he'd be with you."

"No—but he'll be here for breakfast."

"Breakfast! Do you know what the time is?...Anyway, he was supposed to be here: I'd set up a breakfast meeting for him. Remember? I'm his agent."

Brigitte said, "Of course." But it was true—she really had forgotten about this connection between Shoki and Ralph. Maybe she had even forgotten that Shoki was here for any other purpose than to be with her. She asked, "Do you and he often have breakfast meetings?"

"Well. Most days. I'm trying to help him, Brigitte." She could hear Ralph trying to choke down his anxiety. He said, "Have you any idea where he spends the night? You think he's in his room, don't you, but have you ever checked?" His voice rose. "Don't you ever wonder?" he asked, angry with her now.

Actually, she did wonder sometimes—not as Ralph evidently did, with anguish, but with curiosity, even pleasure. She knew it was not possible for Shoki to restrict himself to people he liked but who, by virtue of their age, were barred from one whole potent side of his nature. For that he did need—she freely admitted it—those as young as himself, and as gay (possibly in both senses). But to Ralph she only said, "What's happening with his screenplay?"

241

"It still needs work." He swept aside the irrelevant subject. "The fact is, he needs someone to take charge, be a bit strict with him—"

"You mean to make him work?"

"Yes yes that too. Now listen, Brigitte, we need to talk—"

"Oh," she said quickly, "there's someone at the door. That may be he."

But it was Frances. Brigitte went back to the phone: "No, it's my sister. She's here from New York."

"Do you realize he was not in his room, not at midnight, not early this morning?"

"My sister and I are going out now. This minute. We have a dental appointment."

When Brigitte was off the phone, Frances said, "I don't know why you have to tell people lies all the time."

"That's not fair, Frankie." But she reflected for a while: "It's mostly to save their feelings."

Frances was silent; she drew in her lips. "Don't ever think you have to save mine."

After a moment of surprise, "Of course not!" Brigitte said. "Why should I think that? Why should anyone?" But in her heart she thought, yours most of all. A rush of love and pity filled her, and she kissed her sister.

There was a very brief knock—for courtesy, not permission—and then Shoki came in. It was exactly the time he appeared every day. Wherever he might have been all night and this morning, now he was fresh, rested, smiling, and terribly pleased to meet Brigitte's sister. As for Frances, whatever prejudice she might have had was entirely swept away: It was as if she herself was swept clean of all negative thinking. If she had come to assess the situation, she would have to start all over again with entirely different premises.

✳

How to explain anything to Marshall? He had never in all their life together been so attentive with phone calls; and never had she been so negligent in return. It was the first time she had actually enjoyed Los Angeles. Before, on her visits to Brigitte, she had disliked being here, and so had Marshall, though he had insisted on coming with her. Everyone they met—the actors, agents, producers, publicists— appeared to them to be social flotsam. The town itself was flotsam, its houses ready to be razed as quickly as they had been put up, or collapsing into the earth quaking beneath them. But now that she was having fun with Brigitte and Shoki, all that was changed for Frances.

Shoki had accepted Frances completely. He loved the idea of family, and a sister was something almost sacred to him. With the intimacy that came so naturally to him, he at once adopted Frances and became the only other person besides Brigitte to call her Frankie. "Doesn't Frankie look marvelous?" he would say about some new outfit. Between them, he and Brigitte had decided to change Frances's style; and although Brigitte herself loved brilliant orange and purples, for Frances they chose discreet and lighter colors, with a hint of California playfulness. Accompanying them to a boutique, Shoki sat outside the dressing rooms chatting up the sales girls; and when Frances emerged, he said, very thrilled, "It *suits* you." Then her years dropped away from Frances.

She confided to Brigitte that, with Shoki, it was like being with another sister—though at the same time he was so manly, in the best way. Unlike other men, he was not hard and insensitive but the opposite. "He must have grown up with a lot of sisters," she guessed, "that's how he knows about women, what we have to put up with."

Brigitte agreed, but she too was guessing. Although Shoki had a high regard for the notion of family, he hardly ever mentioned his own. When he did, it was with a wistful, almost sad air. They specu-lated with each other—perhaps he was too homesick, perhaps the subject was too sacred for him. But Ralph said it was because he was too damn secretive.

Ralph: For Frances he had become as disturbing an element as was Marshall with his constant phone calls. Ralph often turned up in one of the restaurants where they had booked a table for three. "May I?" Ralph said, having already drawn out a chair for himself. He knew a lot of people there and sometimes he took Shoki away to introduce him to a useful contact. This was very irritating to Frances—"Shoki is with *us*," she complained. But Ralph was dissatis-fied too, as if it wasn't enough for him to be professionally useful to Shoki. Shoki was always as nice to him as he was to the two sisters and seemed anxious that all of them should be comfortable and happy with one another. But Ralph rarely was. He talked too much, telling some insider anecdote that made him laugh or sneer. He became brittle, malicious, assuming a role that perhaps belonged to his pro-fession but was not in his nature. Sooner or later, and sometimes before he had even finished laughing at his anecdote, he became gloomy and was silent. When Shoki tried to cheer him up, Ralph brushed this good-natured attempt aside. Instead he said something that the two sisters could not and Shoki perhaps would not hear. Then all three avoided looking at Ralph, the way a squeamish person avoids looking at someone in pain.

Marshall asked questions over the telephone: "So what's he like—the little friend? The lover?"

"There's nothing like that."

"Come *on*."

There was always some threat in his attitude to her that prevented Frances from holding out when he wanted something. "He's only a boy, Marshall."

"A substitute son? I knew she'd pick one up sooner or later . . . What about you?"

"I have a son," Frances said with dignity. Marshall hadn't spoken to their son for two years and gritted his teeth when he had to write out checks for him and his dependents from various relationships.

In a thoroughly bad mood now, Marshall told her, "Just get yourself back here. I don't want you hanging around there. In that *atmosphere*."

Atmosphere! Frances thought to herself. What about the home, the heavy empty costly apartment he wanted her to come back to and live there with him? And as if guessing the new desire arising in her heart, that same day Shoki suggested, "Wouldn't it be great if you stayed with us?" He turned to Brigitte: "Wouldn't it?"

Brigitte said, "Frankie's husband really needs her. They've been married for—how many years is it, Frankie?"

"32." Frances said, and Shoki made a gallant joke: "I don't believe it. You're not a day over 32 yourself."

"My son is 30. And Gilberte, my daughter, is 28. They're both married. And divorced."

Brigitte said, "He twice, and now he's in Hong Kong with another girlfriend. And Gilberte? We don't know about Gilberte. The last time we heard she was in Buenos Aires, and that was almost six months ago. So at least she doesn't need money—unlike her brother who needs lots. He even comes to me for it."

"I wish he wouldn't," Frances said, speaking as freely before Shoki as when she and her sister were alone.

Brigitte laughed: "He knows I'm loaded."

"This is the family today," Shoki commented. But although they waited, he still did not speak about his own family. Instead he said, "That is why everyone is making their own arrangements."

As though aware of this subversive conversation, Marshall arrived the next day. He had taken an early flight and went straight to his wife's suite in the hotel. Brigitte and Shoki had started on their room-service orders—neither of them could ever wait for meals; that day it was not Frances who joined them but Marshall. "What a surprise," Brigitte said, calmly continuing to eat her croissant. But Shoki leaped to his feet, in deference to an older man. He appeared flustered, not emotionally but socially, like a hostess with an extra guest. "Should we send for more coffee?" He lifted the lid to peer in: "Frankie needs at least three cups."

Marshall's eyebrows went right up: "Frankie?" Then they went down again: "Frances has a headache."

"Then there's enough." Shoki was already pouring for Marshall. "But Brigitte has finished the entire bread basket. So *greedy.*"

"It's all right," Brigitte said. "Marshall has to watch his weight."

Marshall was certainly a weighty man. This was never so obvious at home in New York, or in his office, or at his club lunches with other weighty men. But here in Brigitte's hotel suite, where the furniture was gilded and frail and the flowers seemed to float without support of vases in a cloud of petals, Marshall in his thick business suit imposed a heavy burden.

He didn't consider Shoki worth addressing, so it was Brigitte he asked, "Is he an actor?"

Of course Brigitte knew that to identify anyone as a possible actor was, in Marshall's view and intention, to insult him. Shoki however answered as though he had been paid a compliment; and it was regretfully that he admitted he wasn't—although, he added, he had done some acting in college. "What college?" Marshall said, asking an idle question to which no adequate answer was expected. Anyway, Shoki apparently didn't hear, he went straight on—"Just smaller roles in student productions, but the experience was very helpful to me as a writer."

"You're a writer?" Marshall spoke like one picking up an unattractive insect between pincers.

Shoki began to bubble over with enthusiasm. He spoke of his screenplay, which his agent was placing for him—at the moment it was with Fox who were showing interest. Of course it was a difficult subject, he confided to Marshall, partly symbolic and partly historical. The history reflected contemporary events so it was very topical, though one did have to know something of India's past as well as of her not-always-perfect present. Marshall consulted his watch and shifted his big thighs where he sat. He tried to catch Brigitte's eye, the way he always did, had done through all their past together, to communicate the fact that he desired her and wished to be alone with her. Shoki appeared completely oblivious of this tension—he carried on expounding his story as though Marshall's sole intention in traveling to Los Angeles was to listen to it.

But sooner or later, Brigitte knew, Marshall would create the opportunity of being alone with her. He might give the impression of being unwieldy, but he was also subtle at least in mental calculation. By next morning he had discovered the arrangement that his wife and sister-in-law had made with Shoki for their morning meal together. By the time Frances woke up, he was fully dressed and on the point of going out.

"I need fresh air," he told her. "A stroll by the ocean." He didn't usually tell her his plans, so she didn't think it worth mentioning how far they actually were from the ocean. "How's your headache?" he said. "You had a headache. You'd better stay in bed and rest."

"Who is he anyway? Your little friend?" was his first question to Brigitte. After opening the door to him, she had gone back to bed and he sat by the side of it, the vast hotel bed with the padded satin backrest.

"He's a prince. From one of those old Indian princely families. What do they call them? Maharajas." She had only just thought of this but it made sense.

"Yes and look at you: a Maharani."

She did look royal, leaning against her pillows, one side of her silken nightie slipped down from her broad shoulder—divine even, a goddess emerging out of a flood of rumpled shiny satin sheets. He murmured to her in a voice that had gone thick, so that she knew that soon he would be climbing in next to her, and she would let him. It had happened before in their many years together as in-laws, and the only thing surprising to her was that it should still be happening.

"Frankie will be here any minute," she said afterward to Marshall, who showed every indication to stay right where he was next to her.

"My wife has a headache and I advised her to rest." But he was good-natured about letting her push him out of bed and smirked a bit as he climbed back into his trousers.

Then he became practical. He said he wanted her to return with them to New York—why wait? Everything was ready for her arrival.

"Oh you bought it, did you? The apartment Frankie was talking about?"

"You don't need an apartment...We have one. It's enormous. It's big. Much too big for just two people now that the kids are—where are they?"

"In Hong Kong."

"Yes and Buenos Aires. What are Frances and I supposed to do rattling around by ourselves in a place that size? It's ridiculous." He frowned at the impracticality of it, and she laughed at his impudence.

"So you and I would be like this every day of our lives from now on?"

"It makes perfect sense. We shouldn't be wasting time, having to commute from one apartment to another, secret rendezvous and all that nonsense." He spoke with the decision of a man of business, the chairman of the board. She smiled a bit, but she said, "You really have to leave now."

He took his time about it, strolled around the suite, stood at a window to frown at the city of Los Angeles and its giant billboards: "I don't know how you can live in a place like this. No climate. No history."

"I didn't know you cared about history."

"Only my own. Grandmothers and so on. Great-grandmothers. New York."

"What about Poland and Russia?"

"That's too far back. By the way, I saw him this morning: your princely friend."

"He has a room in the hotel."

"He doesn't seem to have spent the night in it. I'm just guessing of course—but he looked like someone sneaking in after a night on the tiles."

"What would you know about tiles, Marshall?"

"Nothing. And I won't have to, if we make this arrangement I mentioned to you. No sneaking out, or back in."

✳

On his third and last evening in Los Angeles, Marshall hired a limousine to take his two ladies to dinner. The restaurant he had chosen was one known to other East Coast bankers and to West Coast attorneys from old established family firms. It was very different from the ones Brigitte usually went to, but she didn't mind; it was Frances who said, "Why do we have to come here? We might as well have stayed in New York."

Brigitte was surprised: She had never heard a note of rebellion from Frances in the face of any decision made by Marshall. And what was also surprising was that Marshall did not wither her with one of his looks but concentrated on reading the menu.

"Don't you hate it?" Frances asked her sister. "I hate it." She was actually sulking, and still Marshall continued to read the menu.

The restaurant was a fantasy of an opulent New York eating place recreated by earlier settlers in the Californian desert. It was dark with antique lamps throwing insufficient light and thick carpets and velvet drapes shutting out the rest of it. There was a buffet table overloaded with silver dishes and with giant fruits and flowers that appeared to be a replica of those in the varnished still-lifes on the walls.

"Lobster," Marshall said, returning the menu to the waiter. This waiter was no out-of-work actor but an elderly professional, Italian or Swiss, who had been with the restaurant for over 40 years and would soon be mourning its closing. He hovered over Frances who was unable to make a choice of dishes, but when Marshall said, "You could have the lobster too," she quickly ordered a green salad with a light dressing.

"You know what?" she said to Brigitte. "He's let that apartment go. And it would have been so perfect for you! Now where are you supposed to live in New York? In another hotel? Then you might as well stay in Beverly Hills—I should think you'd want to stay here. My goodness, who wouldn't. And I don't suppose it's occurred to anyone that I'd like to be near my sister. That I'm sick of having her live at the opposite end of the world."

"Not the world, darling," Brigitte said. "Just the country."

"Frances has always been a dunce in geography," Marshall said. He tried to sound playful but was too saturnine. He had tucked his table napkin under his chin and was expertly excavating the meat from a lobster claw. He ate and drank the way he had done throughout his life and would continue till he could do so no more. It was natural for a man like him to be companioned by a handsome woman, even by two of them.

These two were no longer discussing the pros and cons of living in New York or Los Angeles but whether Shoki was a prince. Brigitte had raised the question and Frances had taken it up with such pleasure that Marshall felt he had at once to squash it. He said, "They don't have princes anymore. They've been abolished. They're all democratic now, whatever that might mean. And they're all poor. No more jewels and elephants."

"Money's got nothing to do with it," Frances said. "Anyone can have money. Anyone. But look at the graceful way he moves."

"And the delicate way he eats."

Marshall wiped the butter from his chin. He said, "It's time I took you two back to New York."

"I found a lovely apartment for Brigitte and you let it go."

Brigitte felt Marshall nudge her knee under the table. She was used to this gesture from him, though today it was another kind of plea. She denied it in her usual way, by moving her knee out of his reach. But she said, "Why don't you tell her your grand plan."

"It's simple common sense," Marshall said, losing no ounce of authority. "Our apartment is big enough for ten people, let alone three."

After a moment of shock, "You're completely insane," Frances told him. She turned on her sister: "And you listened to him? You sat and listened and didn't say a word to me?"

She pushed back her chair, rushed from the table. No one looked up from their plates; even when she stumbled against their chairs, the diners carried on dining. The waiters too kept their eyes lowered, so did the maitre d' while guiding her toward the ladies room, where he opened and held the door for her.

"Ah the pièce de résistance," Marshall said as their waiter came toward them bearing the chocolate soufflé. The critical moment of its departure from the oven had now been reached and it rose above its dish in a splendidly browned dome.

Brigitte said, "You are a fool, Marshall."

"Today is not my lucky day," Marshall said. "She calls me crazy, you call me a fool. Why fool? How fool? She's always telling me how she misses you, and you I guess miss her. Sisters, after all...I wonder how they get it to this consistency; I suppose that's why it has to be ordered in advance."

Brigitte, too, was enjoying every bit of the soufflé, but she said, "I'm going to see how she's doing."

"Explain it to her: how it's best for everyone."

"Best for you." Under the table she moved her knee further away. "I'll explain that to her; after all these years maybe she ought to know."

"Did you ever tell Louis?"

"Tell on you? He'd have laughed. He knew how I wouldn't give you the time of day."

"Sometimes you give it to me. The time of day." Over the table his lips curved in a smile, under it his knee went in pursuit of hers.

"I'd better go. This table is not big enough for you and me."

"But the apartment is enormous, as I keep saying. Have a second helping, be a devil. Well I will then," he said and was already digging his spoon in when she left.

A tiny old oriental attendant welcomed Brigitte into her pink kingdom. Brigitte could see Frances's elegant shoes and ankles under a stall so she took an adjoining one. She said, "It's me."

"I know. I can see your feet, and I wish you wouldn't wear those kind of teen-age sandals." Frances's voice was steady; she had not been crying but she had been thinking, and now she announced her decision: "I'm not going back with him. I'm staying with you." But when Brigitte said nothing, Frances's voice was less firm: "I'm staying with you and Shoki." She pulled the lever in her stall and went out.

From inside, Brigitte could hear the excited birdlike voice of the attendant communicating with Frances in what sounded like Chinese but could not have been for Frances was able to respond. When Brigitte emerged, the attendant addressed her in the same birdsong, offering fragrant soap and towel. Frances was already wiping her hands on hers, and since neither of them spoke, the little attendant took over the conversation. They gathered that she was distressed about her job, which she had held for 20 years and now they had been informed by the management that the restaurant was closing. Suddenly she was crying, tiny tears ran down her wizened cheeks, slightly rouged. Brigitte made comforting noises at her.

Frances was staring at herself in the mirror. Her eyes were dry, her face was set. She said, "You can't send me back with him because I won't go."

"Who's sending you back?"

"I haven't heard you say stay."

Brigitte was using her towel to wipe away the attendant's tears. She told her: "You'll find another job. Anyone would like to have you in their home."

The attendant praised Brigitte for her kindness. She went on to explain that she was not weeping for herself but for the others, the old men whom no one would ever again want to employ. She herself had a son and a daughter, both of whom did not want her to work anymore. She took the towel wet with her own tears and gave Brigitte a fresh one.

"You don't need to feel sorry for the whole world," Frances said. "And you heard her—she has a son and a daughter who care for her."

"Of course I want you to stay," Brigitte said. "I don't know what gave you the idea I don't. Shall we go back now?"

"I don't want to see him."

"I mean go back to the hotel. He's all right. He's having another helping of chocolate soufflé." She found a 50-dollar bill in her purse and put it in the tactful little saucer. "That's too much," Frances said outside, though she herself, usually more careful, over-tipped the valet who whistled up a cab for them.

One evening a few weeks later Shoki gave Brigitte a lovely surprise. He came to her suite dressed up in a high-collared jacket of raw silk— Indian, but he had had it made in Beverly Hills. "I showed them exactly what to do, how to cut it—you really like it?"

"Love it, love it; love you," and she kissed his cheek in the beautiful way of friendship they had with each other.

He had been invited to a charity premiere and he asked her to come along. He assured her his host had taken a table for 12.

"Ralph?"

"No someone else, another friend." There was sure to be room, someone or other always dropped out.

"What about Frankie?"

"Of course; let's take Frankie."

Frances said she was waiting for a call but might join them later. Her call came exactly when she was expecting it. Marshall telephoned the same time every evening. It was always when he was home from the office or a board meeting and was having his martini by the fireplace in the smaller drawing room (called the library, though they had never had many books). She imagined him wearing slippers and maybe his velvet housecoat; or if he was going out, he might have begun to dress.

"Isn't tonight the Hospital Benefit?" When he yawned and said he didn't feel like going, she urged, "Marshall, you have to. You're on the board."

"I guess I have to. But to turn up there by myself—" He always left such sentences unfinished. She waited; perhaps tonight he would say more. Instead he became more irritated. "Marie can't find any of my dress shirts—do you think she drinks?"

"Marie! After all this time!"

"Who knows. Servants need supervision. Someone to make them toe the line." Perhaps suspecting that she had begun to preen herself, he said, "I'll send from the office to buy some new ones. What about you? You want any of your stuff sent out there?"

She hesitated: It was true that she was running short of the underclothes that were specially made for her by a Swiss lady in New York. But the subject of her underclothes was not one she ever intruded on her husband, so she murmured, "I'm all right for now."

"For now? What's that supposed to mean?" She was silent, and then he almost asked, though grudgingly, what she was waiting to hear: "Are you intending to stay out there forever or what?"

He sounded so put out—so fed up—and it was her fault. She said, "What can I do, Marshall? Brigitte just likes it better here."

"She thinks she does. She's from New York. She was born here like the rest of us, why would she want to be in that joke place out there? Where is she, by the way?"

"She's gone out. It's a premiere. A big event. She wants me to join her later. Do you think I should?"

"You should do what you want, not what she wants. Though why anyone would want to go to a thing like that. 'A Premiere. A Big Event.' Tcha. You'd be better off at the Benefit with me."

"Marshall? You know my dresser? In the last drawer there are some bits and pieces I might need. If it's not too much trouble. Just some bras. And girdles."

"I didn't know you wore girdles."

"They look like panties but actually they're tummy control." She was glad he couldn't see her face—it was the most intimate exchange they had had in years. "Marie can pack them."

"If she's not too drunk."

"Marie is practically a teetotaler."

"You're the easiest person in the world to fool," he said.

※

Shoki had been right and there were two empty places at his host's table. This host was a powerful studio head but a far more modern type than Louis had been. He was from the mid-West and had been to some good schools in the East; still in his 30s, he was well groomed, well informed, *smart.* The guests at his table were there for their fame, their money, or their youth and beauty. Brigitte's celebrity was in the past but that gave her an aura of historical tradition, and she kept having to raise her cheek for the tribute offered to her by other guests. Each table was ornamented by someone like Shoki, with no claim whatsoever to celebrity. Some were girls, others young men or almost boys, some were very lively, some totally silent—it didn't seem to matter as long as they were visibly there and known to be attached to a powerful member at the table. Shoki and his host hardly acknowledged one another, except that from time to time the older man's eyes stabbed toward the younger, maybe just in an instinctive gesture of checking on the security of possession. He could be entirely relaxed—Shoki gave all his attention to Brigitte next to him and to the matron on his other side, a former star. He was lightheartedly laughing and making them laugh.

But there *was* tension—not emanating from their table but from elsewhere. Her eyes roaming around the room, Brigitte soon discovered Ralph: He was craning in their direction and even half rose in his chair as though intending to leave his place and make his way toward theirs. But it was impossible—the room was packed, each table crowded and the spaces between them thronged with guests still trying to find their place or changing it for a more desirable one, while the servers weaved and dodged among them with their platters and wine bottles.

Although without an invitation card, Frances looked too distinguished not to be let in. But once inside, she had no idea which way to turn to locate Brigitte among this crowd of strangers, strange beings who all knew or knew of one another. She stood there, dazed by the din and glitter. Then she heard her name called: "Are you all right?"

It was Ralph. He settled her into an empty chair beside him and tried to revive her with wine. She preferred water—"For my aspirin," she said, taking her pillbox out of her evening purse.

He laughed: "Are you sure that's what it is?"

"It may be dispirin. For my headache. It's so terribly noisy. How can anyone enjoy being in such a noisy place."

"At least one doesn't have to hear what's going on in his own head. They're over there. No you're looking in the wrong direction."

The reason it took her so long to find Brigitte's table was that all the 84 tables crammed into that space appeared very much the same. Everyone there sat as in a burnished cast of wealth, of costly ornament. It was she, Frances, who was out of place. Although her hair too was professionally dyed, it had a discreet touch of silver; and her jewelry was not like that of others, women and some men, who displayed diamonds and rubies and pearls of a size and quantity that, if this had been any other place, would have been taken for paste. And maybe it was paste, she thought; it couldn't be safe to walk around loaded with such immeasurable riches.

"They're waiting for me," she told Ralph.

"I've been trying to get through myself, but there's such a crush. Maybe after they've served the dessert. Why didn't you come with them?"

"I was on the phone with my husband. He wants me to come back to New York." Again looking around the room, she thought of Marshall at his fundraiser. He too would be with the powerful and rich, but his would be not only physically less brilliant but much more glum than these surrounding her, who were laughing chatting shouting and out-shouting one another as though placed on a stage to impersonate characters having a festive time.

"Brigitte doesn't want to leave. But he wants both of us. They've been having sex together." She found it difficult to say—the words, that is; to herself she still thought of it as "sleeping together." "It's been going on for years. I don't blame her for not wanting to come live with us. She doesn't even like Marshall."

"No. Not the way she likes Shoki. As a friend, that is. They're friends."

"Yes he's my friend too. But I really think I must go home. Of course Marshall will be angry if I come without her. But he's angry at me anyway. It's just that he needs someone with him where he can be any mood he wants. That's the only way he feels comfortable."

Dessert had been served. A master of ceremonies tapped a microphone. Speeches were about to start. Ralph suggested that they should try and squeeze their way toward the other table. He led the way, and when Shoki looked up, he saw them cleaving their way toward them. Shoki told Brigitte that it was very hot inside and maybe they should try to catch some fresh air? She got up at once and he took her elbow to guide her through the crowd. Their host rose in his chair, but they did not appear to see him, or to hear him when he called after them.

Unimaginably, outside the noisy room there was an empty terrace hovering over an expanse of ocean and moonless sky. Although a crowd of brilliant figures could be seen agitating inside, no sound reached through the double-glazing of the walls. Two faces were pressed against the glass trying to peer out into the darkness. Shoki said, "There's Ralph."

"Yes and Frankie."

They sighed as though something was difficult for them. But it wasn't. Nothing was difficult for them. Shoki knew a way down from the terrace to the beach and soon he and Brigitte were walking there, their hands lightly linked. He told her about Bombay where he had also walked on the beach, but it was not the same. For one thing, the sun was too hot, and then, always, there was Bombay—right there on the beach with the coconut sellers, the boy acrobats, and others seeking money for food; and beyond, the whole city of Bombay with its traffic, its slums, its huge heavy Victorian buildings pressing down on the earth and the human spirit. He didn't have to explain much to Brigitte, because in some way it was how she felt about New York where everything was just as oppressive. But here, now, the ocean was very calm and very dark and all that could be seen of it were the white fringes of its waves gliding into the sand. There was absolutely nothing, no world at all between water and sky, and it was inconceivable that, with such fullness available, anyone could be troubled about anything—apartments, desires, attachments, anything.

THE LAST GOOD WAR

BY Maxine Kumin

Pearl Harbor. A scurry to marry. Two brothers
take up with a pair of sweet Southern sisters.
Antebellum manners, mouths that plaster rumors
on the brothers' sister, younger than summer.
They never aspired to the Seven Sisters.
Claim she is sleeping with her professor.
When the pater familias bursts a main artery
leaving a tangled will, read the next chapter
in the lives of two brothers who married two sisters.
Imagine which sister unties the tether,
which couple keeps the house with wisteria
twining the back fence they bought together.
Brothers, oh brothers, how could you go bitter,
go without speaking, one winner, one debtor?
Less than a year fells taker and giver
but the widows remain, their old quarrels fester
as into their nineties they flourish, the sisters
whose sweet Southern manners won them two brothers.

I NEEDED TO TALK TO MY SISTER

BY *Grace Paley*

I needed to talk to my sister
talk to her on the telephone   I mean
just as I used to every morning
in the evening too whenever the
grandchildren said a sentence that
clasped both our hearts

I called   her phone rang four times
you can imagine my breath stopped   then
there was a terrible telephonic noise
a voice said   this number is no
longer in use   how wonderful I
thought   I can
call again they have not yet assigned
her number to another person despite
two years of absence due to death

FROM HAVING OUR SAY: THE DELANY SISTERS' FIRST 100 YEARS

BY *Sarah and A. Elizabeth Delany*

SADIE

One thing I've noticed since I got this old is that I have started to dream in color. I'll remember that someone was wearing a red dress or a pink sweater, something like that. I also dream more than I used to, and when I wake up I feel tired. I'll say to Bessie, "I sure am tired this morning. I was teaching all night in my dreams!"

Bessie was always the big dreamer. She was always talking about what she dreamed the night before. She has this same dream over and over again, about a party she went to on Cotton Street in Raleigh, way back when. Nothing special happens; she just keeps dreaming she's there. In our dreams, we are always young.

Truth is, we both forget we're old. This happens all the time. I'll reach for something real quick, just like a young person. And realize my reflexes are not what they once were. It surprises me, but I can't complain. I still do what I want, pretty much.

These days, I am usually the first one awake in the morning. I wake up at six-thirty. And the first thing I do when I open my eyes is smile, and then I say, "Thank you, Lord, for another day!"

If I don't hear Bessie get up, I'll go into her room and wake her. Sometimes I have to knock on her headboard. And she opens her eyes and says, "Oh, Lord, another day?!" I don't think Bessie would get up at all sometimes, if it weren't for me. She stays up late in her room and listens to these talk-radio shows, and she doesn't get enough sleep.

In the mornings, Monday through Friday, we do our yoga exercises. I started doing yoga exercises with Mama about forty years ago. Mama was starting to shrink up and get bent down, and I started exercising with her to straighten her up again. Only I didn't know at that time that what we were actually doing was "yoga." We just thought we were exercising.

I kept doing my yoga exercises, even after Mama died. Well, when Bessie turned eighty she decided that I looked better than her. So she decided she would start doing yoga, too. So we've been doing our exercises together ever since. We follow a yoga exercise program on the TV. Sometimes, Bessie cheats. I'll be doing an exercise and look over at her, and she's just lying there! She's a naughty old gal.

Exercise is very important. A lot of older people don't exercise at all. Another thing that is terribly important is diet. I keep up with the latest news about nutrition. About thirty years ago, Bessie and I started eating much more healthy foods. We don't eat that fatty Southern food very often. When we do, we feel like we can't move!

We eat as many as seven different vegetables a day. Plus lots of fresh fruits. And we take vitamin supplements: Vitamin A, B complex, C, D, E, and minerals, too, like zinc. And Bessie takes tyrosine when she's a little blue.

Every morning, after we do our yoga, we each take a clove of garlic, chop it up, and swallow it whole. If you swallow it all at once, there is no odor. We also take a teaspoon of cod liver oil. Bessie thinks it's disgusting. But one day I said, "Now, dear little sister, if you want to keep up with me, you're going to have to start taking it, every day, and stop complainin'." And she's been good ever since.

As soon as we moved to our house in 1957, we began boiling the tap water we use for our drinking water. Folks keep telling us that it's not necessary, that the City of Mount Vernon purifies the water. But it's a habit and at our age, child, we're not about to change our routine.

These days, I do most of the cooking, and Bessie does the serving. We eat our big meal of the day at noon. In the evening, we usually have a milk shake for dinner, and then we go upstairs and watch "MacNeil Lehrer" on the TV.

After that, we say our prayers. We say prayers in the morning and before we go to bed. It takes a long time to pray for everyone, because it's a very big family—we have fifteen nieces and nephews still living, plus all their children and grandchildren. We pray for each one, living and dead. The ones that Bessie doesn't approve of get extra prayers. Bessie can be very critical and she holds things against people forever. I always have to say to her, "Everybody has to be themselves, Bessie. Live and let live."

Bessie can be very kind, though she usually saves her kind side for children and animals. She has a little dog who belonged to someone in the neighborhood who didn't want him anymore. He's part Chihuahua and I don't know what else, and he has some nasty habits, but Bessie loves him. She never eats a meal without saving the best piece for her little dog.

I'll tell you a story: Not long ago the Episcopal bishop of New York had a dinner to honor me and Bessie. A couple of days beforehand, Bessie announced that she was going to bring a doggie bag to the dinner. I said, "Whaaaat? Why, Bess, people will think you're a peculiar old woman." And she said, "So what, maybe I am a peculiar old woman. I hear they're having prime rib, and I would die of guilt if I had prime rib and didn't save any for my little dog."

Sure enough, when they served the dinner, Bessie took a bag out of her pocketbook and started to cut off the nicest part of the meat.

And the bishop, who was sitting right there, asked her what she was doing. Next thing I knew, the bishop was cutting off a piece of *his* prime rib and wrapping it in a napkin for Bessie's little dog, and everybody else started doing the same thing, because the bishop did.

When we got home, Bessie was so excited she was almost giddy. She kept saying, "I've got enough prime rib to feed my little dog for a week!" I said, "Well, I certainly hope he enjoys the bishop's dinner."

Before Bessie got her little dog, we had a stray cat we named Mr. Delany, since we don't have a man in the house. He had been run over by a car, and had crawled up on our doorstep. So we brought the kitty in the house, rubbed salve into his cuts, and splinted him up. We fed him by hand and fussed over him, day and night, for two weeks. And you know what? He was just fine. But one day, he ran off. Bessie's still grieving for that old cat. She says, "I know he must be dead, or he would have come back."

If only I could get Bessie to be as sweet to people as she is to her animals. Bessie can be a little bit nasty sometimes, you know. She thinks it's her God-given duty to tell people the truth. I say to her, "Bessie, don't you realize people don't want to hear the truth?"

One time, there was a woman in our neighborhood who was furious at her granddaughter for moving in with a boyfriend. This woman was running around the neighborhood complaining to anyone who would listen. I was sort of sympathetic but Bessie said to her, "You shouldn't be running all around bad-mouthing your own kin." Of course, Bessie was right. But that poor lady was embarrassed and has avoided us ever since.

Another time, a priest was over here visiting us and I noticed he'd put on a little weight. I thought to myself, Uh-oh, I bet she says something to him. Well, when he was leaving, Bessie said, "Now, Father, it seems to me you are getting fat. You've got to lose some weight!" He laughed and said, yes, he knew he needed to go on a diet. When he left I said to Bessie, "What did you have to go and say that for?" And she said, "I care about people's health, and sometimes people need somebody to give it to 'em straight."

Bessie does not mince words, and when she has a strong opinion—especially when it involves me—she's not shy! Not long ago, one of our nieces died, and somebody was over here describing the place where she died. It was called a hospice, and it sounded awfully nice. I said, "Well, maybe when my time comes, y'all should take me to a hospice." But Bessie got real mad. She said, "You ain't dying in no hospice. You ain't dying nowhere but upstairs in yo' bed!"

Over the years, we've buried a lot of people. Even the generation younger than us is starting to die off. I don't know why I'm still here and they're not, but I don't fret over it. It's in God's hands.

You know, when you are this old, you don't know if you're going to wake up in the morning. But I don't worry about dying, and neither does Bessie. We are at peace. You do kind of wonder, when's it going to happen? That's why you learn to love each and every day, child.

Truth is, I've gotten so old I'm starting to get a little *bold*. Not long ago, some young men started hanging out in front of our house. They were part of a gang from the Bronx, and they just thought our dead-end street here was a good spot to play basketball and do drugs and I don't know what-all.

Well, Bessie said to me, "I'll go out there and get rid of them." And I said, "No, Bess. For once, I'm going to handle it. You stay in the house."

I went out the backdoor and around to the sidewalk where they were hanging out. And I said, "You boys better get out of here."

They were kind of surprised. And then one of them said, "You can't make us leave. This is a public street."

And I said, "Yes, it's a public street, but it's not a *park*, so get moving."

And this fella said to me: "Just how do you think you're going to make us go?"

I pointed to my house. I said, "My sister is inside and she has her hand on the phone to call the police." Of course, this was a little white lie because we don't have a phone, but they didn't know that.

So the leader of this group laughed at me and he said, "You think the police are gonna come when some old *nigger woman* calls them?"

I said, "Yes, they will come. Because I own this property here, and I own this house, and I pay my taxes. They *will* come, and they will boot you on out of here."

Well, they grumbled and complained, and finally they left. They came back about a week later, and our neighbor ran them off. And they never did come back.

Bessie was kind of surprised that I took those boys on like that. To tell you the truth, so was I.

⚜

BESSIE

I was mighty proud of Sadie for taking on those no-good fellas and running them on out of there. It just goes to show she can be tough when she puts her mind to it. I said to her, "Sadie, our Grandpa Miliam surely would have been proud."

I was just thinking about Mr. Miliam this morning. There was a cute little squirrel in my yard, and I said, "Oh, you better be glad Mr. Miliam and his gun ain't around. Cause he'd shoot you and fry you up for his breakfast."

You know how when you come up on a squirrel, it'll run around to the other side of the tree? Well, Mr. Miliam would send one of us grandchildren to chase the squirrel back around to his side, and he would shoot it dead while the child stayed hid behind the tree. But don't worry. Mr. Miliam was an excellent shot, and nobody ever got hurt.

I wonder what Mr. Miliam would think of his granddaughters living this long. Why, I suppose he'd get a kick out of it. I know he'd have lived longer if Grandma hadn't died and it broke his heart. Sometimes, you need a reason to keep living.

Tell you the truth, I wouldn't be here without sister Sadie. We are companions. But I'll tell you something else: Sadie has taken on this business of getting old like it's a big *project*. She has it all figured out, about diet and exercise. Sometimes, I just don't want to do it, but she is my big sister and I really don't want to disappoint her. Funny thing about Sadie is she rarely gets—what's the word?—depressed. She is an easygoing type of gal.

Now, honey, I get the blues sometimes. It's a shock to me, to be this old. Sometimes, when I realize I am 101 years old, it hits me right between the eyes. I say, "Oh Lord, how did this happen?" Turning one hundred was the worst birthday of my life. I wouldn't wish it on my worst enemy. Turning 101 was not so bad. Once you're past that century mark, it's just not as shocking.

There's a few things I have had to give up. I gave up driving a while back. I guess I was in my late eighties. That was terrible. Another thing I gave up on was cutting back my trees so we have a view of the New York City skyline to the south. Until I was ninety-eight years old, I would climb up on the ladder and saw those tree branches off so we had a view. I could do it perfectly well; why pay somebody to do it? Then Sadie talked some sense into me, and I gave up doing it.

Some days I feel as old as Moses and other days I feel like a young girl. I tell you what: I have only a little bit of arthritis in my pinky finger, and my eyes aren't bad, so I know I could still be practicing dentistry. Yes, I am sure I could still do it.

But it's hard being old, because you can't always do everything you want, exactly as *you* want it done. When you get as old as we are, you have to struggle to hang onto your freedom, your independence. We have a lot of family and friends keeping an eye on us, but we try not to be dependent on any one person. We try to pay people, even relatives, for whatever they buy for us, and for gasoline for their car, things like that, so that we do not feel beholden to them.

Longevity runs in the family. I'm sure that's part of why we're still here. As a matter of fact, until recently there were still five of us, of the original ten children. Then, Hubert went to Glory on December 28, 1990, and Hap, a few weeks later, in February 1991. That leaves me, Sadie, and Laura, our baby sister who moved to California with her husband.

Now, when Hubert died, that really hurt. He was just shy of ninety years old. It never made a bit of difference to me that Hubert became an assistant United States attorney, a judge, and all that. He was still my little brother.

Same way with Hap. You know what? Even when he was ninety-five years old, Sadie and I still spoiled him. When he didn't like what they were cooking for dinner at his house, he would get up and leave the table and come over here and we'd fix him what he liked to eat.

Good ol' Hap knew he was going to Glory and he was content. He said, "I've had a good life. I've done everything I wanted to do, I think I've done right by people." We Delanys can usually say that, when our time comes.

You know what I've been thinking lately? All those people who were mean to me in my life—all those *rebby boys*—they have turned to dust, and this old gal is still here, along with sister Sadie.

We've outlived those old rebby boys!

That's one way to beat them!

That's justice!

They're turning in their graves, while Sadie and me are getting the last word, in this book. And honey, I surely do love getting the last word. I'm having my say, giving my opinion. Lord, ain't it good to be an *American*.

Truth is, I never thought I'd see the day when people would be interested in hearing what two old Negro women have to say. Life still surprises me. So maybe the last laugh's on *me*.

I'll tell you a little secret: I'm starting to get optimistic. I'm thinking: *Maybe I'll get into Heaven after all.* Why, I've helped a lot of folks—even some white folks! I surely do have some redeeming qualities that must count for something. So I just might do it: I just might get into Heaven. I may have to hang on to Sadie's heels, but I'll get there.

Two years of my sister's bitter illness;

the wind whips the river of her last spring.

I have burned the beans again.

Muriel Rukeyser, "TWO YEARS"

Dedications to Sisters

✳

ELEANOR LAZARUS *thanks* MEG *for being her twin sister—together, wherever, forever.*

SALLY MONTGOMERY *celebrates sisters and cousins* SARAH, MARTHA, RHEA, VIVIAN, MARGARET, CHARLOTTE, HAZEL, *and* AMY.

JEANNE ROSLANOWICK *celebrates her sister of the heart,* RUTH.

BETSEY HARRIES *and* ESTHER WANNING *celebrate the Andrews sisters: grandmother* ROSE, *her sisters* LOUISE *and* ESTHER, *and the '40s singers.*

ANNE GOLDSTEIN *and* PHIL TEGELER *give a shout out to the amazing Delventhal sisters—*MARIE, EMILIE, *and* DOROTHEE.

LAURA *and* MELANIE SLAP-SHELTON *celebrate their "found" sisters here and abroad!*

ALLISON RYAN *salutes her Radcliffe housemate sisterhood —*ANNE, EMILY, JACKIE, ANNE—*bonded after 40 years.*

ELIZABETH DOMINIQUE *and* RICHARD ARTHUR *love and celebrate their sister* DEBORAH MAY!

AMELIA STEVENS *honors the memory of her sister,* MARGARET.

ALISON BERNSTEIN *celebrates* EMMA *and* JULIA*'s special relationship. Love,* MOM.

PATSY ROGERS *celebrates her sisters* KATHIE, BETSY, LUCILLE, CAROL, *and* MICAELA.

ROBIN BECKER *honors the memory of* JILL WENDY BECKER, *1953–1986.*

BRIDGETTE SHERIDAN *rejoices in all that is* SHELLY, KATHY, MARY, *and* JENNY: *sisterly love.*

SUSAN *and* PAUL WOJCIK *toast their favorite sisters,* MOLLY *and* EMILY.

JOYCE FLUECKIGER *celebrates the richness of life with five sisters.*

MOLLY WOJCIK *is forever grateful to her sister* EMILY *for showing her the way.*

For JENNY TSAI, *and in loving memory of* CINDY TSAI,
from SEJIN CHUNG.

JUDY GIBSON *celebrates her sister* SUSAN, *who taught her to read, and her daughters* EMILY *and* MOLLY.

POLLY LONGSWORTH *rejoices in her four incredible daughters, all sisters.*

KAREN KUKIL *remembers her sister-in-law*
DIANE HEMPHILL VALUCKAS, *with affection.*

LEE LINEN *and* JEAN BEARD *toast their sister* PAM CLARKE *on her 65th birthday!*

MICHAEL SHERIDAN *honors* MARINA *and the* SHERIDAN WOMEN AND GIRLS: *wife, sisters, nieces, and great-nieces.*

PAULA WINOKUR *sends wishes for peace to* MARCY SLATER, *who she misses and loved like a sister.*

JEN BENKA *celebrates the* KELLY *sisters.*

BETH JOHNSON *honors the memory of* GREGGIE. *You were the big sister I never had.*

MELINDA WATSON *sends love and gratitude to* NELDA KAY,
BETSY SYLVIA, *and* MARIELENA ELIZABETH.

RHONDA COPELON *celebrates cousin-sister* TERRY BLUM, *and her fierce, beloved sisters around the world.*

JEFF FARRELL *honors his six sisters, here and gone.*

FRED LAZARUS *honors his three independent sisters:* ELLIE, MEG, *and* BETSY.

CARLA FREEMAN *thanks sisters* JAN *and* NANCY, *and* IZZY *and* ALICE, *without whom life would be unimaginable.*

BRUCE SLATER *honors the unique relationship between his mother* MARTHA *and her sister* ALICE.

WO SCHIFFMAN *celebrates* CHRISTINE, ELANA, JAN, JILL, JOAN, JULIA, KATY, LILL, LESLIE, SARAH, TERRI.

BETSY STONE *blows kisses to her sisters* SALLY *and* SUKI, *and her kindred spirit* LIZ.

JOAN HASTINGS *celebrates* WENDY WALKER, *an innovative writer and editor for Prototypes Press.*

JANET BATTEY *sends much love and admiration to her sister* ELLEN.

ROSEMARY AHERN *thanks (and loves)* CLAIRE AHERN MASSIMO, *sharer of memories and laughs.*

JUDY EISENBERG *celebrates* PATCHES, *spending days at Innisfree, nights at Dell O' Four.*

MARCIA RANDOL *honors her "sister"* MARCY. *Friends are the family we choose for ourselves.*

SUSAN STRICK *and* LILY SALTZBERG *celebrate our sister-friend,* CAROL EPSTEIN. *All the love and laughter shared.*

BARBARA PLETZ *celebrates her sister,* JUDY, *and her nieces* LAURA *and* SARAH.

DIANE KAUDERS *and* JANE BLUMENFELD—*sisters and friends forever! We toast our wonderful family—past and present.*

BABARA *and* ED BECKER *celebrate the memory of* CELIA HERMAN, *a joyful reader.*

JANE LUND *sends luscious Libra love to her sister* CARLA LUND.

TIM SCHAFFNER *celebrates* ELIZABETH BRYHER SCHAFFNER *and the* MALEY *sisters:* ANNE, CAROL, *and* JOAN.

GAIL, KATHERINE, PAMELA, KIM, CHRISTINA: *what if we didn't have each other?*—CAROL MACCOLL

ELAINE FREEMAN *celebrates her sister,* LILA, *her three daughters, and three granddaughters!*

275

ABOUT THE AUTHORS

Joyce Armor is a former television writer for *The Love Boat, WKRP in Cincinnati,* and *Remington Steele;* author of several books, including *Letters From a Pregnant Coward;* and a columnist, newspaper, and magazine writer.

Margaret Atwood is the author of more than fifty books of poetry and prose, including the Booker Prize-winning *Blind Assassin, Moral Disorder,* and *The Year of the Flood.* Her work has been translated into more than forty languages.

Joan Baez is a singer-songwriter and activist, with over thirty albums spanning her career. She is the recipient of multiple awards, including the 2007 Lifetime Achievement Grammy.

Claire Bateman has published five books of poetry, most recently *Leap.* She has taught at the Fine Arts Center in Greenville, South Carolina, Clemson University, and Chattanooga State University.

Robin Becker is the author of six books of poetry, most recently *Domain of Perfect Affection.* She is a professor of English at Penn State University, and a Contributing Editor and Poetry Editor for *The Women's Review of Books.*

Jane Bowles (1917–1973) published a novel, a play, and a short-story collection— as well as *The Collected Works of Jane Bowles.* Her expanded collected works, *My Sister's Hand in Mine,* and two volumes of her letters and stories, were published posthumously.

Gwendolyn Brooks (1917–2000) is the author of more than twenty books of poetry. In 1950, she became the first African American writer to win the Pulitzer Prize, for *Annie Allen.* She was Poet Laureate of Illinois in 1968, and was Consultant of Poetry to the Library of Congress in 1985.

Lan Samantha Chang is the author of the novel *Inheritance,* and *Hunger: A Novella and Stories.* She is a professor of English and the director of the Iowa Writer's Workshop at the University of Iowa, and serves as the fiction editor for the *Harvard Review.*

Marilyn Chin is the author of six books of poetry, most recently *Revenge of the Mooncake Vixen,* and editor of two anthologies. She is the winner of the PEN/Josephine Miles Award and four Pushcart Prizes, and is Director of the MFA program at San Diego State University.

Catherine Chung recently completed her first novel, *Forgotten Country*. She received her MFA from Cornell University and lives in New York City.

Lucille Clifton is the author of eight books of poetry, including the National Book Award-winning *Blessing the Boats: New and Selected Poems 1988-2000*, and over twenty children's books. She is the recipient of the 2007 Ruth Lilly Poetry Prize, and a Chancellor of the Academy of American Poets. She was Poet Laureate of Maryland in 1979, and is Distinguished Professor of Humanities at St. Mary's College.

Clare Coss is a playwright, psychotherapist, and activist who lives and works in New York City. Her plays include *Emmett, Down in My Heart*, *Love and Defiance: Ten Scenes from the 20th Century*, and *The Star Spangled Banner*.

Edwidge Danticat is the author of seven books of fiction and memoir, including the American Book Award-winning *The Farming of Bones* and the National Book Critics Circle Award-winning *Brother, I'm Dying*. She is the editor of *The Butterfly's Way*, an anthology of Haitian-American writing, and she was awarded a MacArthur Fellowship in 2009.

Sarah "Sadie" Delany (1889–1999) and **A. Elizabeth "Bessie" Delany** (1891–1995) are the authors, with Amy Hill Hearth, of *Having Our Say: The Delany Sisters' First 100 Years*. Sadie Delany was the first African American to teach domestic science in the New York City public high schools; Bessie Delany was the second African American woman licensed to practice dentistry in New York.

Rita Dove is the author of over twenty books, including the Pulitzer Prize-winning *Thomas and Beulah* and *Sonata Mulattica*. In 1993 she was appointed U.S. Poet Laureate, and served as Virginia's Poet Laureate from 2004–2006. She is Chair of the English Department at the University of Virginia.

Delia Ephron is a novelist, screenwriter, playwright, and film producer. She is the co-author of the play *Love, Loss, and What I Wore* with her sister, Nora Ephron. She has published ten books for adults and children, including *Hanging Up* and *The Girl With the Mermaid Hair*, and seven screenplays, including *Sisterhood of the Traveling Pants*.

M.F.K. Fisher (1908–1992) is known for her writing about food. She published over thirty books and memoirs, including *Consider the Oyster* and *Last House: Reflections, Dreams and Observations*. The M.F.K. Fisher Award, given biennially by Les Dames d'Escoffier, honors exceptional women culinary writers around the world.

Julia Glass is the author of three novels: the National Book Award-winning *Three Junes*, *The Whole World Over*, and *I See You Everywhere*. She is the recipient of numerous fellowships and awards, including the Tobias Wolff Award.

Barbara L. Greenberg is a poet and fiction writer. She is the author of four books, including *What Nell Knows* and *Late Life Happiness*. She is affiliated with the Women's Studies Research Center at Brandeis University.

Jane Hirshfield is the author of six books of poetry, most recently *After,* and the editor and co-translator of three collections of poetry by women. In 2004, she received the Academy Fellowship for Distinguished Poetic Achievement from the Academy of American Poets.

Cynthia Hogue has published three collections of poetry, including *Flux,* and is co-editor of *We Who Love to Be Astonished: Experimental Women's Writing and Performance Poetics.* She is the Jonathan and Maxine Marshall Chair in Modern and Contemporary Poetry at Arizona State University.

Beverly Jensen (1954–2003) is the author of the linked short-story collection, *The Sisters From Hardscrabble Bay,* two plays, and numerous short stories. Her story "Wake" was included in *2007 Best American Short Stories.*

Ruth Prawer Jhabvala is the author of nearly fifty novels, short-story collections, and screenplays, including the Booker Prize-winning novel *Heat and Dust,* and the Academy Award-winning screenplays for *A Room With a View* and *Howard's End.*

Ana Maria Jomolca is a Cuban-American writer, producer, and director. Her plays have appeared Off Broadway and her film *everygirl* was screened at film festivals in New York City and Chicago. Her most recent play, *Chiquitina,* debuted in New York in 2009.

Mary Karr is the author of three memoirs, including the PEN/Martha Albrand Award-winning *The Liars' Club* and *Lit,* and three books of poetry. She is the Jesse Truesdell Peck Professor of Literature at Syracuse University.

Marie Luise Kaschnitz (1901–1974), a German poet, essayist, and short-story writer, is the author of six books of poetry and eight collections of short stories. Kaschnitz received the Georg Büchner Prize and the Georg Mackensen Literature Prize.

Tsipi Keller is the author of eight books, including the novels *Retelling* and *Jackpot.* She is the translator and editor of *Poets on the Edge: An Anthology of Contemporary Hebrew Poetry* and *The Hymns of Job & Other Poems* by Maya Bejerano.

Barbara Kingsolver is the author of twelve books of fiction, essays, and poetry, including *The Poisonwood Bible* and *Animal, Vegetable, Miracle: A Year of Food Life.* She received the National Humanities Medal in 2000. Her work has been translated into nineteen languages.

Maxine Kumin is the author of more than forty books of poetry and prose, including the Pulitzer Prize-winning *Up Country: Poems of New England* and *Always Beginning: Essays on a Life in Poetry*. She is the recipient of the Ruth Lilly Poetry Prize, the Pulitzer Prize and Robert Frost Medal. She served as U.S. Poet Laureate in 1981.

Jeanne M. Leiby is the author of *Downriver: Short Stories*. She is the editor of *The Southern Review*, and is an associate professor of English at Louisiana State University.

Audre Lorde (1934–1992) is the author of eighteen books of poetry and prose, including *The Black Unicorn*, the National Book Award-winning *A Burst of Light*, and the *Collected Poems*, which was published posthumously. She served as the poet laureate of New York from 1991–1992.

Grace Paley (1922–2007), a poet, short-story writer, and essayist, published eleven books, including *The Little Disturbances of Man* and *Fidelity*, her final collection of poetry, which was published posthumously. She served as New York's first state author, from 1986–1988, and was poet laureate of Vermont from 2003–2007.

Dorothy Parker (1893–1967), a poet, screenwriter, and short-story writer, published many collections of poems and short stories, and wrote or contributed to nearly forty screenplays. She was a member of the Algonquin Roundtable in New York City, and spent much of her life in Los Angeles and traveling abroad.

Martha Rhodes is the author of three poetry collections, including *Mother Quiet*. She is the Director of Four Way Books, a literary press in New York City, and teaches at Sarah Lawrence College and at Warren Wilson College.

Muriel Rukeyser (1913–1980) is the author of fifteen books of poetry and prose, including *The Life of Poetry*, *The Orgy*, and *The Collected Poems*. She received the Copernicus Award from the Academy of Arts and Letters and the Shelley Memorial Award, and served as president of PEN/American Center from 1975–1976.

Myra Shapiro is the author of *I'll See You Thursday* and a memoir, *Four Sublets: Becoming a Poet in New York*. Her poems have appeared in *The Best American Poetry* 1999 and 2003. She teaches at The International Women's Writing Guild.

Ali Smith is a Scottish writer and author of four collections of short stories, a play, and four novels, including *The Accidental*, winner of the 2005 Whitbread Novel Award, and *Girl Meets Boy*.

Misty Urban is a short-story writer, whose work has been published in *Roanoke Review*, *Quarterly West*, and *Front Range Review*. She is an assistant professor of English at Lewis-Clark State College in Lewiston, Idaho.

Alice Walker is the author of over twenty-five books of poetry and prose, including *A Poem Traveled Down My Arm, Possessing the Secret of Joy*, and *Now Is the Time to Open Your Heart*. She is the recipient the Pulitzer Prize, the American Book Award, and was inducted into the California Hall of Fame in 2006.

Wendy Wasserstein (1950–2006) is the author of five plays, including *The Heidi Chronicles*, for which she received both a Tony Award and the Pulitzer Prize. She published several books of essays, including *Shiksa Goddess: Or, How I Spent My Forties*. Her novel *The Elements of Style* was published posthumously.

C.D. Wright is the author of ten books of poetry, including *Cooling Time: An American Poetry Vigil* and *Rising, Falling, Hovering*. She has received the Lannan Literary Prize, a MacArthur Fellowship, and the Griffin Poetry Prize. Wright was the Poet Laureate of Rhode Island from 1994–1999. She is an editor for Lost Roads Publishers and professor of English at Brown University.

Daisy Zamora is a Nicaraguan poet and author of six collections of poems, including *The Violent Foam: New and Selected Poems*. She is the editor of an anthology of Nicaraguan women poets. She served as Vice-Minister of Culture for Nicaragua in 1979, and received the Mariano Fiallos Gil National Poetry Prize from the University of Nicaragua. Her poems have been translated into thirteen languages.

ACKNOWLEDGMENTS
AND PERMISSIONS

Paris Press offers gratitude to the many individuals and foundations who have offered support to the Press and to *Sisters: An Anthology*. We thank those whose generous contributions to *Sisters: An Anthology* through their Dedications to Sisters helped to make it possible for Paris Press to bring this book into the world. And we are deeply grateful for the bountiful support of Margery Adams, Diane Bernard, Sara and Jon Budish, Fay Chandler, Daniel Hellerstein, John Jacob, Martha Richards, Eva Schocken, Nan Schubel, Charlotte Sheedy, and Richard Van Demark. Immense thanks to the Massachusetts Cultural Council, Olaf J. and Margaret L. Thorp Fund of the New York Community Trust, the Shapiro Family Foundation, the Fred Lazarus Jr. Foundation, and the Astraea Fund. Thanks also to the organizers of 11/11 Art Night, and to the artists who donated their work to the auction, which benefited *Sisters: An Anthology*.

Joyce Armor, "Sweet Dreams," copyright © 1991 Joyce Armor. Reprinted from *Kids Pick the Funniest Poems* by permission of Meadowbrook Press.

Margaret Atwood, "The Headless Horseman" from *Moral Disorder and Other Stories* by Margaret Atwood, copyright © 2006 O.W. Toad, Ltd. Reprinted with permission of Nan A. Talese, an imprint of The Doubleday Broadway Publishing Group, a division of Random House, Inc. Included in Electronic and Audio editions by the permission of the author.

Joan Baez, excerpt from *Daybreak* by Joan Baez (Avon, 1969), copyright © 1966, 1968 Joan Baez. Used by permission of the author.

Claire Bateman, "Reprieve" from *Clumsy* by Claire Bateman (New Issues Poetry & Prose, 2003), copyright © 2003 Claire Bateman. Used by permission of the author.

Robin Becker, "Borderline" from *Domain of Perfect Affection* by Robin Becker, copyright © 2006 Robin Becker. Used by permission of University of Pittsburgh Press.

Jane Bowles, "A Quarreling Pair," copyright © 2005 Jane Bowles. Used with permission from Farrar, Straus and Giroux, LLC, and The Wylie Agency, LLC.

Gwendolyn Brooks, "Sadie and Maud," copyright © Gwendolyn Brooks. Used by consent of Brooks Permissions.

Lan Samantha Chang, "The Eve of the Spirit Festival" from *Hunger* by Lan Samantha Chang, copyright © 1998 Lan Samantha Chang. Used by permission of W.W. Norton & Company, Inc.

Marilyn Chin, "Parable of the Cake" from the forthcoming *Revenge of the Mooncake Vixen* (W.W. Norton, 2009). Copyright © 2009 Marilyn Chin. Used by permission of the author.

Catherine Chung, "Hannah" from *Forgotten Country*, copyright © 2009 Catherine Chung. Used by permission of the author.

Barbara Kingsolver, excerpt from pp. 475–483 from *The Poisonwood Bible* by Barbara Kingsolver, copyright © 1998 Barbara Kingsolver. Used by permission of HarperCollins Publishers.

Maxine Kumin, "The Last Good War," copyright © 2009 Maxine Kumin. Printed by permission of the author.

Jeanne M. Leiby, "Docks" from *Downriver* by Jeanne M. Leiby, copyright © 2007 Jeanne M. Leiby. Used by permission of the author.

Audre Lorde, "A Family Resemblance" from *First Cities* (Poets Press, 1968), republished in *Undersong: Chosen Poems Old and New* (W.W. Norton, 1992), copyright © 1968 Audre Lorde. Used by permission of the Charlotte Sheedy Literary Agency.

Grace Paley, "I Needed to Talk to My Sister" from *Fidelity* by Grace Paley, copyright © 2008 The Estate of Grace Paley. Reprinted by permission of Farrar, Straus and Giroux, LLC.

Dorothy Parker, "To Helen Rothschild Droste" from *The Portable Dorothy Parker* by Dorothy Parker, edited by Marion Meade. Copyright © 1928, renewed © 1956 by Dorothy Parker; copyright © 1973, 2006 by The National Association for the Advancement of Colored People. Used by permission of Viking Penguin, a division of Penguin Group (USA) Inc.

Martha Rhodes, "Without Gloves" from *Perfect Disappearance*, copyright © 2000 Martha Rhodes. Reprinted with permission of New Issues Press. All rights reserved.

Muriel Rukeyser, "Two Years" from *The Collected Poems of Muriel Rukeyser*, copyright © 1973 Muriel Rukeyser. Reprinted by permission of International Creative Management, Inc.

Myra Shapiro, "Basque Guide," copyright © 2009 Myra Shapiro. Printed by permission of the author.

Ali Smith, from *Girl Meets Boy* by Ali Smith, copyright © 2007 Ali Smith. Used by permission of Grove/Atlantic, Inc., and Random House of Canada.

Misty Urban, "A Lesson in Manners." First published in *Quarterly West* (Winter 2005). Copyright © 2005 Misty Urban. Reprinted by permission of the author.

Alice Walker, "Everyday Use" from *In Love & Trouble: Stories of Black Women*, copyright © 1973 Alice Walker. Used by permission of Houghton Mifflin Harcourt Publishing Company.

Wendy Wasserstein, from *Shiksa Goddess* by Wendy Wasserstein, copyright © 2001 Wendy Wasserstein. Used by permission of Alfred A. Knopf, a division of Random House, Inc.

C.D. Wright, "Yellow Dresses" from *Translations of the Gospel Back Into Tongues* by C.D. Wright (SUNY Press, 1982), copyright © 1982 C.D. Wright. Reprinted by permission of the author.

Daisy Zamora, "Letter to a Sister Who Lives in a Distant Country" from *The Violent Foam: New and Selected Poems* by Daisy Zamora, trans. George Evans. Copyright © 2002 Daisy Zamora. Used by permission of the author and Curbstone Press.

ABOUT THE EDITORS

Jan Freeman is the director and founder of Paris Press. She is the author of three books of poetry, *Simon Says, Hyena, Autumn Sequence*, and a new manuscript, *Blue Structure*. She lives in Ashfield, MA; her younger sisters live in Atlanta and New York City.

Emily Wojcik is the assistant editor of Paris Press. She is completing her doctorate in English at the University of Connecticut, where she teaches writing and American Literature. She lives in Northampton, MA; her younger sister lives in New York City.

Deborah Bull has spent her career in publishing, most recently as director of Photosearch, Inc./Fair Street Productions, which produced illustrated books, including anthologies on a variety of subjects. She lives in New York City; her younger sister lives in Los Angeles.

284

ABOUT PARIS PRESS

Paris Press is a not-for-profit, 501(c)(3) independent press that publishes litera-ture by women writers worthy of greater recognition from readers, educators, and the publishing world. Paris Press values work that is daring in style and in its courage to speak truthfully about society, culture, history, and the human heart. To publish our books, Paris Press relies on support from organizations and individu-als. Please help Paris Press keep the voices of essential women writers in print and known. To contact the Press, please visit www.parispress.org, send an e-mail to info@parispress.org, or write to Paris Press, P.O. Box 487, Ashfield, MA 01330. All contributions are tax-deductible.

Other Paris Press trade books include *Tell Me Another Morning* by Zdena Berger; Bryher's *Visa for Avalon, The Heart to Artemis: A Writer's Memoirs,* and *The Player's Boy;* Muriel Rukeyser's *The Life of Poetry, The Orgy,* and *Houdini: A Musical;* Virginia Woolf's *On Being Ill;* Elizabeth Cady Stanton's *Solitude of Self;* Ruth Stone's *Simplicity* and *Ordinary Words;* Jan Freeman's *Simon Says;* Adrian Oktenberg's *The Bosnia Elegies;* and *Open Me Carefully: Emily Dickinson's Intimate Correspondence with Susan Huntington Dickinson,* edited by Martha Nell Smith and Ellen Louise Hart. Virginia Woolf's *On Being Ill* is available as a letterpress, hand-bound limited edition of 100. To order Paris Press books, please visit our website at www.parispress.org or your online or local booksellers.

The text of this book is composed in Mrs. Eaves.
Cover and text design by Judythe Sieck.
Calligraphy on cover and in text by Judythe Sieck.
Typesetting by Linda Weidemann, Wolf Creek Publishing Services.
Collage on cover, "Sisters Dresses," by Jane Lund,
copyright © 2009 reproduced with permission.
Photograph of "Sisters Dresses" by Stephen Petegorsky.
Printed by The Studley Press.

285